Praise for *White And Black*

"Sabaaneh's illustrations are intricate and moving—stark, striking, and rich with Palestinian visual traditions and symbols. The result is a series of intimate portraits of Palestinian life under occupation that combines history and present day reality. These cartoons are a powerful call to action, both to the international community and to the Palestinian people, serving as a reminder that at the end of the day it is we—Palestinians around the world—who will be the masters of our own destiny."

—LEILA ABDELRAZAQ
author, *Baddawi*

"An eloquent work on the ravages of settler colonialism. Every line in this collection achingly cries 'Palestine, Palestine!' This book is a must for all who care about peace and justice."

—KHALIL BENDIB
author, *Mission Accomplished: Wicked Cartoons by America's Most Wanted Political Cartoonist*

"Being an editorial cartoonist in the world today is a challenging task. First there are the journalistic rigors of keeping abreast of the news big and small, local and international. Then there is the satirical challenge of finding a way for you to employ the many faces of humor in your cartoon commentary. Finally there are the artistic challenges of drawing your satirical commentary in a compelling visual way on short deadlines.

"Mohammad has proven that he can master all the difficult challenges of our unique craft. But what makes Mohammad's place in the world of cartooning so extraordinary is that he performs his art in the world's hottest of political hotspots. There is no place on the planet where the skins are thinner or the fuses shorter than in the Israel/Palestinian conflict. Mohammad bravely uses his great talents as a cartoonist to work in the midst of this political minefield.

"Mohammad has earned the respect and admiration of many in the global cartoon community. I salute Mohammad and his cartoon efforts."

—KAL
editorial cartoonist, *The Economist* (London)
and *The Baltimore Sun*

"If you want to get a smart Palestinan's view of what's happening in the Middle East, you can't do better than look at Mohammad Sabaaneh's cartoons—they tell you more than words can say."

—VICTOR NAVASKY
publisher emeritus, *The Nation*

"Mohammad Sabaaneh has been accused of many terrible things. This is good. The best political cartoonists are always accused of libel, blasphemy and slander. In a part of the world where the conflicts have run so long that the issues seem dreadfully familiar, Mohammad's brutal cartoons about a brutal occupation prompts readers to think about things from a different perspective. A fresh point of view can change the world, and no one's trying harder to do that than Mohammad Sabaaneh."

—TED RALL
editorial cartoonist

"Mohammad Sabaaneh is one of the most talented Palestinian cartoonists working today. His haunting figures, rendered in black, white and grey, show us a vivid Palestinian perspective on the Israeli-Palestinian conflict, protest, injustice, and human rights. Sabaaneh avoids the stereotypes so often encountered in cartoons about Israel made by Arab cartoonists, making his message that much stronger."

—TJEERD ROYAARDS
cartoonist, editor-in-chief of Cartoon Movement

"Despite working at a very complicated crossroads of ideology and political pressures, Mohammad Sabaaneh continues to produce sharp, incisive cartoons. His tenacity and courage is an inspiration for cartoonists around the world."

—MATT WUERKER
Pulitzer Prize-winning editorial cartoonist, *Politico*

Just World Books

Timely Books for Changing Times

Just World Books exists to expand the discourse in the United States and worldwide on issues of vital international concern. We are committed to building a more just, equitable, and peaceable world. We uphold the equality of all human persons. We aim for our books to contribute to increasing understanding across national, religious, ethnic, and racial lines; to share more broadly the reflections, analyses, and policy prescriptions of pathbreaking activists for peace; and to help to prevent war.

To learn about our existing and upcoming titles or to buy our books, visit our website:

www.JustWorldBooks.com

Also, follow us on Facebook and Twitter!

Our recent titles include:

- *Condition Critical: Life and Death in Israel/Palestine*, by Alice Rothchild
- *The Gaza Kitchen: A Palestinian Culinary Journey*, by Laila El-Haddad and Maggie Schmitt
- *Lens on Syria: A Photographic Tour of its Ancient and Modern Culture*, by Daniel Demeter
- *Never Can I Write of Damascus: When Syria Became Our Home*, by Theresa Kubasak and Gabe Huck
- *America's Continuing Misadventures in the Middle East*, by Chas W. Freeman, Jr.
- *Arabia Incognita: Dispatches from Yemen and the Gulf*, edited by Sheila Carapico
- *War Is a Lie*, by David Swanson
- *The People Make the Peace: Lessons from the Vietnam Antiwar Movement*, edited by Karín Aguilar-San Juan and Frank Joyce

WHITE AND BLACK

This book is dedicated first to my mother for saving my drawings when I was a child; my father, for taking me by the hand to my first drawing competitions; my siblings, my greatest supporters; and to Athar Hodali and dear Salma, for putting up with my absences both while I was preparing this book and when I was in prison.

WHITE AND BLACK

Political Cartoons from Palestine

Mohammad Sabaaneh

Just World Books
Charlottesville, Virginia

Just World Books is an imprint of Just World Publishing, LLC

Images on p. ix: Seth Tobocman
Development editing: Ida Audeh
Project management and proofreading: Marissa Wold Uhrina
Typesetting: PerfecType, Nashville, TN
Cover image: Mohammad Sabaaneh
Cover design: MTW Design

Publisher's Cataloging-In-Publication Data
(Prepared by The Donohue Group, Inc.)

Names: Sabaaneh, Mohammad.
Title: White and black : political cartoons from Palestine / Mohammad Sabaaneh.
Other Titles: Political cartoons from Palestine
Description: Charlottesville, Virginia : Just World Books, an imprint of Just World Publishing, LLC, [2017]
Identifiers: LCCN 2016954453 | ISBN 978-1-68257-067-8
Subjects: LCSH: Palestine--Politics and government--1948---Caricatures and cartoons. | Israel--Ethnic relations--Political aspects--Caricatures and cartoons. | Political prisoners--Palestine--Caricatures and cartoons. | Political cartoons. | LCGFT: Humor.
Classification: *LCC DS119*.76 .S23 2017 | *DDC 320.9569402/07--dc23*

CONTENTS

SABAANEH'S SOCIAL SURREALISM

Foreword and cartoons by Seth Tobocman

Can there be an accurate depiction of an insane situation? Why should we draw in perspective when the world has lost its perspective? When reality becomes bizarre, social realism gives way to social surrealism.

Mohammad Sabaaneh is a young Palestinian artist who joins a long tradition of Arab political cartoonists. For over a hundred years, the Arab countries have had newspapers in which the issues of the day are hotly debated. Such newspapers do not pretend to be neutral or polite. This is a partisan political press. These papers are often punctuated with illustrations. The intention of such drawings is not decorative but deeply didactic. It is the job of the cartoonist to explain complex political problems in such a way that the simplest person can understand them. The artist deploys an arsenal of well-understood symbols that speak to the history of the nation. He tries to combine them in new ways to describe a continually changing contemporary situation. But this is more than an intellectual exercise. This is a form of militant activism, and it has its risks.

Naji al-Ali, perhaps the most famous Palestinian cartoonist, was assassinated in 1987. His popular cartoons provide an accurate picture of Israel's persecution of the Palestinians, but he also called out corruption among Arab leaders, and so it has never been clear who was responsible for his execution. More recently, Syrian cartoonist Ali Ferzat had his hands broken by thugs for satirizing President Assad. Ahmad Nady has been

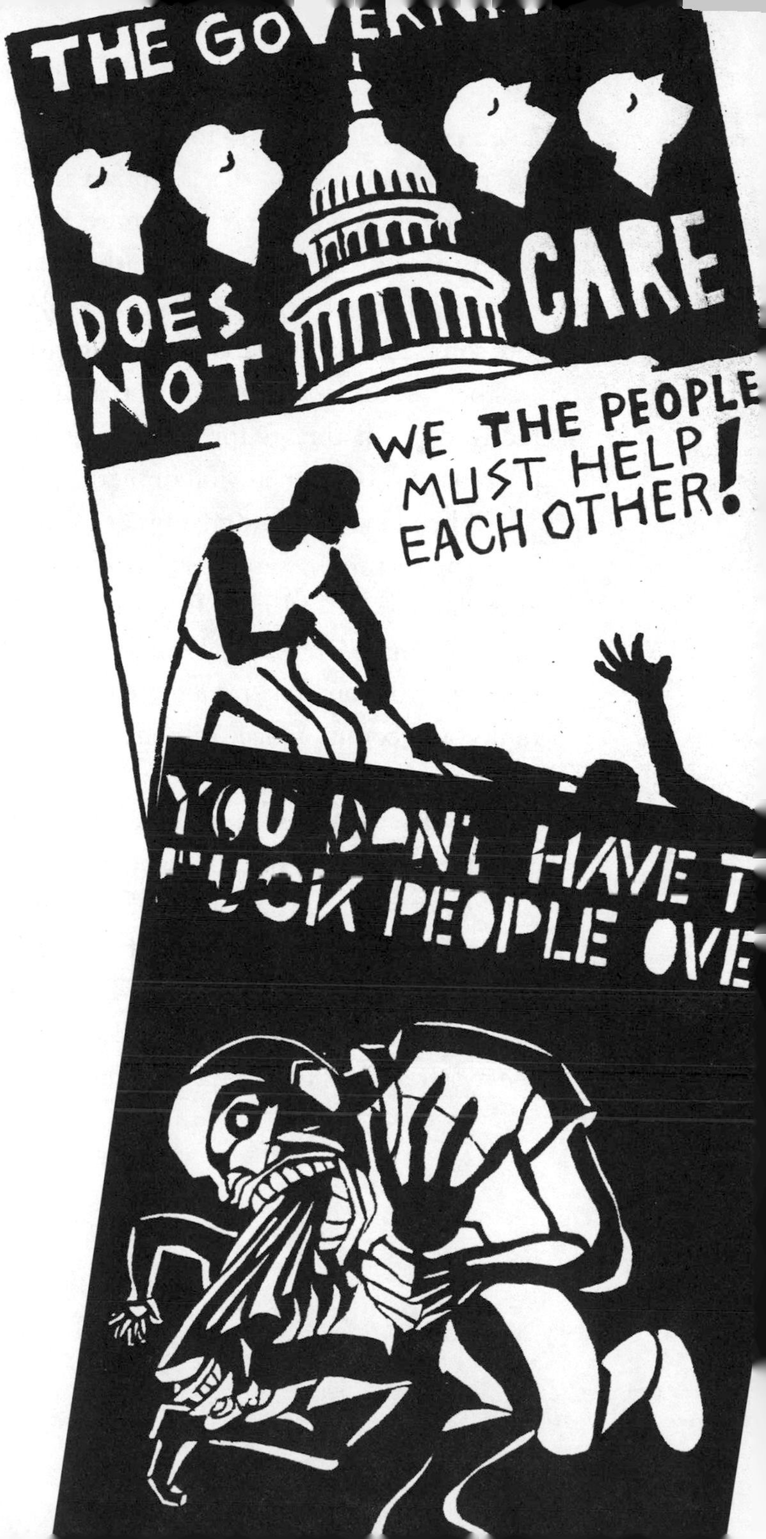
DOES NOT
CARE
WE THE PEOPLE MUST HELP EACH OTHER!

jailed over and over again for cartoons critical of successive Egyptian regimes. As the Egyptian military dictatorship consolidates power, more and more Egyptian cartoonists prefer to publish anonymously rather than risk arrest.

So it is not surprising at all that Mohammad Sabaaneh did some of his best artwork during the six months he was held in an Israeli prison, or that he has more recently received death threats for publishing an entirely positive portrait of the Prophet Mohammad.

When I look at the drawings of Mohammad Sabaaneh, I see the tortured, compressed, and crowded space that is everyday life for ordinary Palestinians. His cartoons capture this maze of walls, checkpoints, 24-hour-a-day curfews, and prison cells punctuated by bombings, soldiers, tanks, and commonplace killings in a way that photo journalism fails to.

To describe this impossible landscape, Mohammad Sabaaneh draws on the language of 20th-century cubism. The distortion of urban space of Braque and Picasso. But the modernists were not sure if the technological world would be a curse or a blessing. There was the geometric beauty of Picasso's nudes and still life paintings as well as the hysteria of his *Guernica*. Sabaaneh's drawings are closer to the *Guernica* for sure. But even the *Guernica* seems to explode outward into space while Mohammad's world implodes, trapped in the crammed frame. Mohammad shows us children inside a prison inside a city that grows from a tired man's back, and this tired man is also inside a prison. "This," Sabaaneh tells us, "is Palestine!"

Even Sabaaneh's comic strips employ a pattern of painfully narrow panels, arranged like the spaces between prison bars. It is uncomfortable to view the world through this tiny slit. Mohammad never lets us forget where he is or how hard it is to be there.

It is hard to look at. It should be. This is angry art, ruthless and relentless. And who has more right to be angry than the children of Palestine? Born into a box, without the human and democratic rights many of us take for granted. This is the landscape that the West has created through almost a hundred years of political and military intervention. This is a man-made wilderness. A world we made, which reflects our own madness. In the words of Colin Powell, "You broke it, you own it." I am glad this collection is being published and made available to people in the United States and Europe. Everyone needs to see these drawings.

PREFACE

The idea for this book began to take shape during the two weeks or so that I spent in solitary confinement in an Israeli occupation prison. Detained in 2013 for five months, my experience was not that different from that of thousands of other Palestinian detainees; less typical was my placement in solitary confinement following the end of interrogation. I had no idea how long my ordeal might last. I was being held in "administrative detention," a provision of the military laws that Israel has applied continuously since 1967 to the indigenous Palestinians of the West Bank and Gaza. Under these laws, which date back to the days of British rule, detention can be imposed for renewable six-month terms and is in theory indefinite. I spent the long hours thinking about creating a book that would depict all aspects of Palestinian life through snapshots of both the heroic and the ordinary, which like a mosaic becomes whole when one sees all the pieces together.

In Cell 28, in the interrogation center at Jalama, my "home" while I was in solitary confinement, I came to realize that we Palestinians have a duty to show ourselves in a realistic light—not quite as ordinary people (because people who are able to live in the conditions of the life they face are anything but ordinary), but not quite as legendary heroes either. What is challenging about the Palestinian experience is that a rational Palestinian cannot identify with either picture. The child who confronts an Israeli tank with a rock or the little girl who leaps with all her might to save her little brother from the arms of the Israeli soldiers—these are indeed acts requiring a measure of courage that cannot and should not be

minimized. On the other hand, the reality of an ordinary detained person commonly glorified in popular culture—a damp cell in which time passes slowly, filled with dreams of going about the routine details of daily life—is anything but heroic.

Placing detainees in isolation was one method of interrogation and psychological torture used with detainees. To fight the isolation, I pretended I was a journalist whose mission it was to convey to the world at large what detention in an Israeli prison is like. I thought of subjects and ideas for cartoons I must draw. During one of my interrogation sessions, I managed to steal some paper and a pencil, and then I listed some cartoon ideas, cramming as many ideas as I could on a single sheet. I hid the sheet of paper from my jailers until I was sent to prison, where I had access to more paper and pencils. I created sketches without any details that would convey that the subject matter was prison life because I was afraid that they might be confiscated. I drew things like the bus that transported prisoners from one facility to another; the transportation was a kind of torture too, because the bus was a metal contraption that was ice-cold in winter and stifling in summer, and transportation could take anywhere from three to seven days. I drew sick prisoners and prisoners who thought constantly about the daily activities of their children and about family visits. I smuggled rough sketches out with every prisoner who was released. When I was released, I collected my sketches and completed the cartoons.

While I was in prison, I lacked the instruments I was accustomed to using, and so I spent months developing a new approach that was based on free-hand drawings. I have been inspired by the work of Kevin Kallaugher, Ann Telnaes, and Seth Tobocman (among the many artists I have had the good fortune to meet) and their commitment to free-hand drawings and the use of recurring characters. For their help and support, I thank Nancy Sadiq, Athar Hodali, Faris Sabaaneh, Thamer Sabaaneh, Dr. Waleed Deeb, Dr. Nahed Habiballah, Miko Peled, and the Arab American University.

INTRODUCTION

My first encounter with Palestine was through my mother's stories of Palestinian *fedayeen* (freedom fighters). Growing up in the Palestinian diaspora in Kuwait, I listened to her stories and constructed fantasy images of a Palestinian hero who struggled for freedom and justice in an idealized Palestine. During the summers, we would go to that idealized land for family visits, and years later when I recalled those visits, the big fig tree that my siblings and I used to play around seemed more luscious and green than any other tree. Other memories are not so benign; upon crossing the bridge from Jordan, I was aware even as a child that those in control were armed and spoke in a foreign language. I remember, too, crouching beneath a window in my grandparents' house where my grandmother hid us when the Israeli army stormed the neighborhood, their helmets visible above the window sill. We returned to our homeland for good just before the second intifada (uprising) began in September 2000. My return enabled me to further develop the image of the Palestinian hero who struggled against injustice, which found expression in my drawings time and time again.

The experiences of political prisoners had already been a theme I addressed in my cartoons. In 2013, I found myself sharing their fate. Arrested by the Israeli occupation forces, I was detained for five months, part of that time in solitary confinement. Like other detainees, I was shuttled from one prison to another and from one cell to another to accommodate the whims of my jailer. In detention, I got to know my heroes and witnessed their agonies; they longed for the banal details of ordinary lives,

such as lighting a cigarette, conversing with a loved one, basking under the heat of the sun, or sipping a cup of coffee as they pleased and not as dictated by a set timetable.

I had drawn thousands of prisoner-heroes in the past, but in prison I felt completely impotent. Unable to portray myself as a hero, I surrendered to my weaknesses, for we all love, miss, fear, and feel pain, and I had to confront the inescapable question: Was everything I drew a lie?

I tried to answer this question through sketches that I drew during the long periods in solitary detention. Through their artistic and literary efforts, the artists, writers, and intellectuals among us have always insisted that Palestinian prisoners are heroes, and prisoners themselves have been willing to adopt this view, I later learned, as a survival tactic to protect our souls from the dehumanizing conditions in which we found ourselves and to safeguard our ability to resist. As a tactic, it was vital in keeping our spirits high.

This book, I hope, presents a candid portrayal of Palestinian life to the wider world. My visualization of the "subject" includes not only Palestinians but also the occupier. I tried to expand my lens to spot the humanity of the occupier, but this effort proved difficult to sustain when an Israeli soldier placed handcuffs around my wrists, or dragged me to an interrogation room, or prevented me from moving from one part of my homeland to the other. With each violation, the occupier denied my humanity in order to justify his violence toward me. Consequently,

I could not make the image of the occupier esthetically pleasing, even when I acknowledge that in the process of exerting his political will, the occupier is also occupied.

In some of my sketches, occupier and occupied are hard to tell apart. I felt ugly when I was in my cell, and I still remember the reflection of my face on the jail truck as I was being transported and my attempt to recognize my features. I used my cell's rough walls to file my nails so I wouldn't look as degraded as the system was designed to make me feel. Ultimately, an awful reality cannot be prettified; our reality includes the bodies of children under the remains of homes bombed by Israeli military planes, and such realities are ugly.

The cartoons in this book are my attempt to tell the story of Palestine pictorially and to place it in a global context, and in so doing to cast light on the human dimension, all too often forgotten in political discussions. The cartoons are grouped into five chapters. The first chapter, "History Matters," depicts almost a century of Palestinian history, beginning with the start of the British Mandate in 1922 and extending to 2016, which saw sustained Israeli assaults on the Palestinian presence in Jerusalem and the Palestinians' unwavering demand for their right of return. These images provide the framework for the materials in the chapters that follow.

The second chapter, "Life in Occupied Palestine," takes as its subject matter the daily life for Palestinians under occupation. These cartoons deal with the distorted facts of daily living: the confinement in smaller spaces, the checkpoints, the wall snaking its way across the landscape, the elevated and armed Jewish-only colonies designed to fragment densely populated Palestinian areas and to assist the army in controlling the indigenous population. Other facts of daily life include the destructive internal divisions between Palestinian political factions and the environmental deterioration, partly caused by the occupation but also by ordinary negligence.

The third chapter, "Palestine and the World," illustrates the similarities between events and conditions in Palestine and those in other parts of the world. The fourth chapter, "Short Stories," is a collection of vignettes, some of which were drawn from my personal experiences; others were inspired by events that have become commonplace. One example among many: few can forget the image of the four little boys playing football on a Gaza beach in the summer of 2014, boys who were killed by the Israeli army; friends in childhood, they are together in death, too. Variations on this theme, unfortunately, are not unfamiliar to most Palestinians.

The cartoons in "Political Prisons" were drawn when I was detained in an Israeli prison and depict the typical experiences of prisoners. Rather than defend the idea of the prisoner as hero, I have tried to dispense with it altogether and instead illustrate the experience of ordinary men contending with dehumanizing conditions.

CHAPTER 1

HISTORY MATTERS

History is written by the victorious, we are told. How would that history read if those who bled and suffered through it had written it? The frieze that is highlighted in this chapter, along with more detailed views of its different sections, illustrates a few key moments from the struggles of the Palestinian people to withstand Zionist efforts to erase them from their landscape and to live in Palestine as a nation in its rightful place.

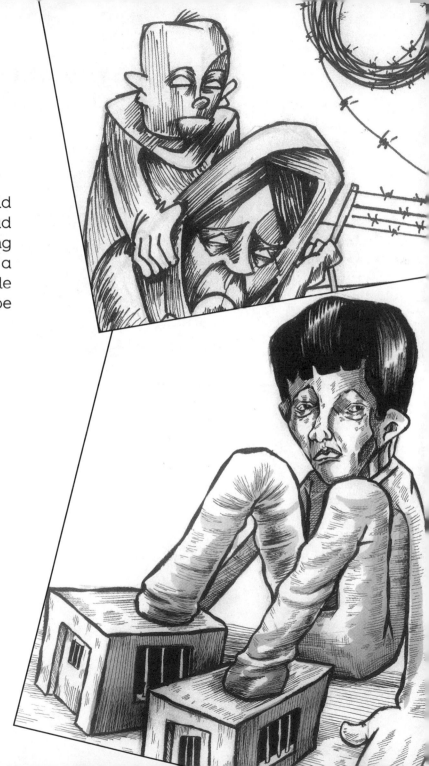

The Story of Palestine: Some Highlights

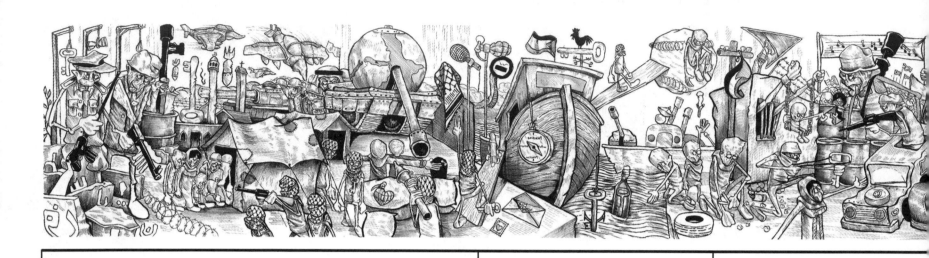

1922–65

The British Mandate,
the Nakba,
and Palestinian
resistance

1982

Israel's invasion
of Lebanon and
expulsion of the
PLO

1987

The start of the first
intifada

1993-2004

The Palestinian
Authority, a new
intifada, Israel's
Apartheid Wall

2004-14

Increased Israeli
control of the West
Bank, assaults on
Gaza

2015-16

Renewed attention
to Jerusalem and
the Right of Return

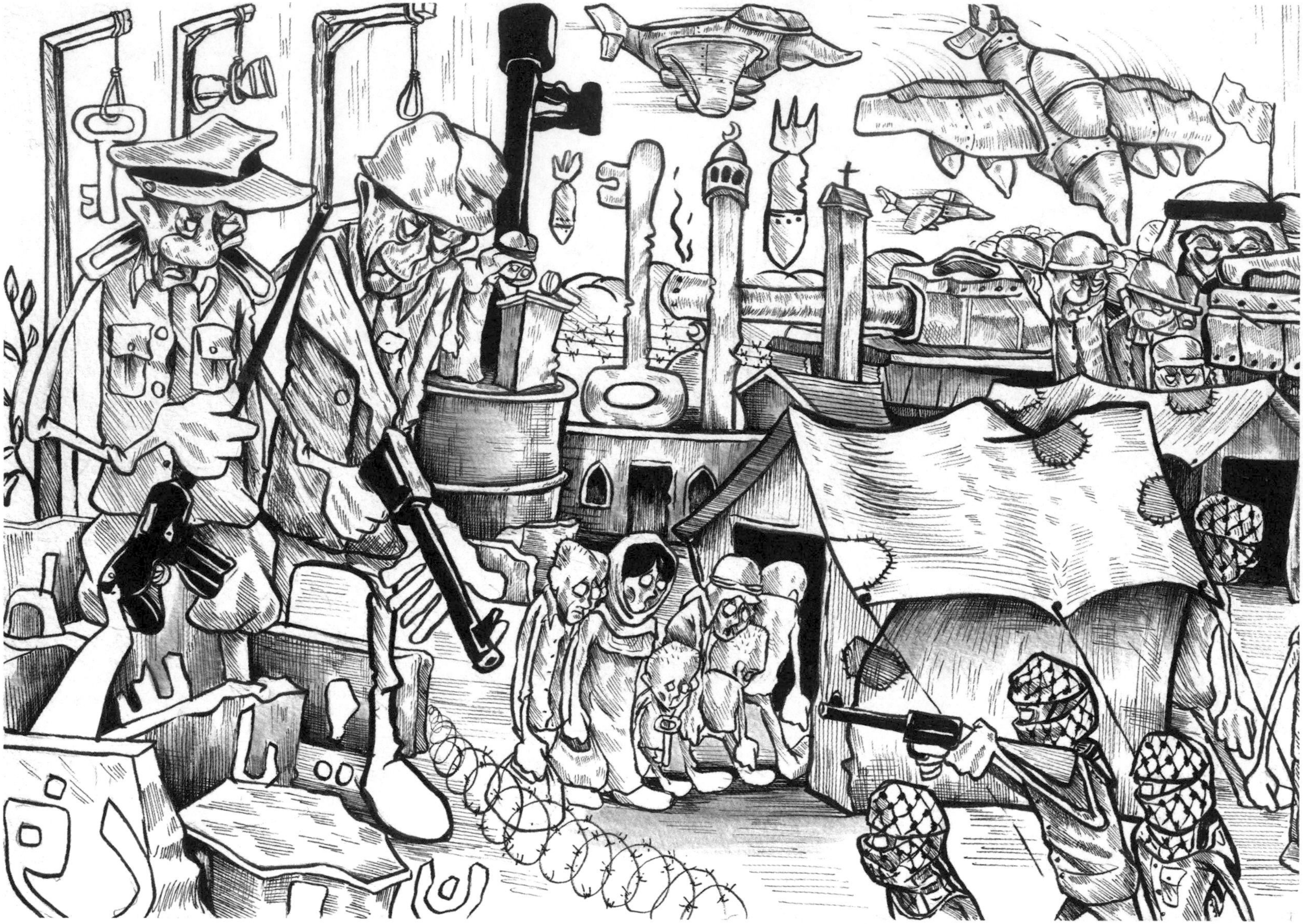

1922–65

The British Mandate, the Nakba, and Palestinian resistance

In 1922, the League of Nations gave Britain a "Mandate" to govern Palestine. Under Britain's rule, Zionist colonization accelerated. When Palestinians resisted, the British military countered with collective punishments, home demolitions, and public hangings. In 1947–48, as the British withdrew, Zionist militias expelled 750,000 Palestinians from the area in which they established a Jewish state, a process that Palestinians refer to as the Nakba, or catastrophe. After many years of hoping that diplomacy would win their UN-promised "Right of Return," exiled Palestinians formed their own liberation movements to achieve this. The keys to their stolen family homes were potent symbols of their Return.

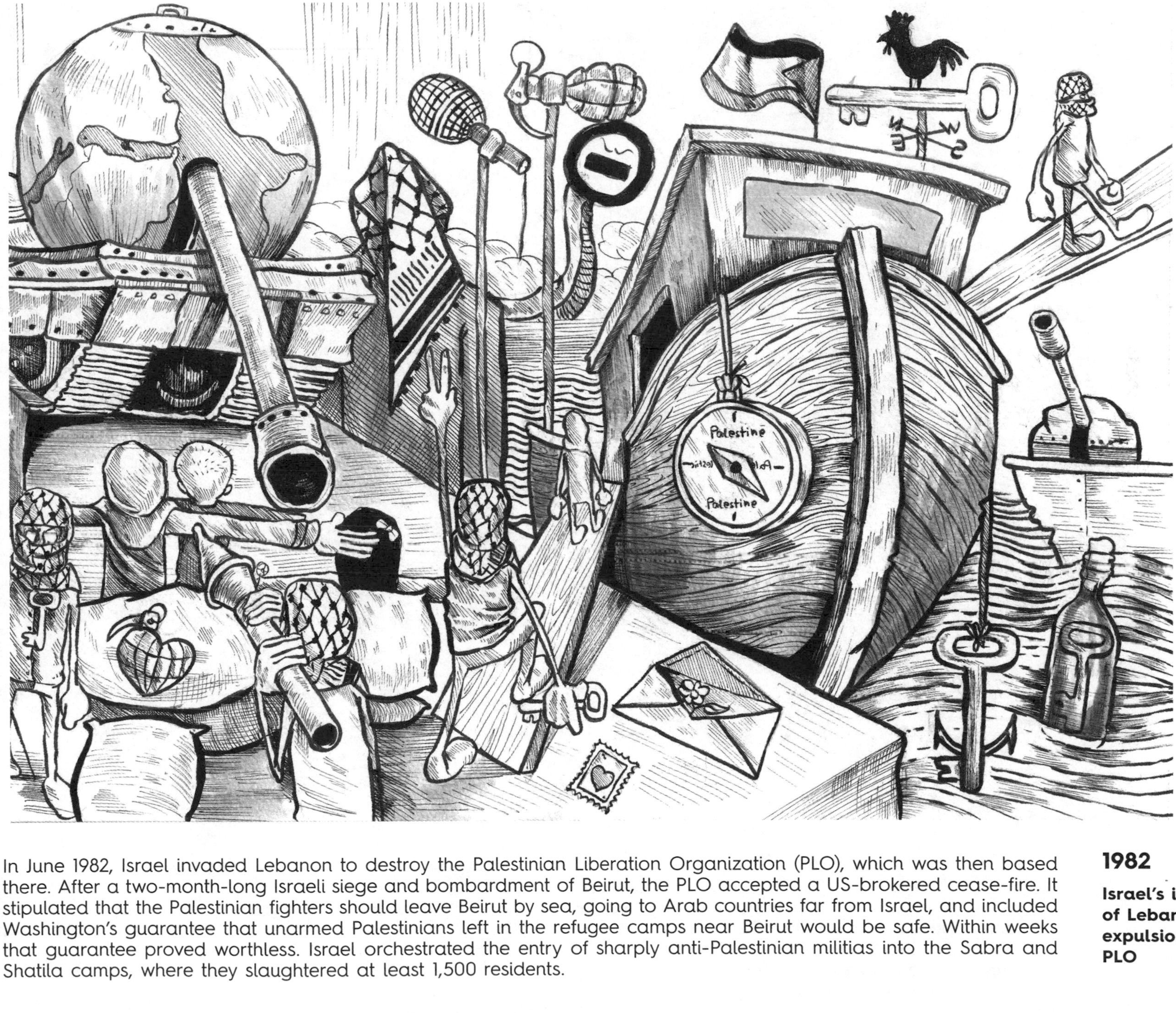
Palestine
Palestine

1982

Israel's invasion of Lebanon and expulsion of the PLO

In June 1982, Israel invaded Lebanon to destroy the Palestinian Liberation Organization (PLO), which was then based there. After a two-month-long Israeli siege and bombardment of Beirut, the PLO accepted a US-brokered cease-fire. It stipulated that the Palestinian fighters should leave Beirut by sea, going to Arab countries far from Israel, and included Washington's guarantee that unarmed Palestinians left in the refugee camps near Beirut would be safe. Within weeks that guarantee proved worthless. Israel orchestrated the entry of sharply anti-Palestinian militias into the Sabra and Shatila camps, where they slaughtered at least 1,500 residents.

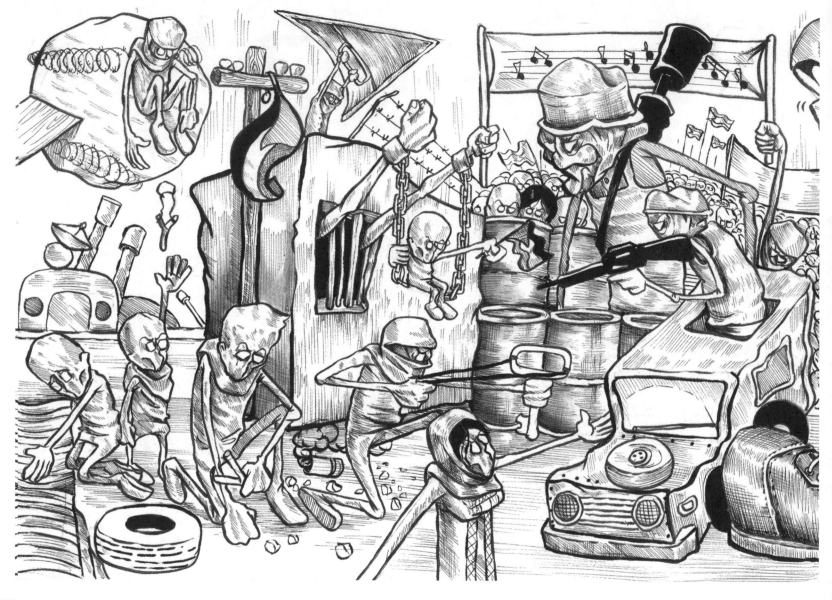

1987

The start of the first intifada

In late 1987, Palestinians in the West Bank and Gaza launched a nearly wholly nonviolent intifada, or uprising, against Israel's 20-year military occupation. They undertook many creative acts of civil disobedience, such as general strikes, mass demonstrations, and boycotts of Israeli products. In response, Israel shot demonstrators, imposed curfews, launched broad campaigns of imprisonment, closed schools and universities, deported suspected ringleaders, and used intentional tactics of "breaking their bones." By the end of the intifada's first year, 405 Palestinians had been killed, 20,000 injured, 20,000 arrested, and 32 deported.

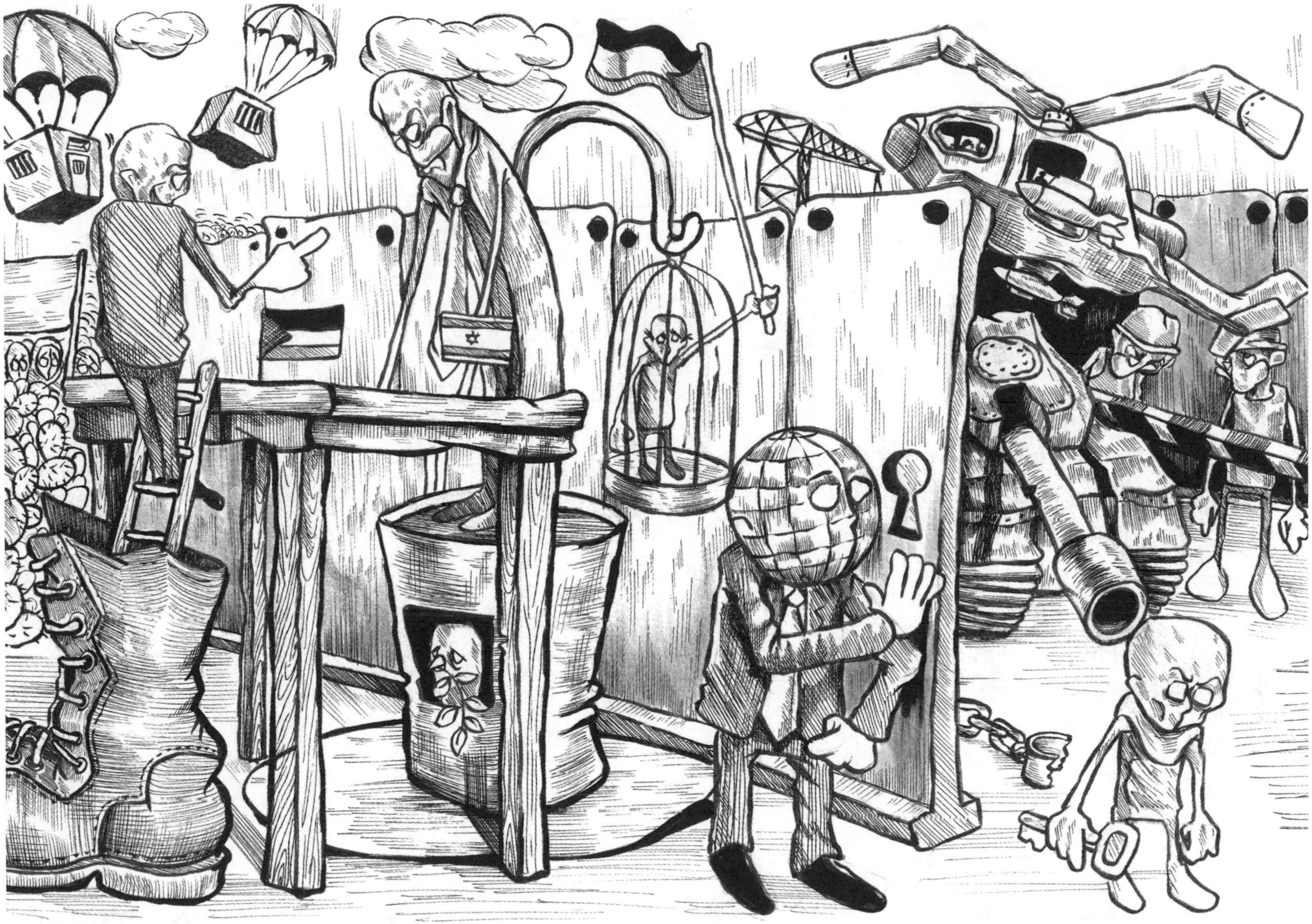

In 1993, the PLO and Israel signed the Oslo Accord. It allowed some PLO leaders to enter the West Bank and Gaza to create an interim "Palestinian Authority" but under firm Israeli control. A final peace was supposed to be negotiated by 1999. But Israel intensified its illegal construction of settlements, and the peace talks led nowhere. In September 2000, Palestinians launched a second intifada. Israel responded with familiar violence. Claiming security needs, Israel started building a massive wall that cut many West Bank Palestinian communities off from each other. The wall, along with Israeli settlements, curfews, and checkpoints, radically constrains Palestinians' daily life and economic activity.

1993–2004

The Palestinian Authority, a new intifada, Israel's Apartheid Wall

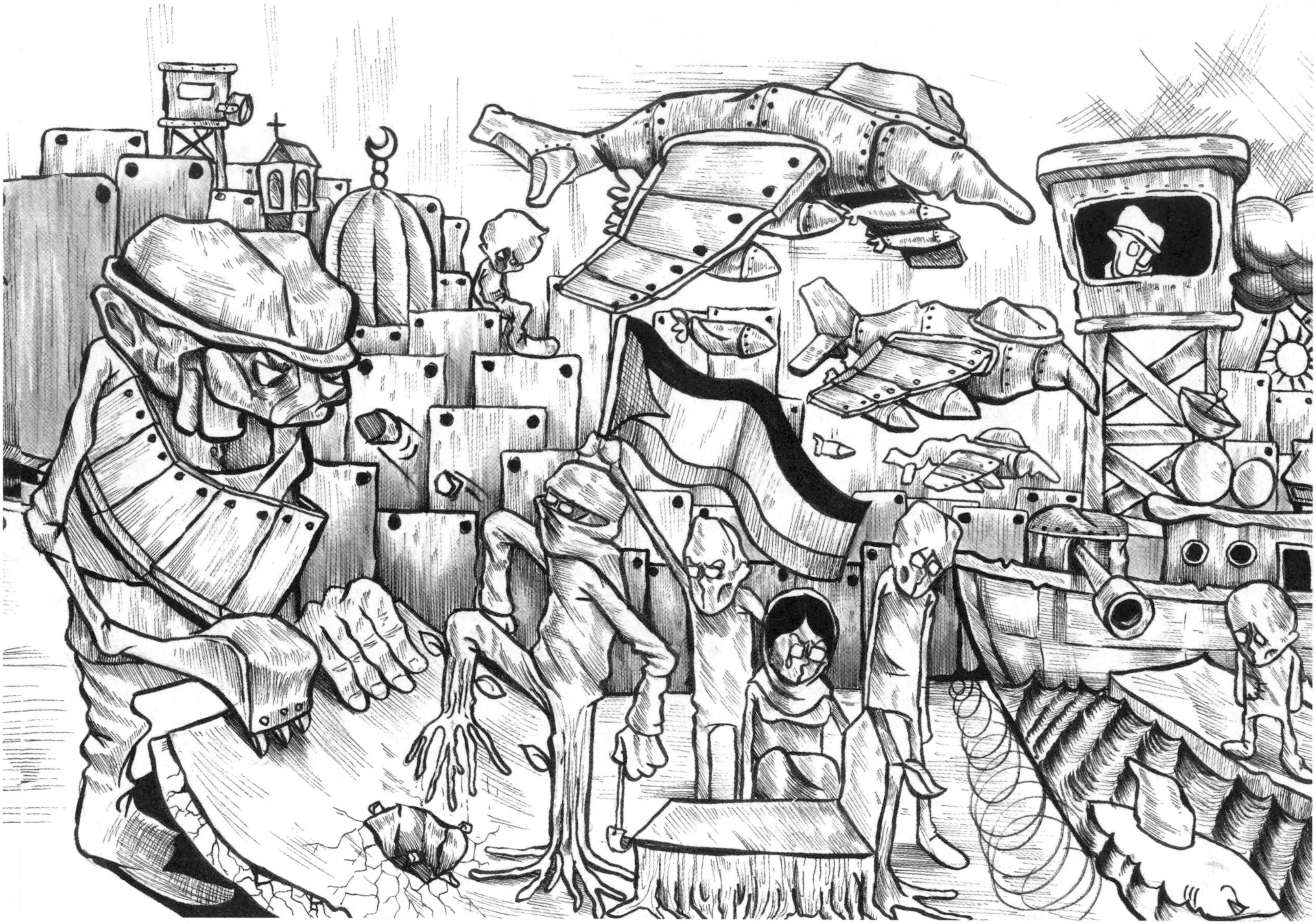

2004-14

Increased Israeli control of the West Bank, assaults on Gaza

Palestinians judge that the Oslo process is dead. They feel trapped in an endless, US-led process that lets Israel do as it pleases. Israel's land confiscation, settlement construction, and wall-building in the West Bank dice the terrain into ever smaller pieces. In 2005, Israel withdrew its settlers and soldiers from inside the Gaza Strip. That allowed it to launch broad, devastating military attacks against the Strip's two million Palestinians, which it did in 2008, 2012, and 2014. Those attacks, along with Israel's tight land and sea blockade of Gaza, have destroyed its economy, pushing many Gaza Palestinians into despair. (Gaza is shown here, adrift on a hostile sea.)

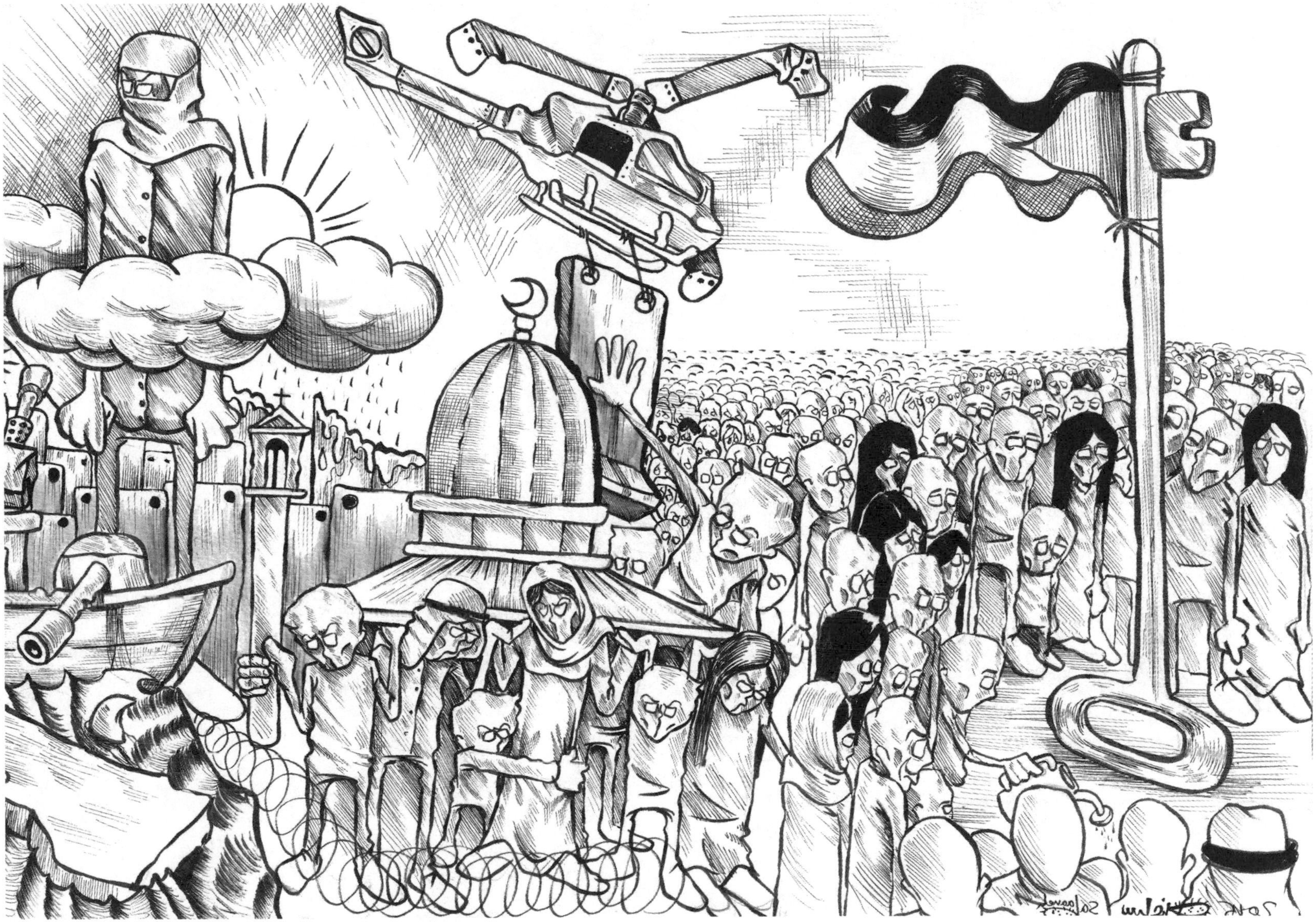

2015-16

Renewed attention to Jerusalem and the Right of Return

Israel accelerates its attacks against Jerusalem's Palestinians, increasing its demolition of their homes and revocation of their residency rights as it builds massive, Jewish-only settlements in and around East Jerusalem. The walling-off of East Jerusalem from its natural hinterland elsewhere in the West Bank continues. The Aqsa Mosque sees ongoing confrontations between Palestinians and Israeli soldiers who seek to restrict Muslim access to it, and increasingly aggressive actions from Zionist extremists aiming to replace it with a Jewish Temple. Meanwhile, Palestinians around the world reject as anachronistic the concept of a Jewish exclusivist state and continue to demand their Right of Return.

CHAPTER 2

LIFE IN OCCUPIED PALESTINE

The cartoons that follow depict Palestinians trying to live their lives despite a crushing colonialist force and internal political strife, while the world watches silently and noncommittally.

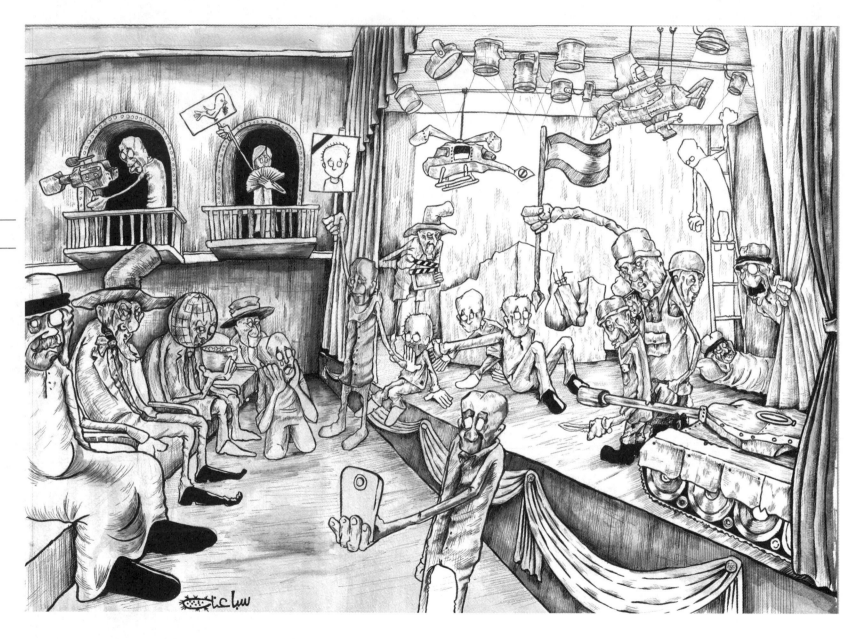

The world watches as the media pursue hidden agendas.

The struggles of life
begin before birth.

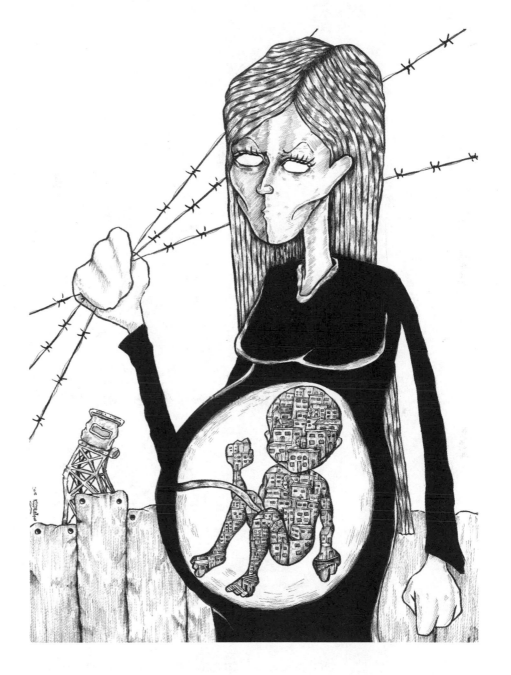

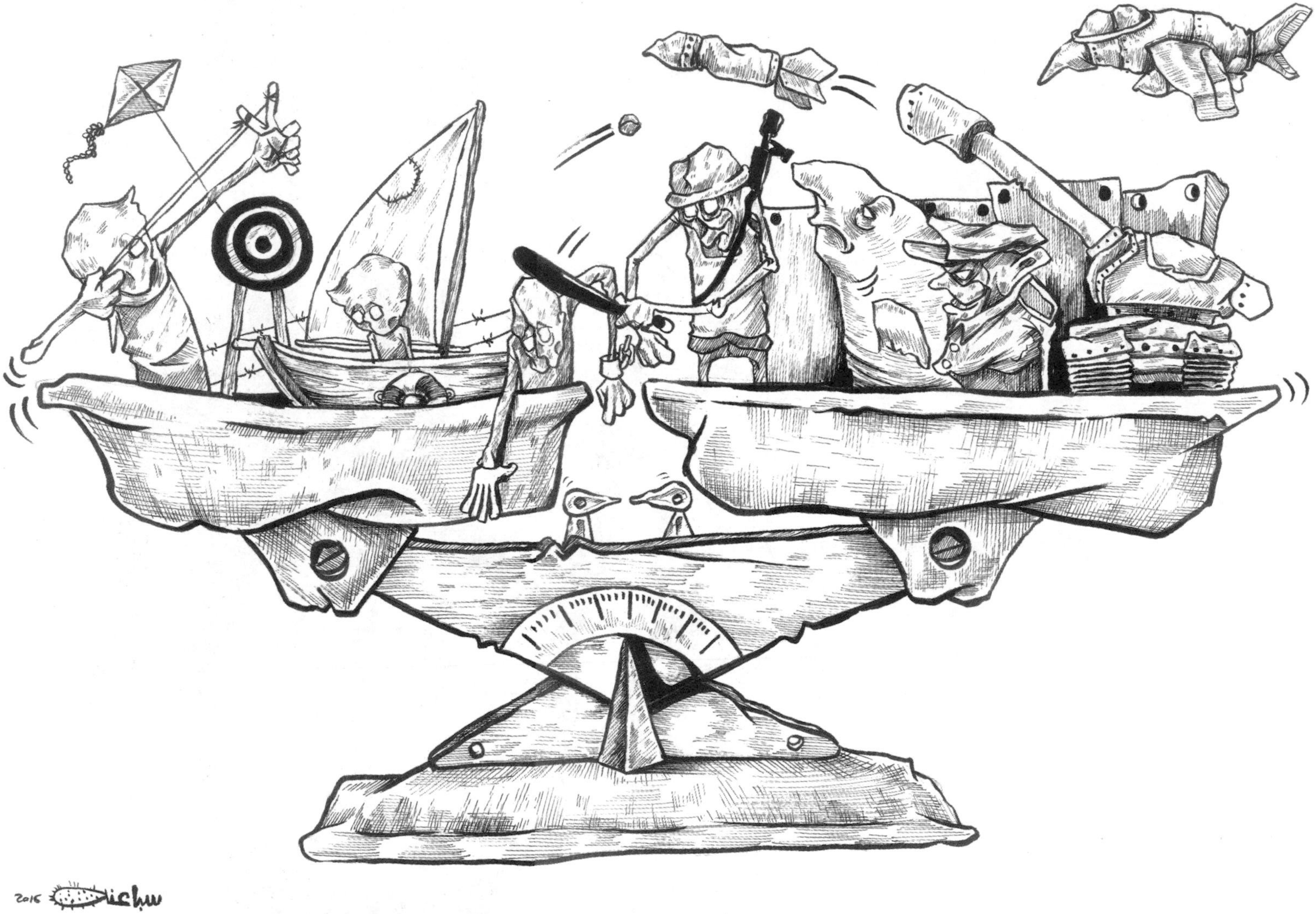

The balance of great military force and the suffering it causes.

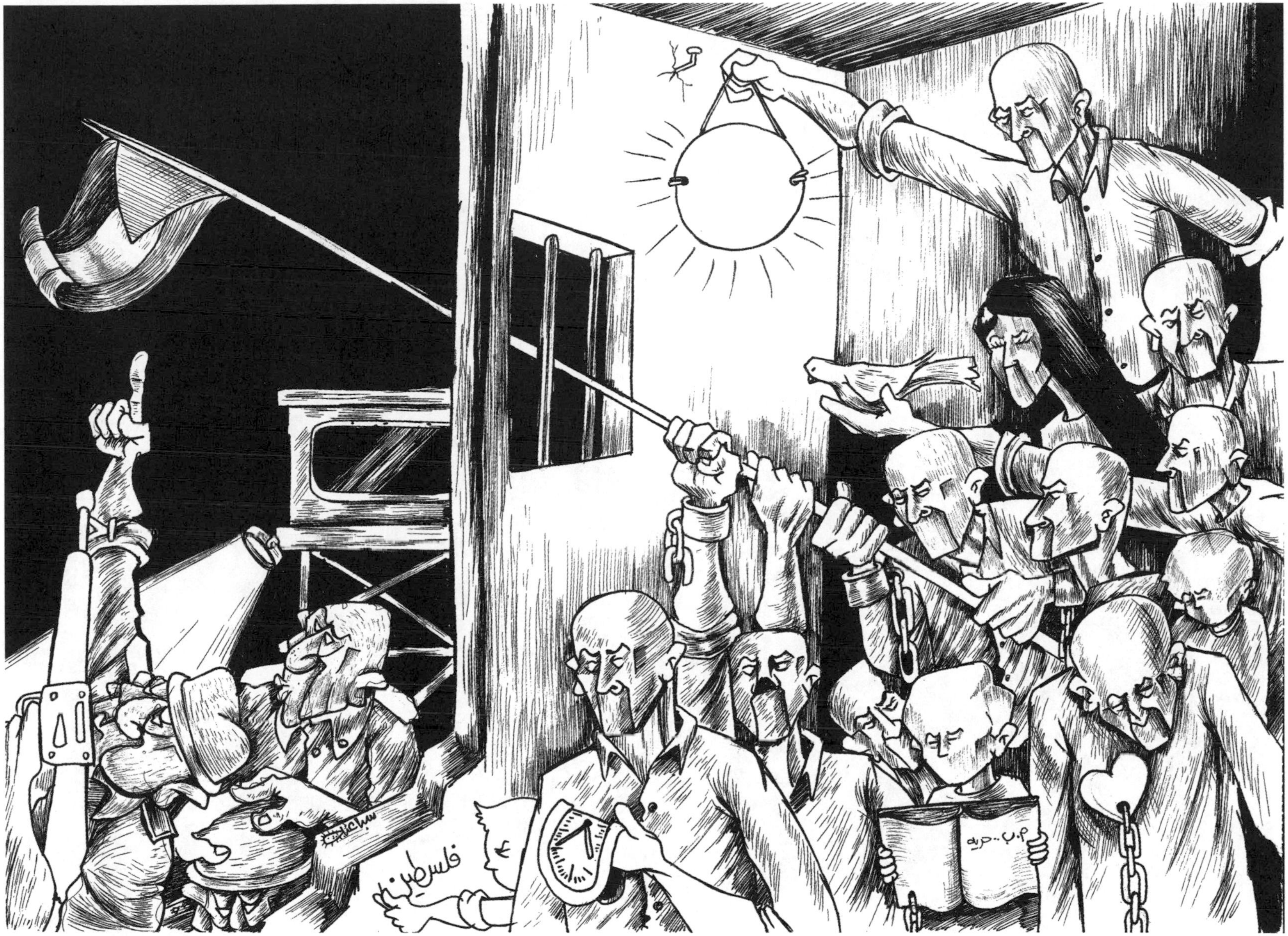
فلسطين

The struggle for justice is a responsibility that political prisoners understand very well.

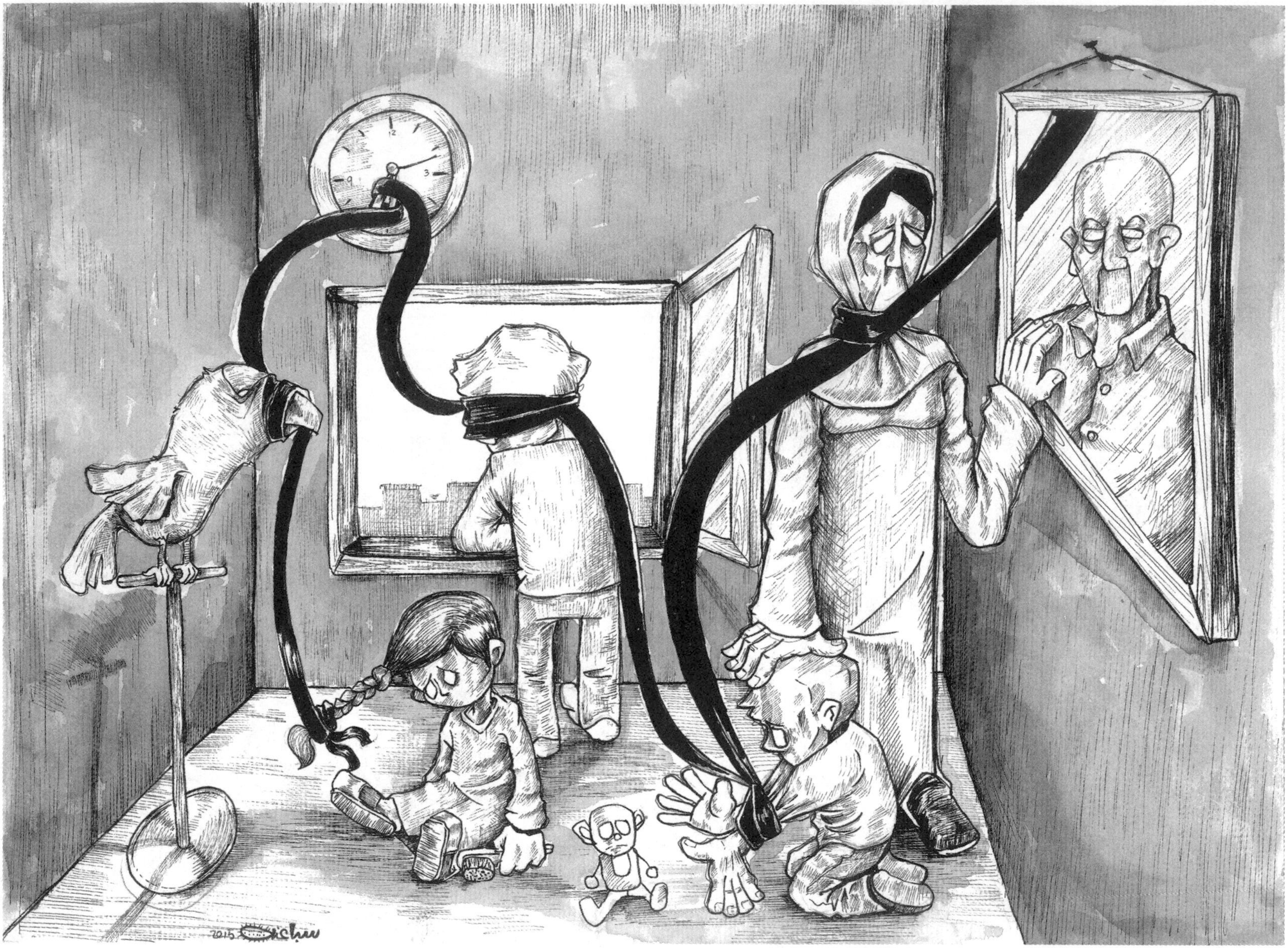

Connecting our stories, dreams, and sorrows.

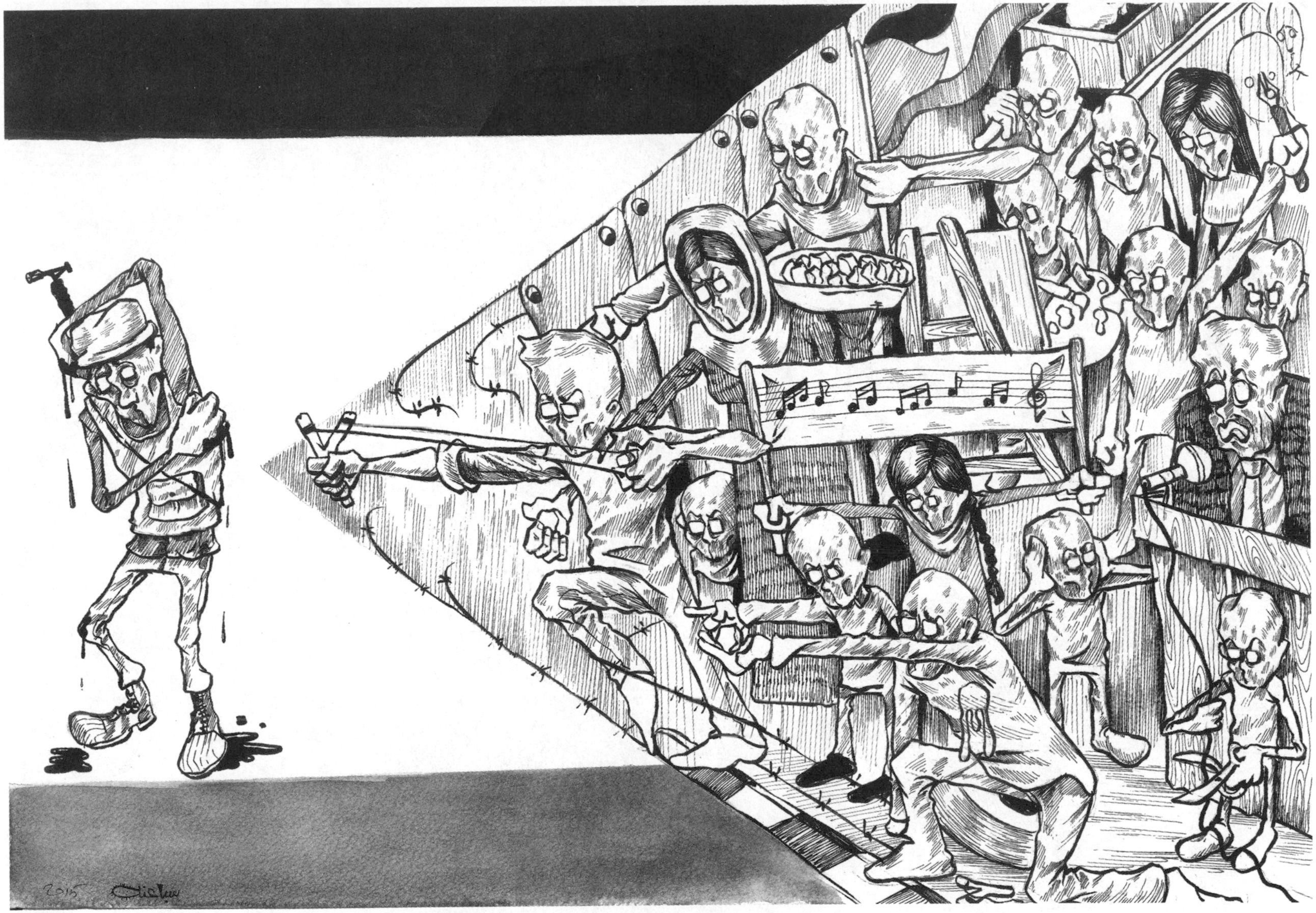

The ongoing struggle for freedom requires unity of purpose and steely determination.

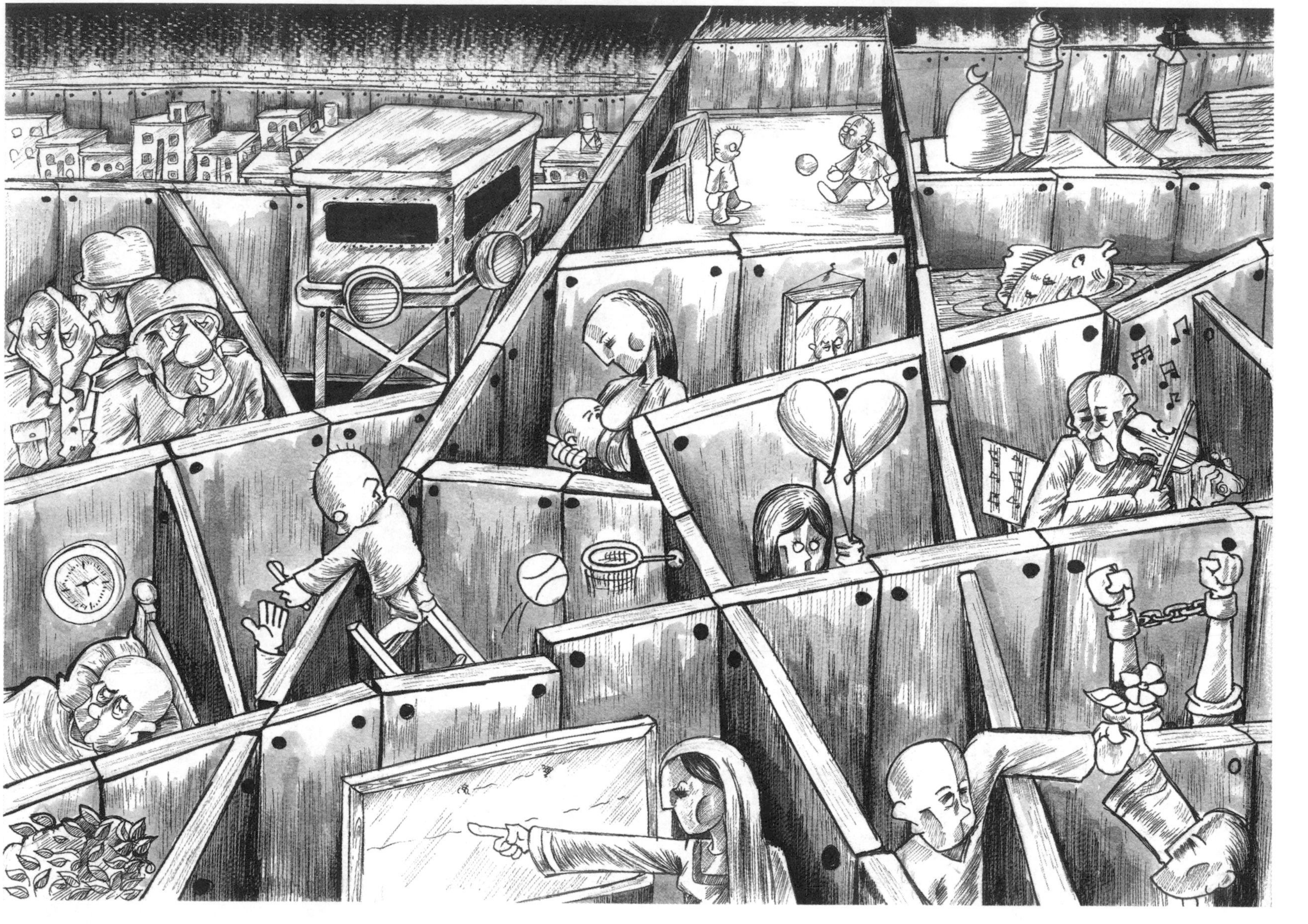

Lives interrupted.

Resilience.

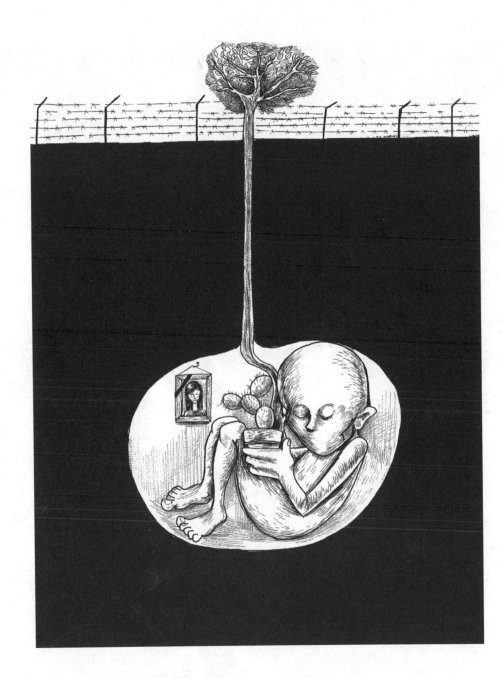

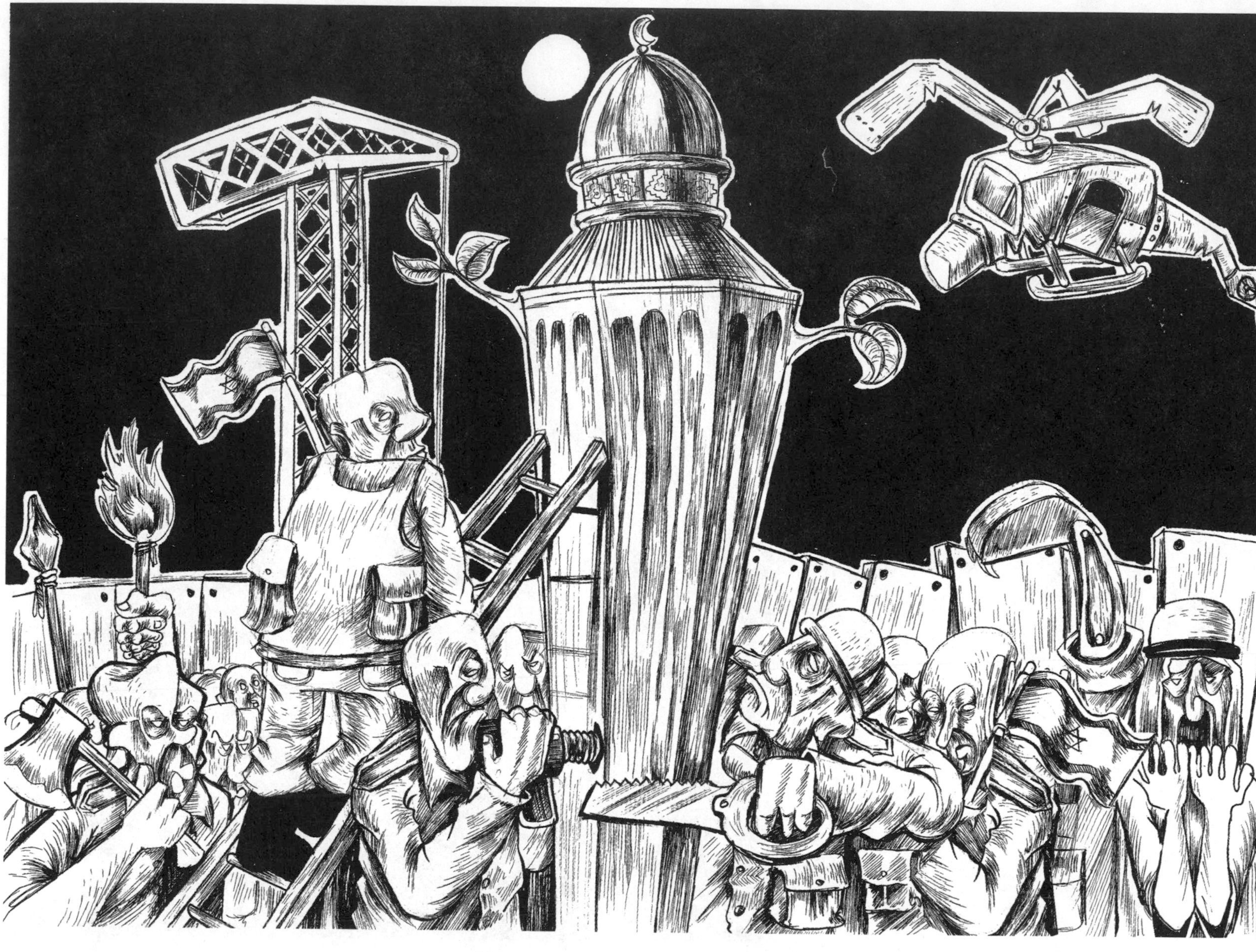

Jerusalem, the Holy Land.

Protect your trees as though
your lives depend on them.

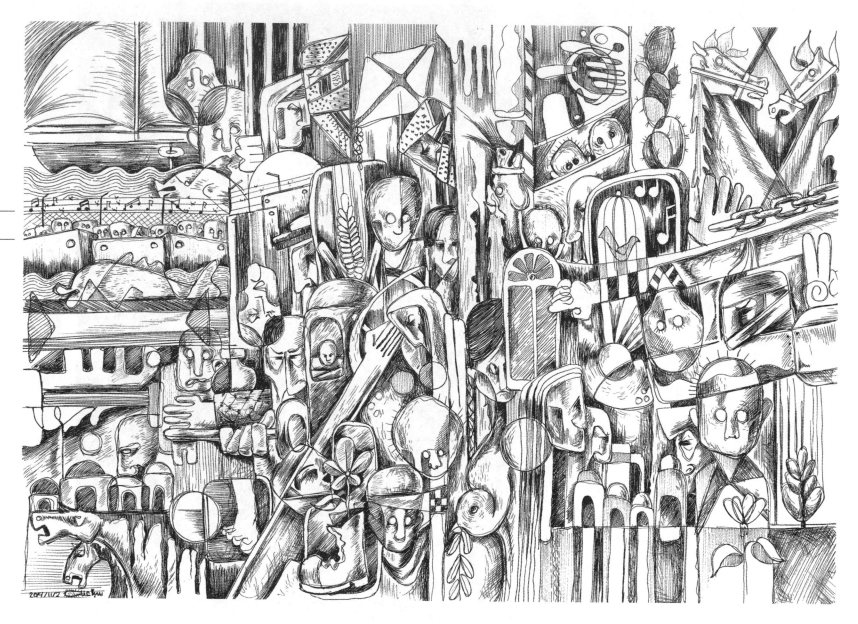

In the end, it's the "us" (and not me or you) that matters.

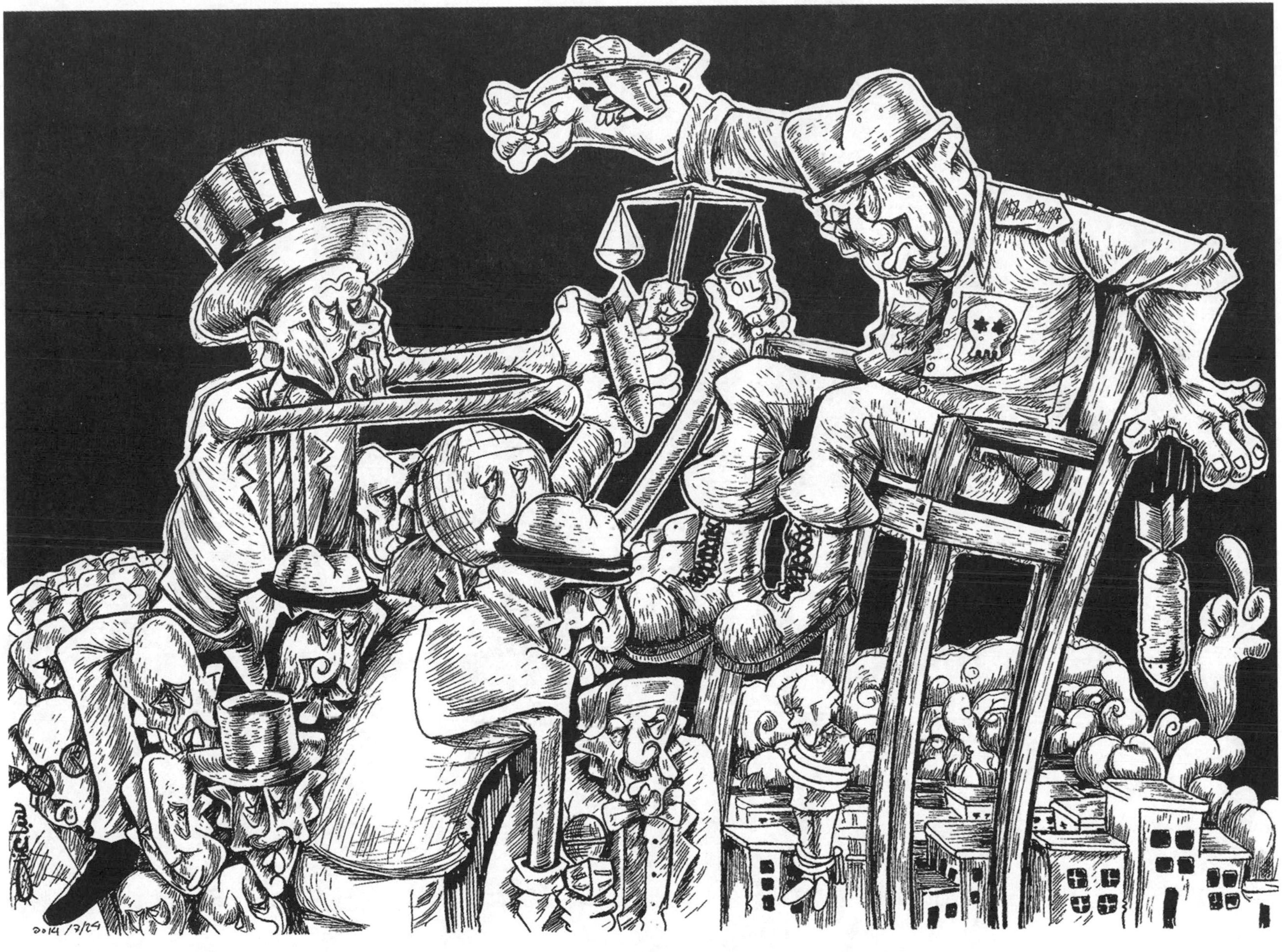
OIL
2014/7/24

Tyrants are created and collectively sustained.

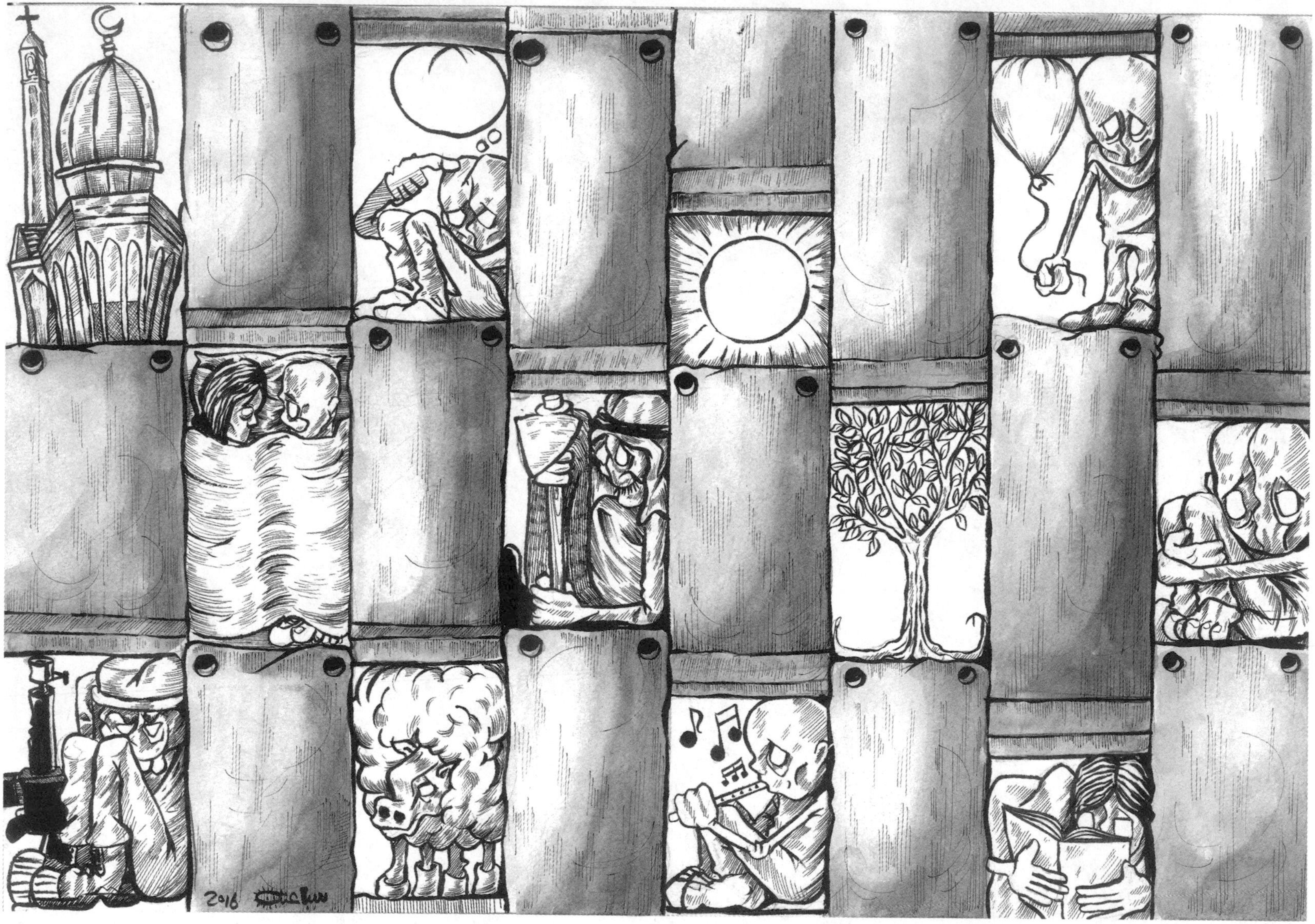
2016

The wall besieges everything.

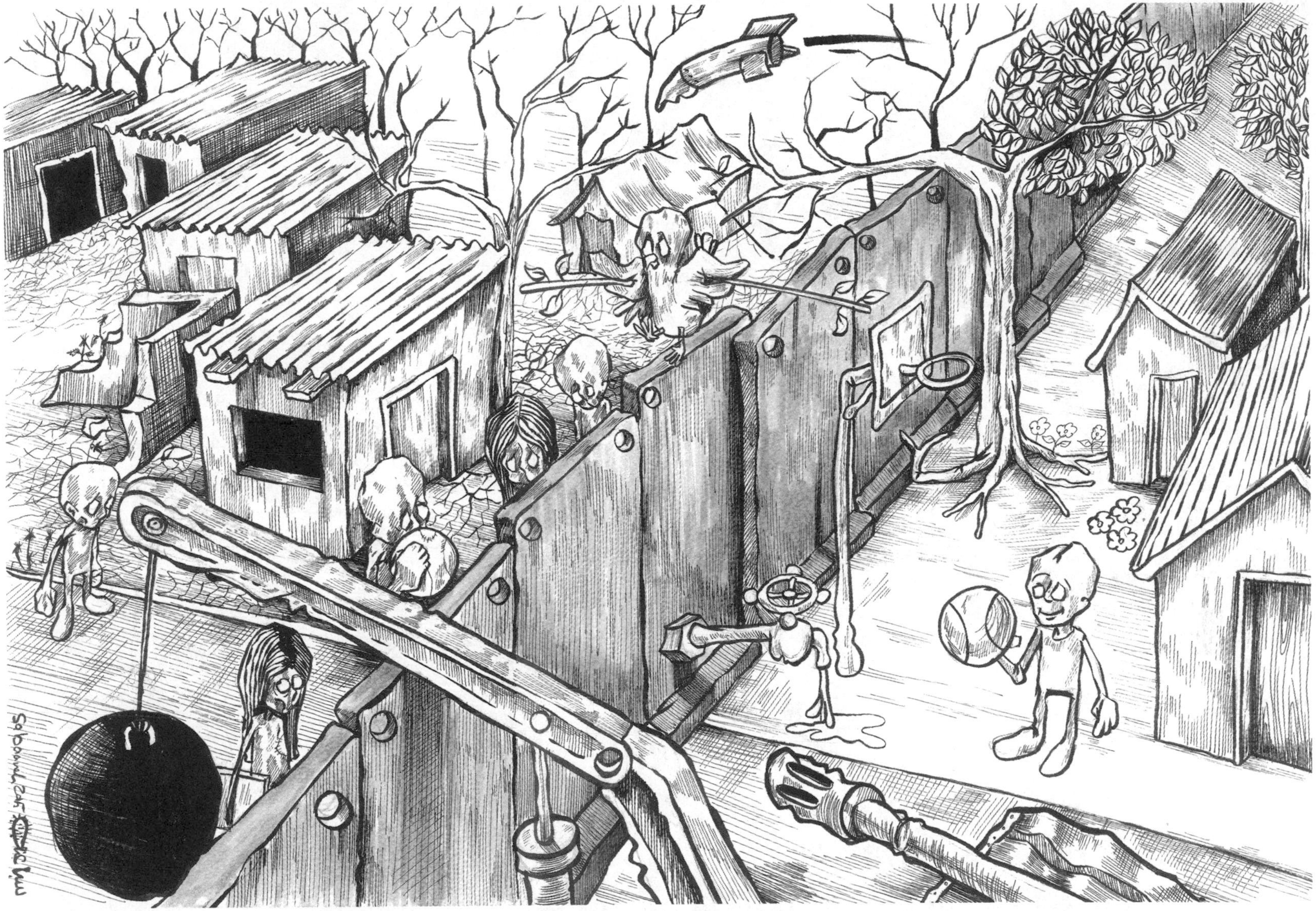

Keeping out the have-nots.

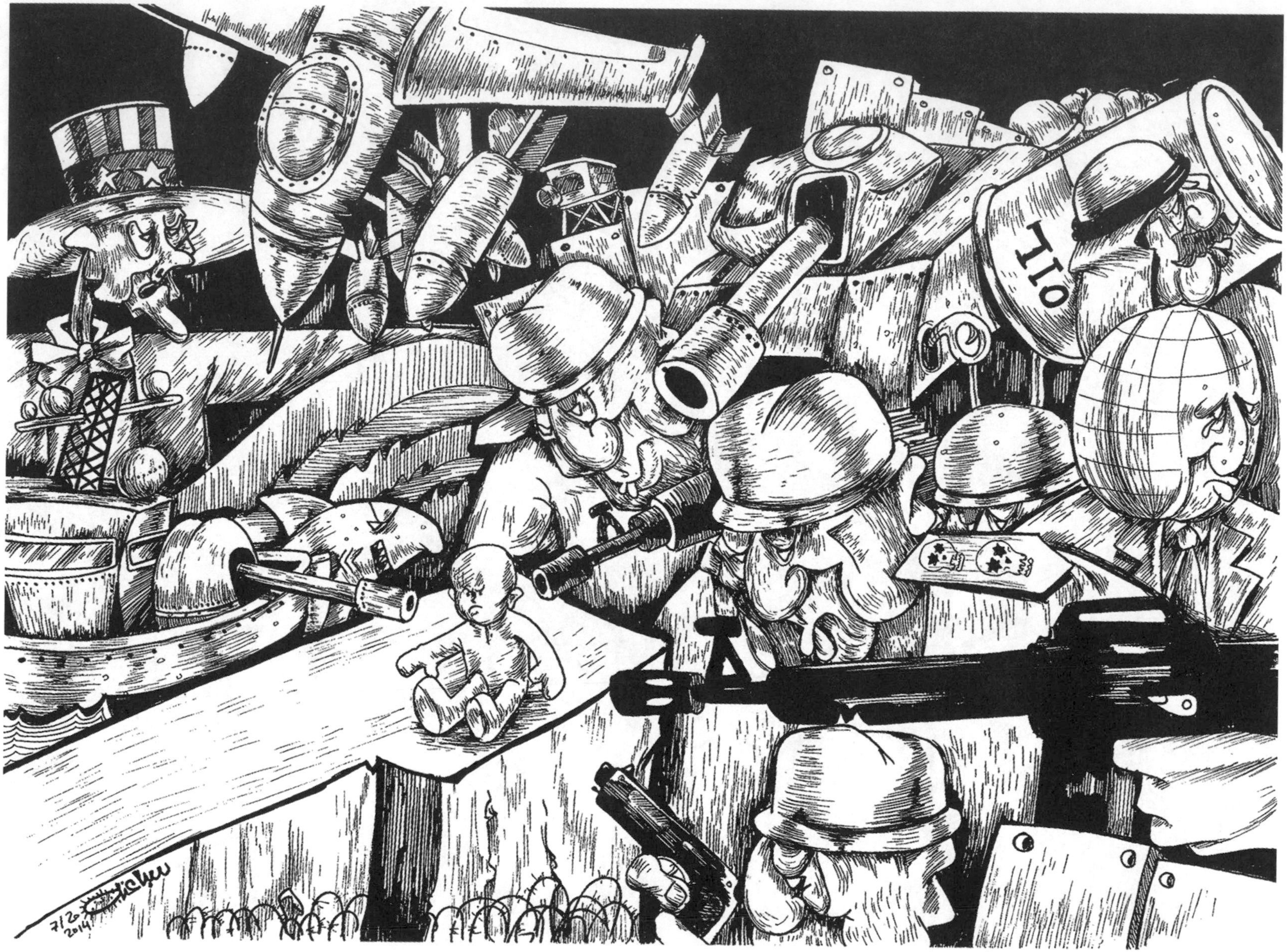
OIL

Confronting an existential threat.

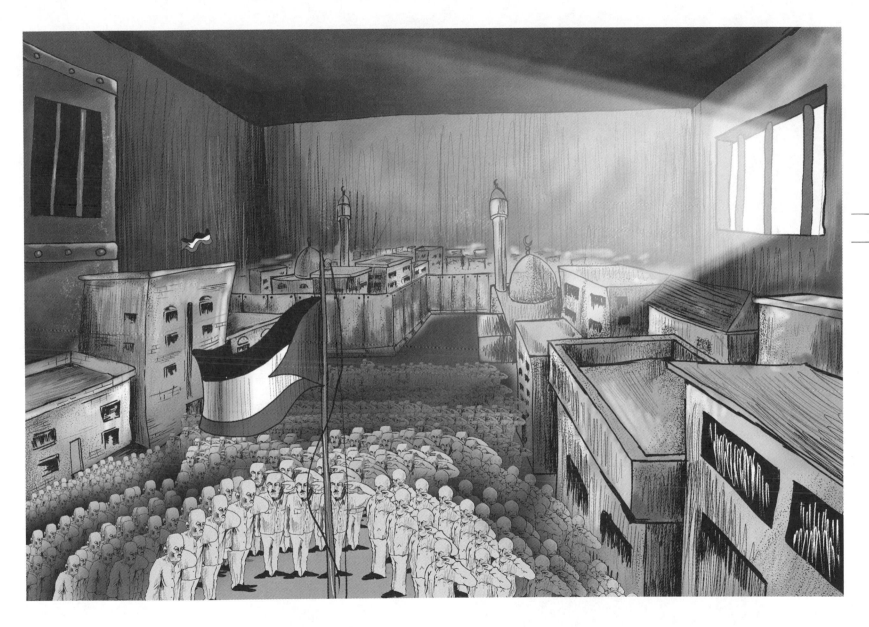

Foreign occupation and national institutions of statehood coexist in confined spaces.

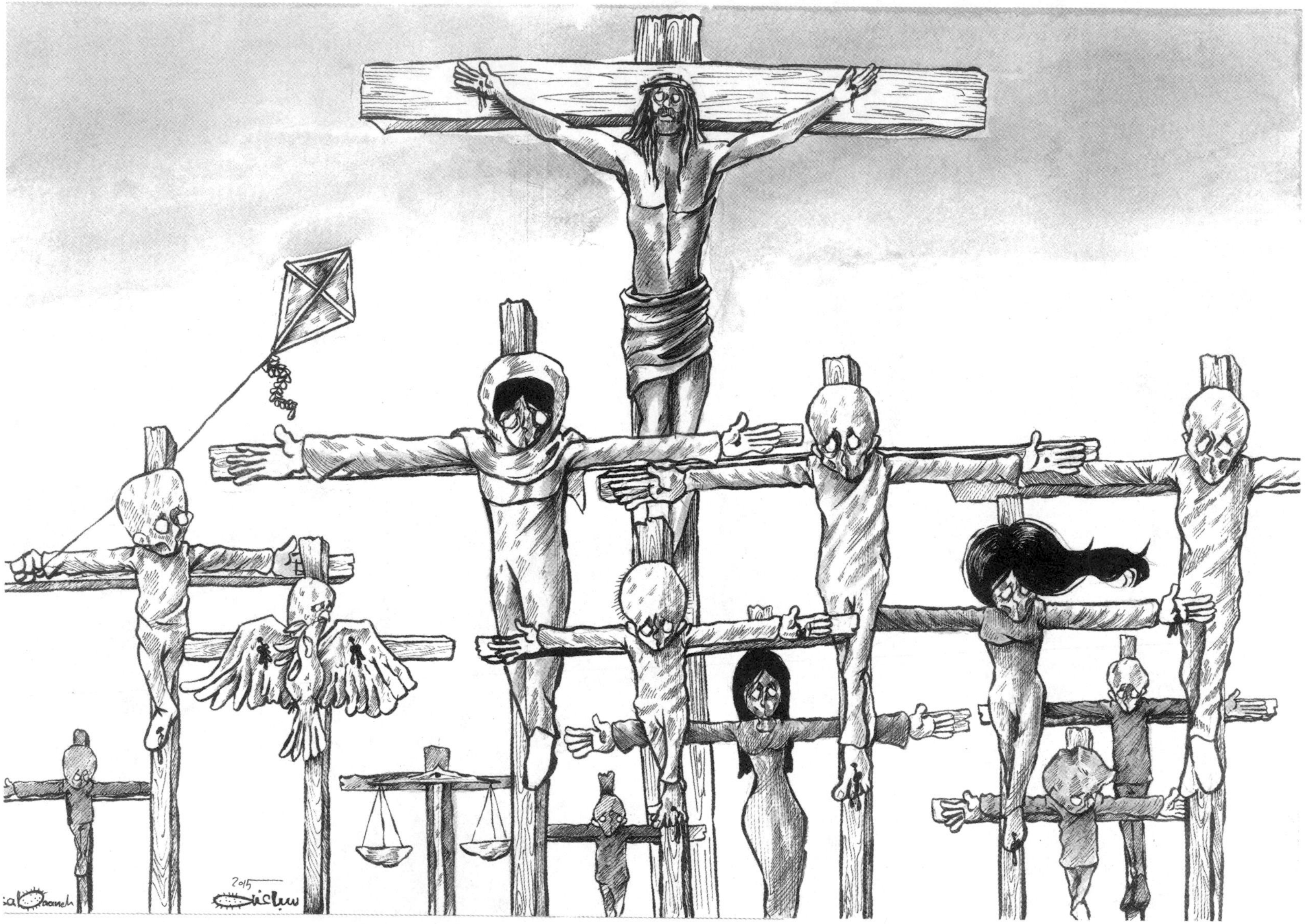

Golgotha today.

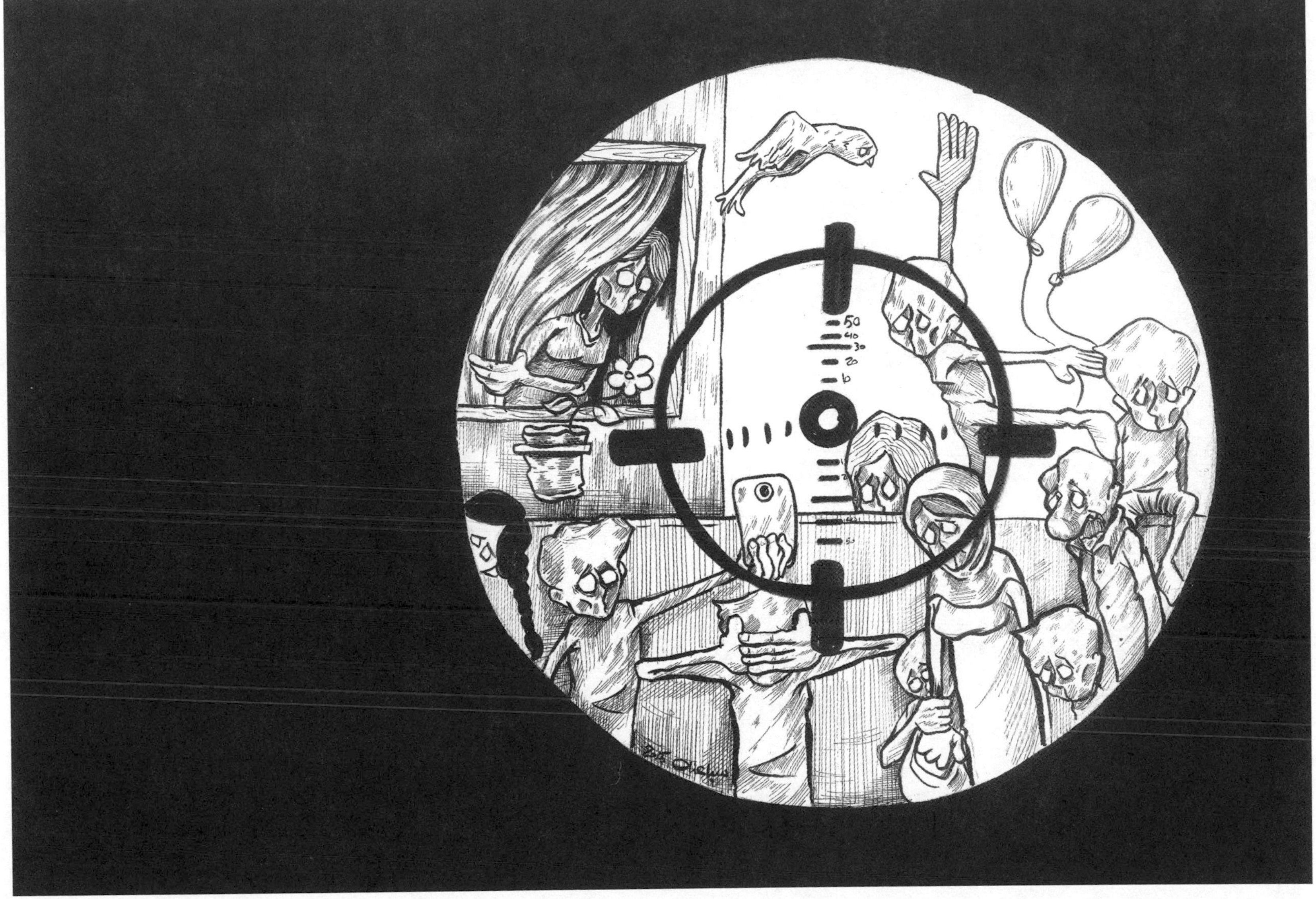

Target: civil society.

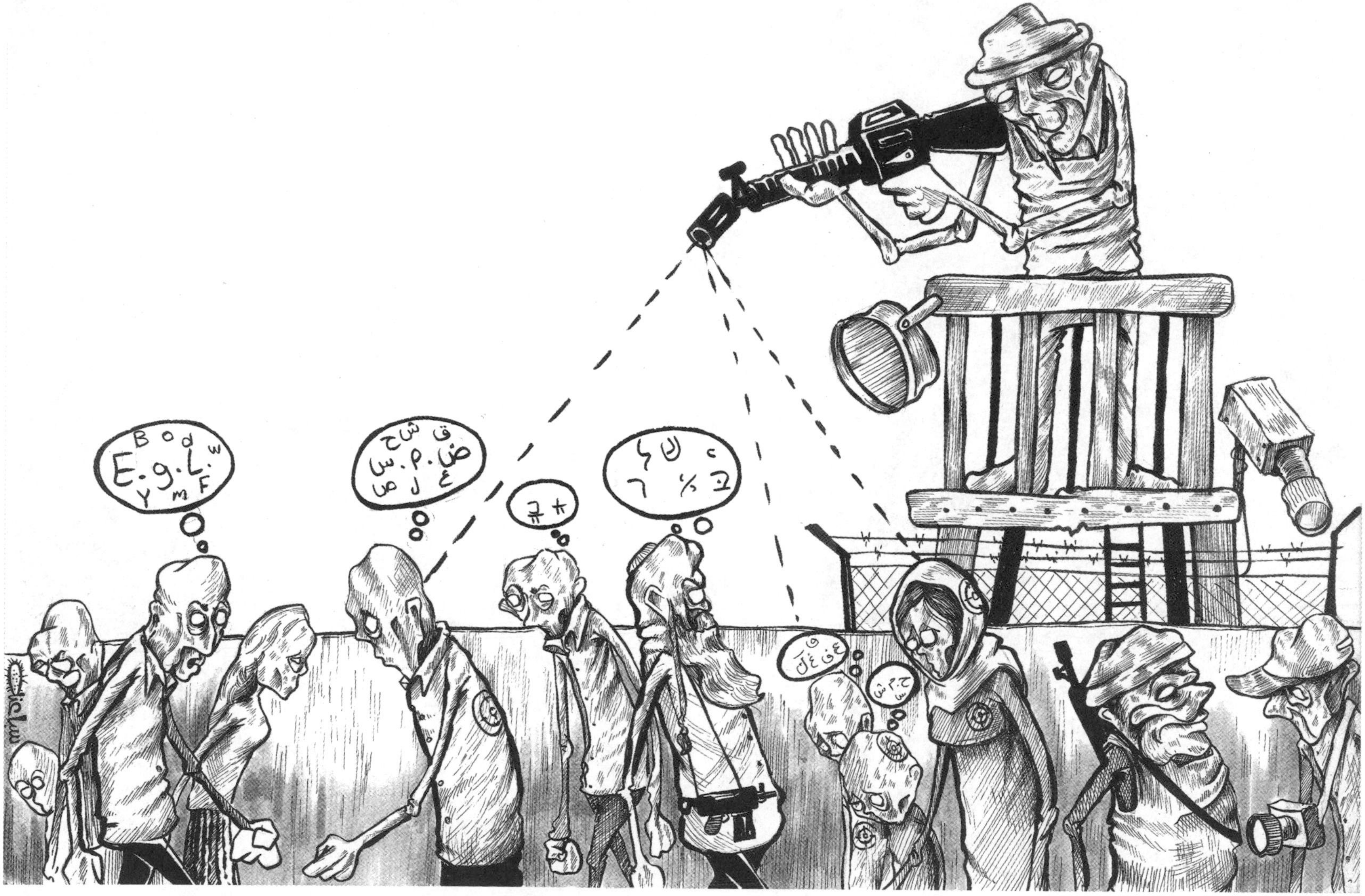

Corralling the natives.

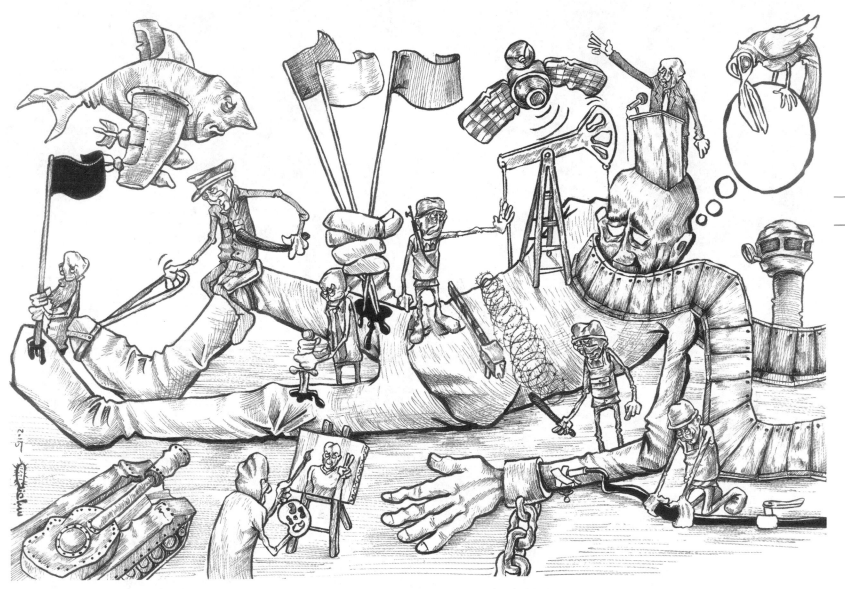

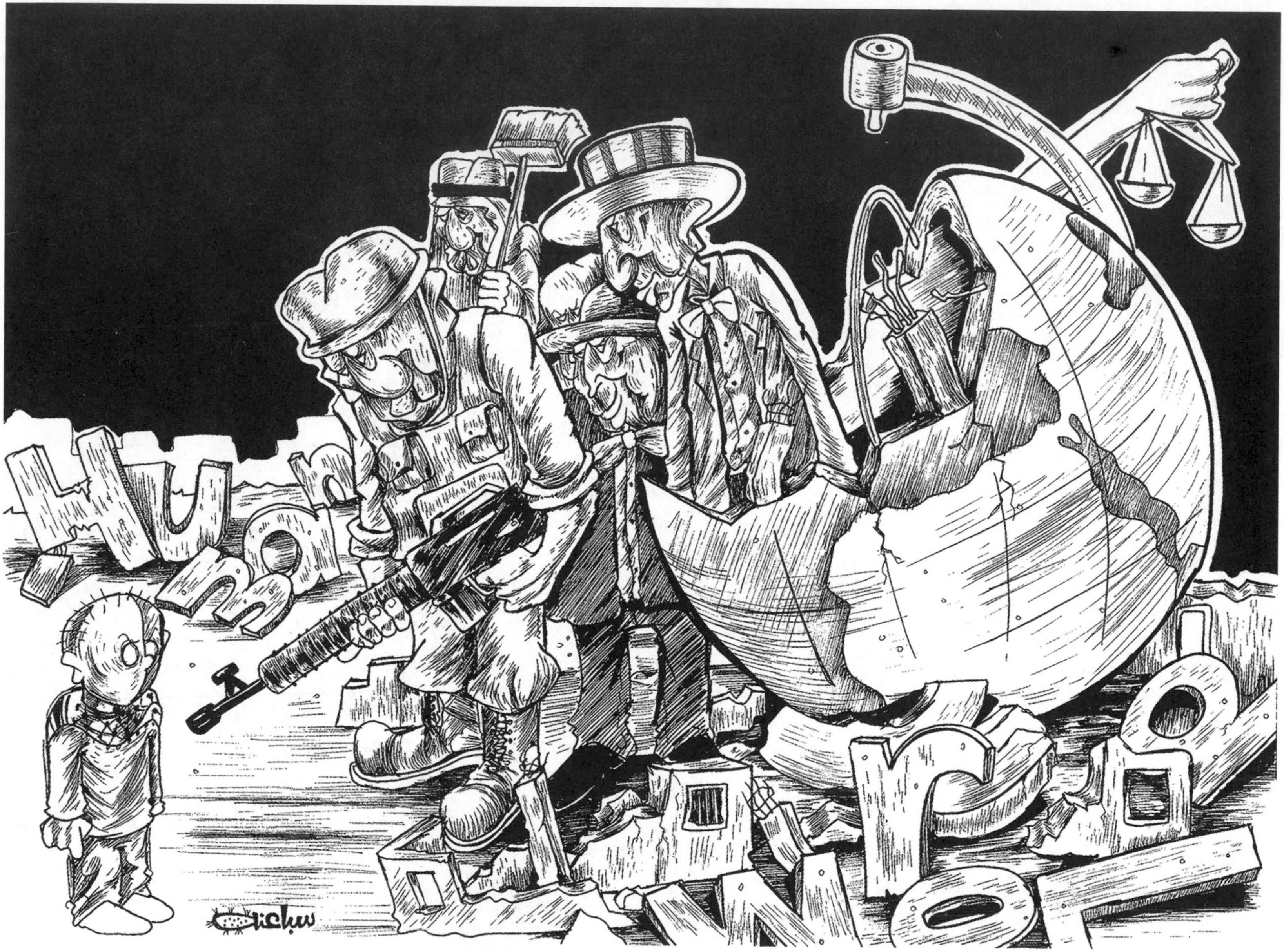

Identifying the real threat.

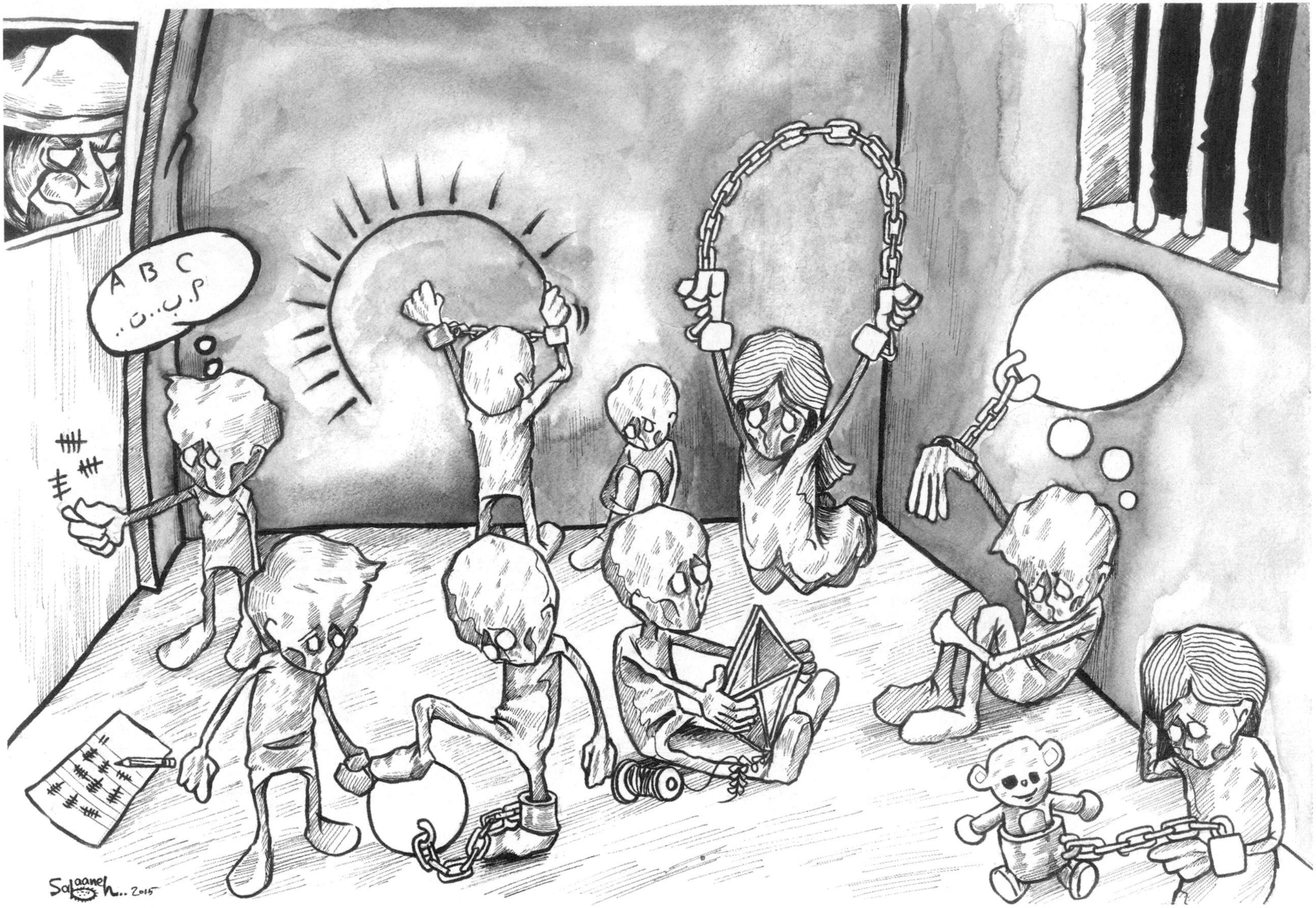
A B C

Children going about their business, even behind prison bars.

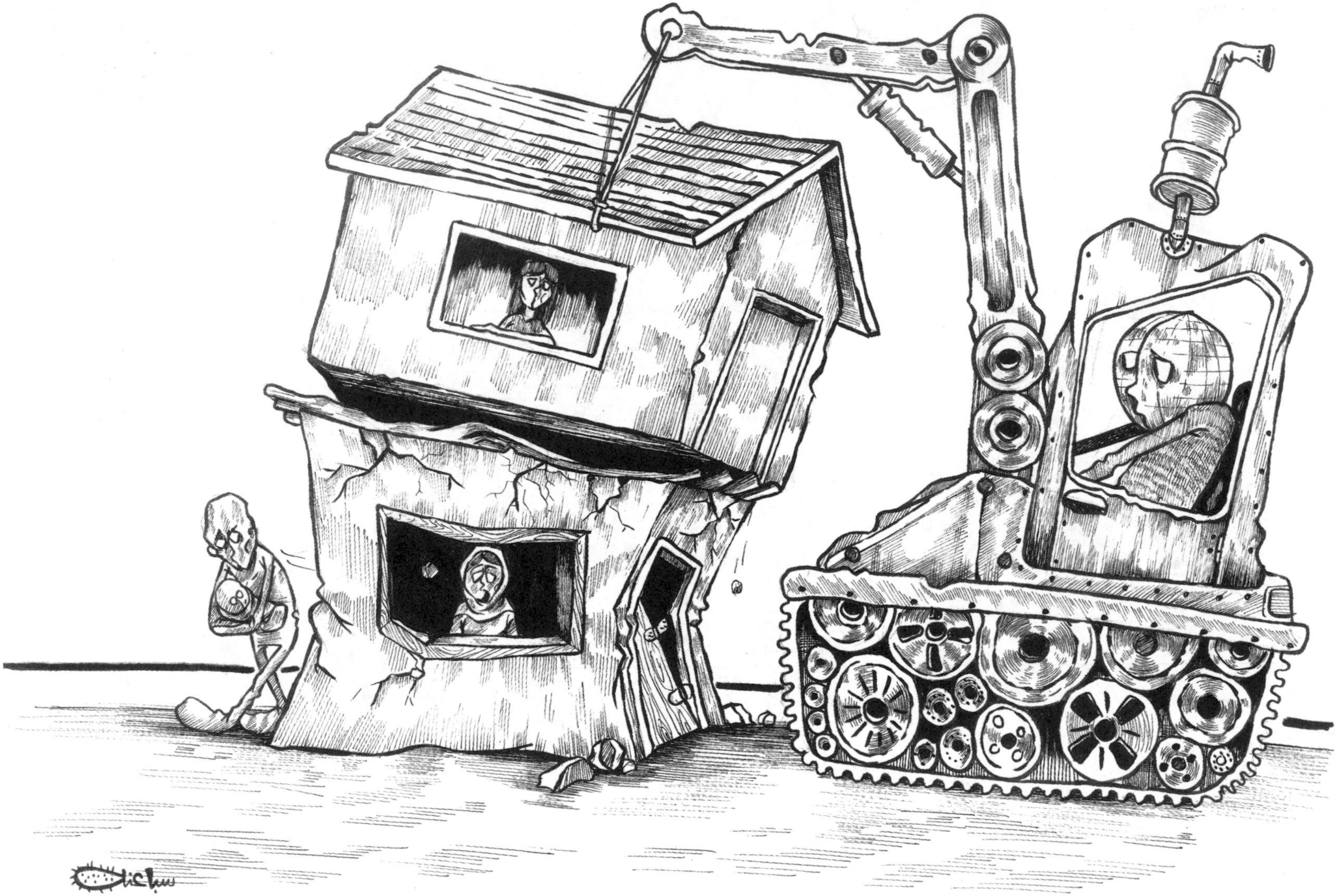

Replacing the indigenous population.

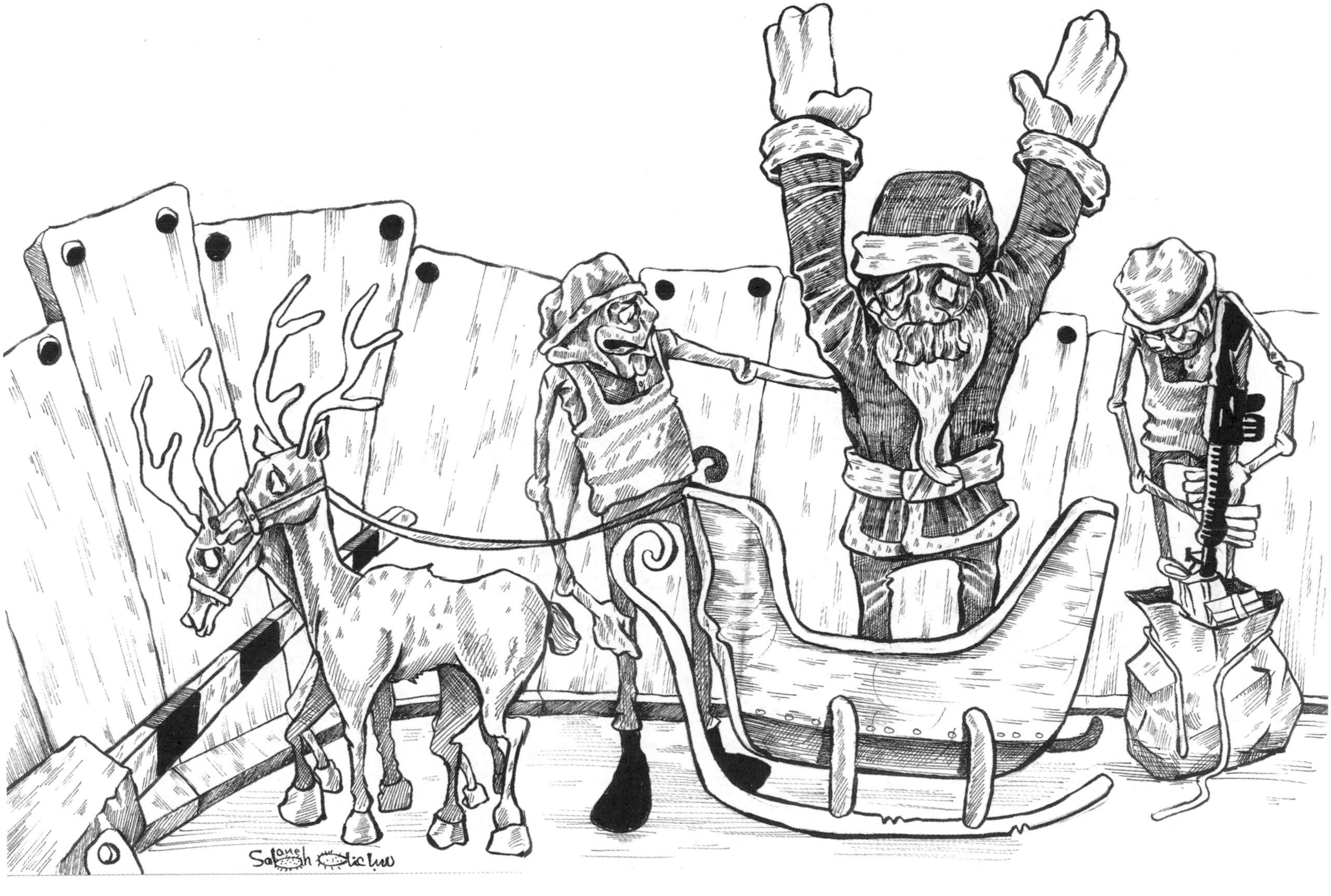

No exceptions.

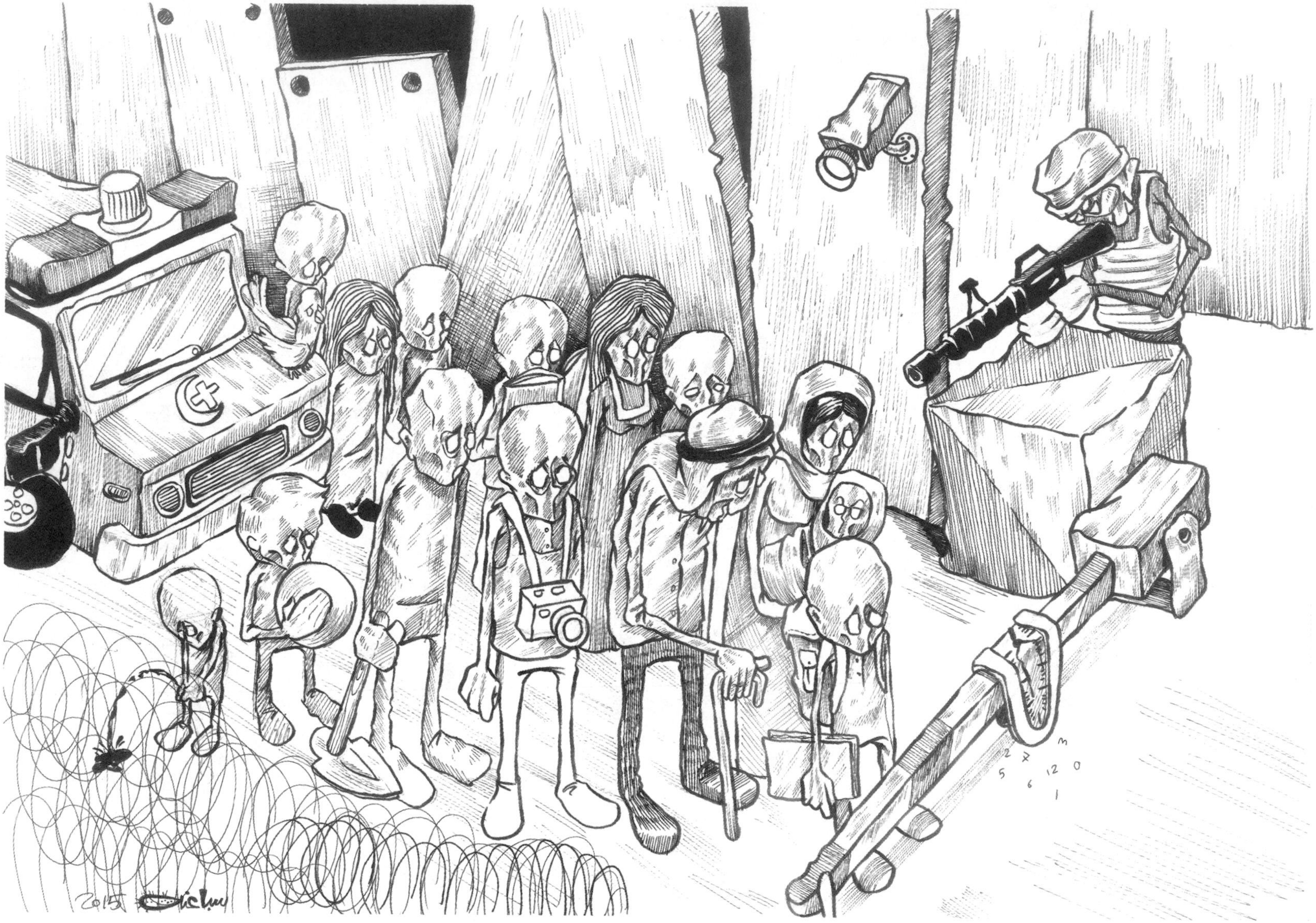

You aren't going anywhere.

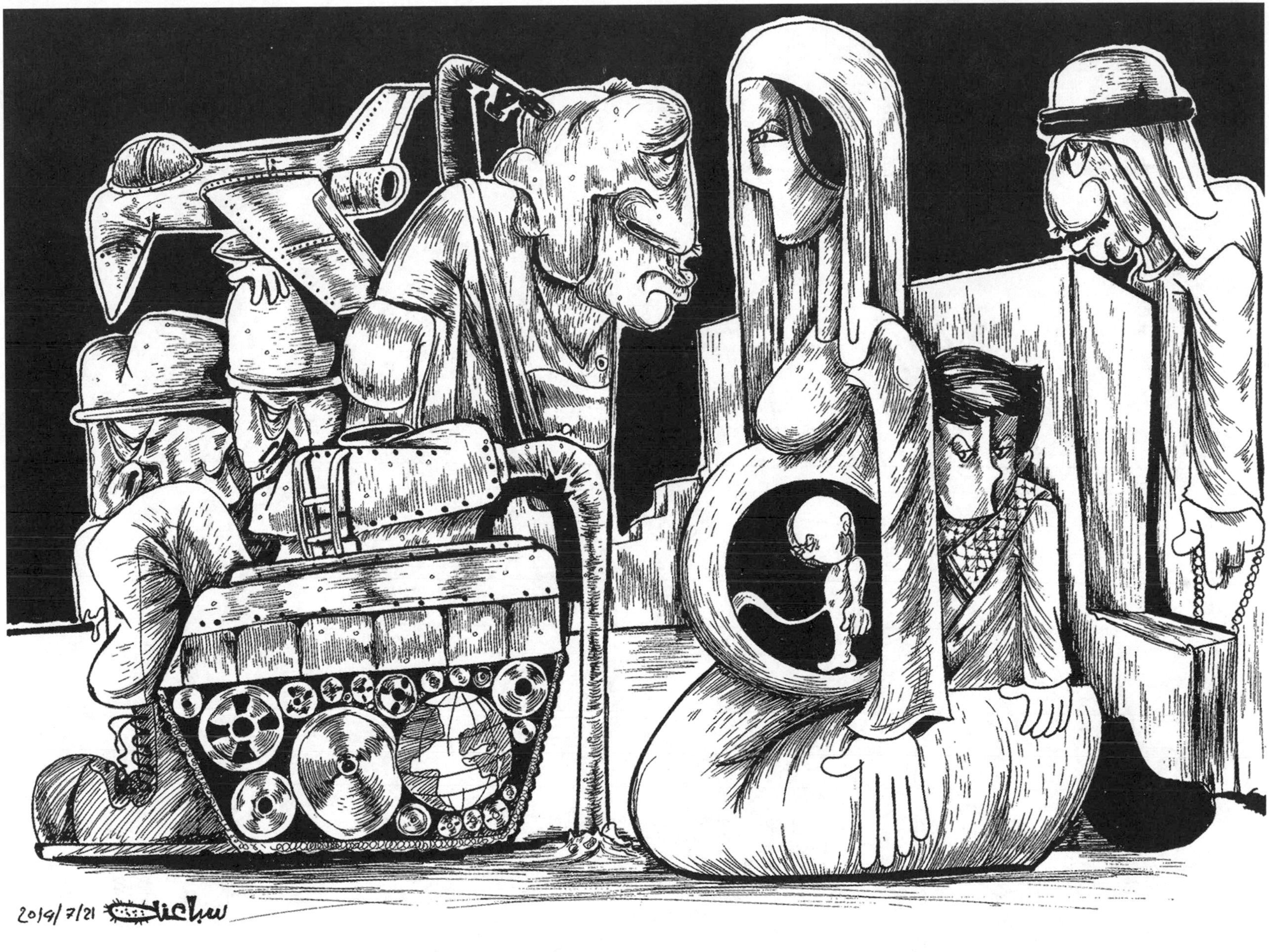
2019/7/21

Survival is the mother of all confrontations.

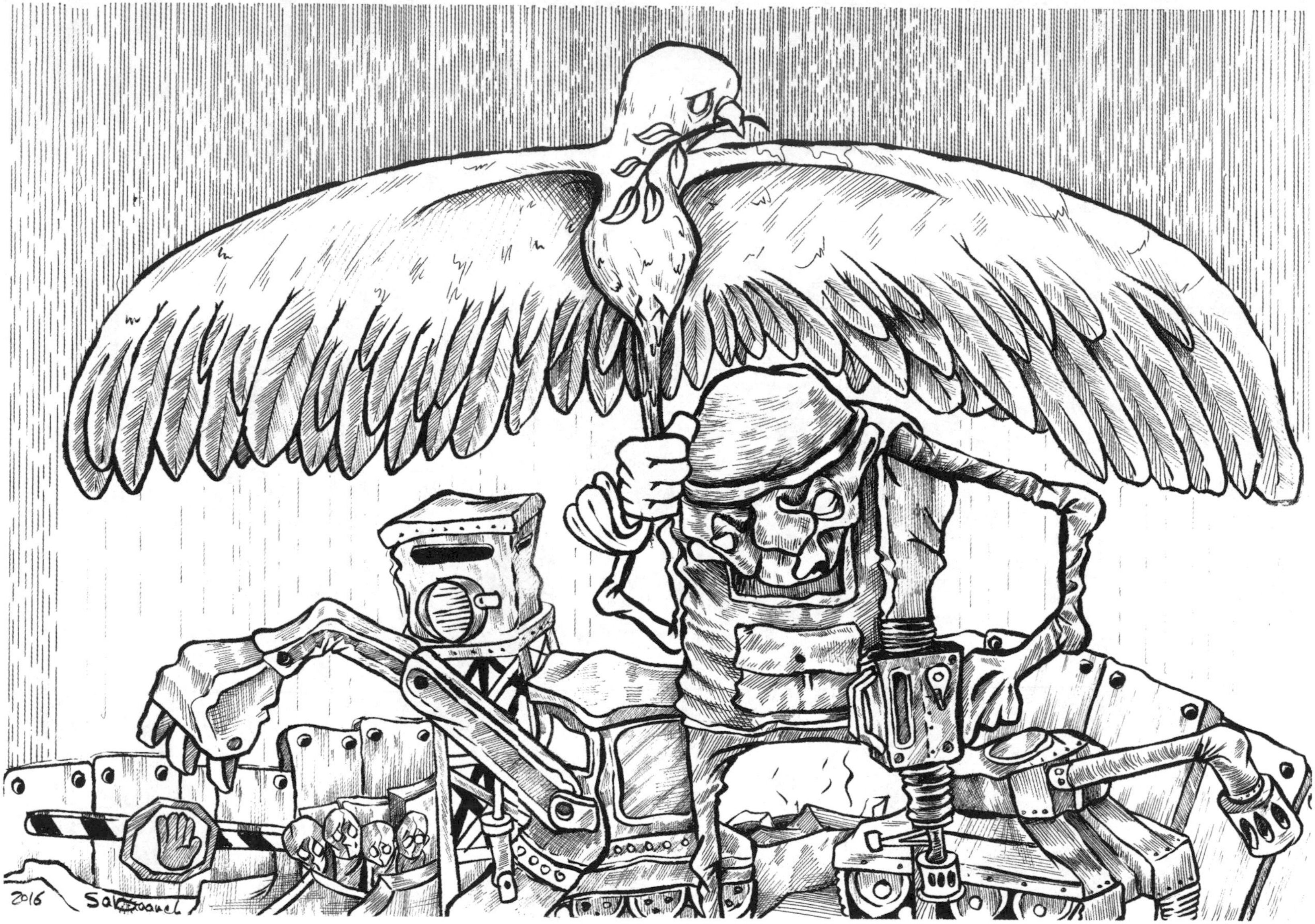
2016

Fig leafs come in all shapes and sizes.

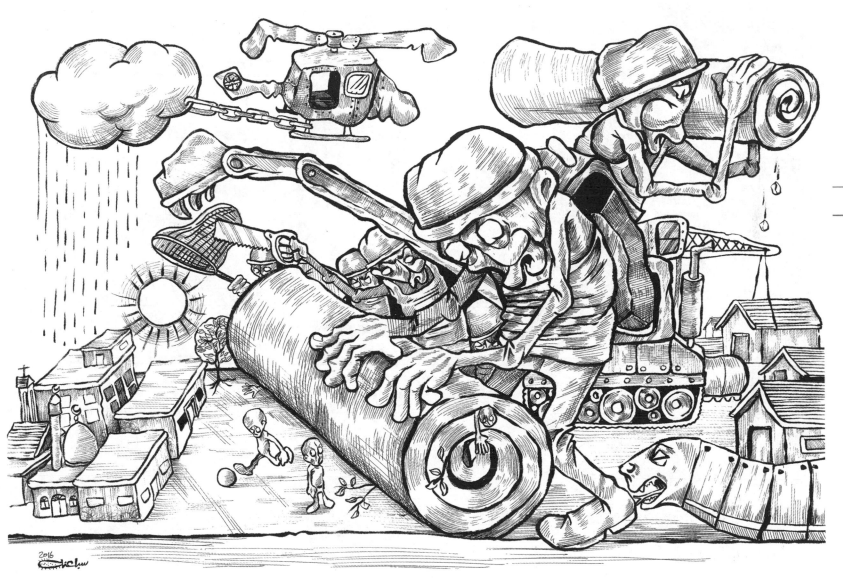

Invaders are oblivious to dreams.

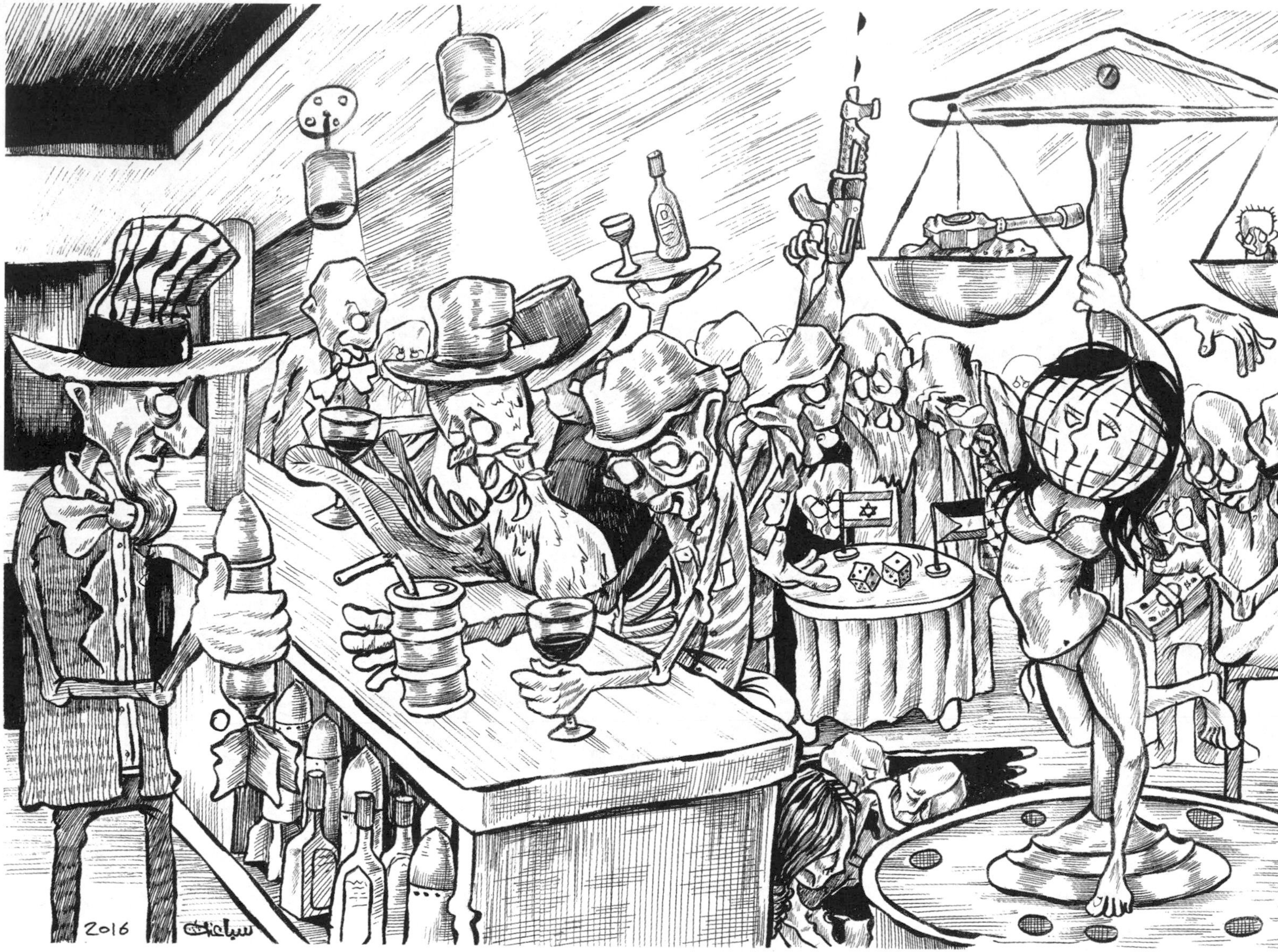
2016

Parties to the "peace process" hit the bar.

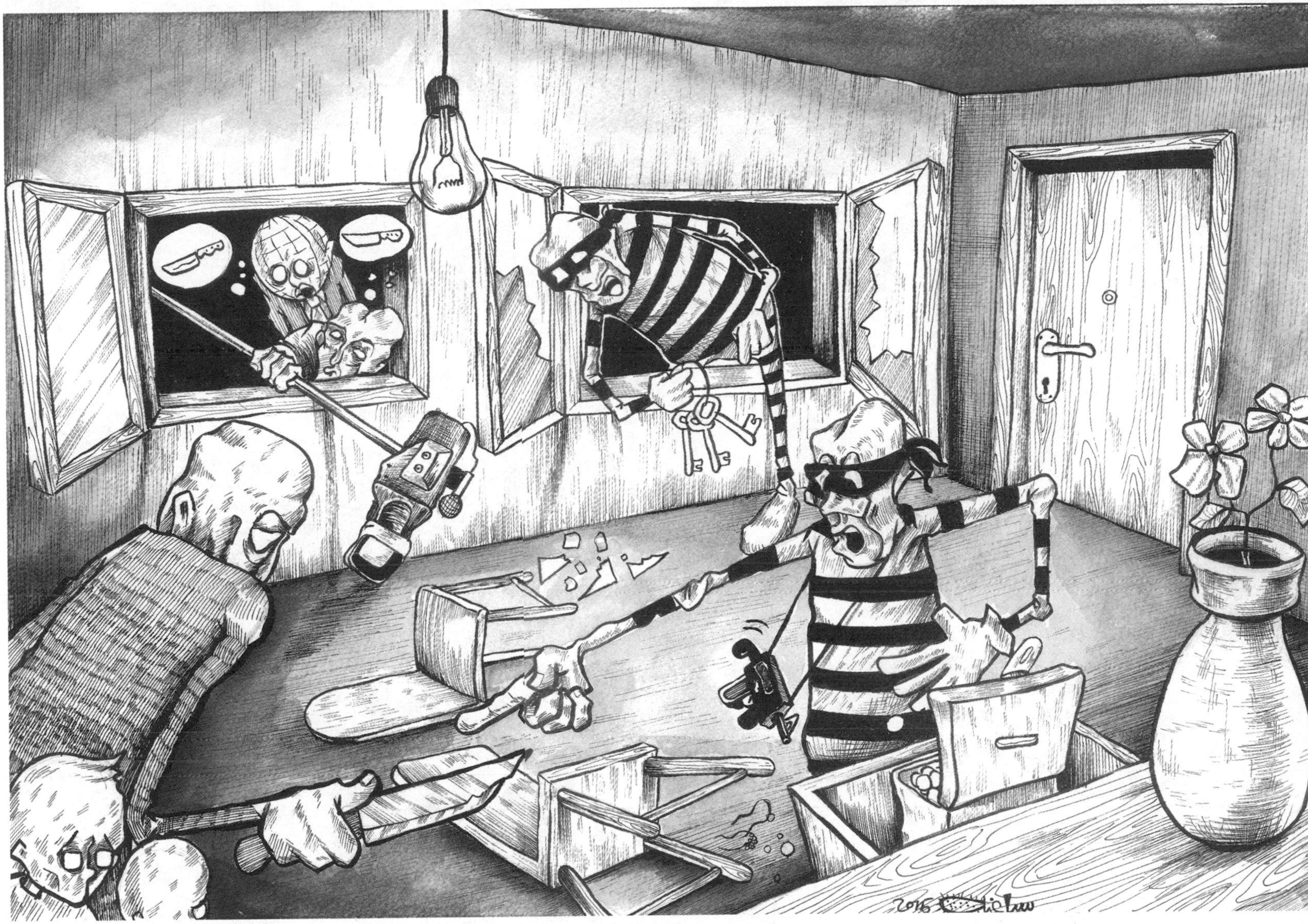

When the media appear, thieves become victims.

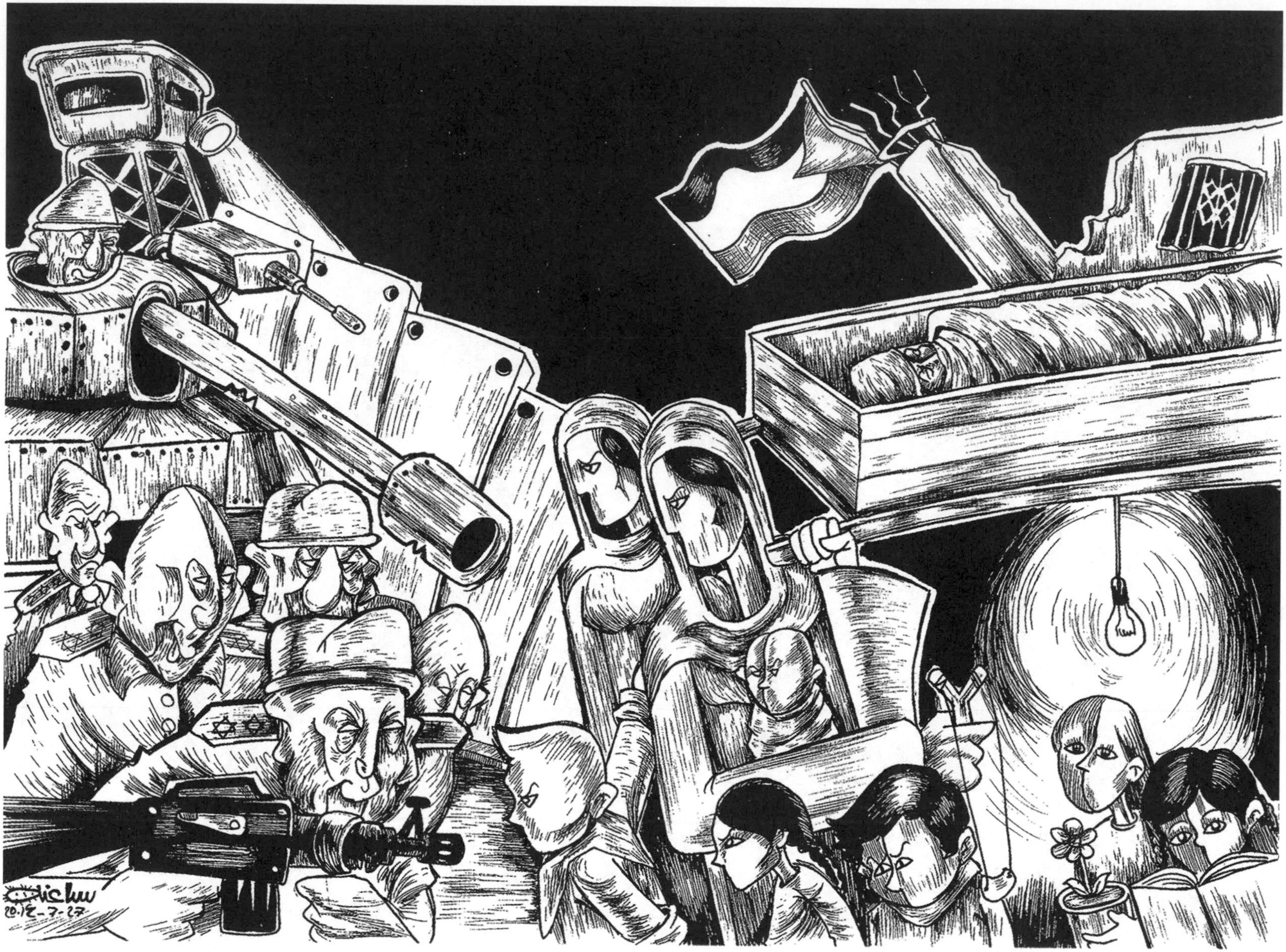

No peace for the dead either.

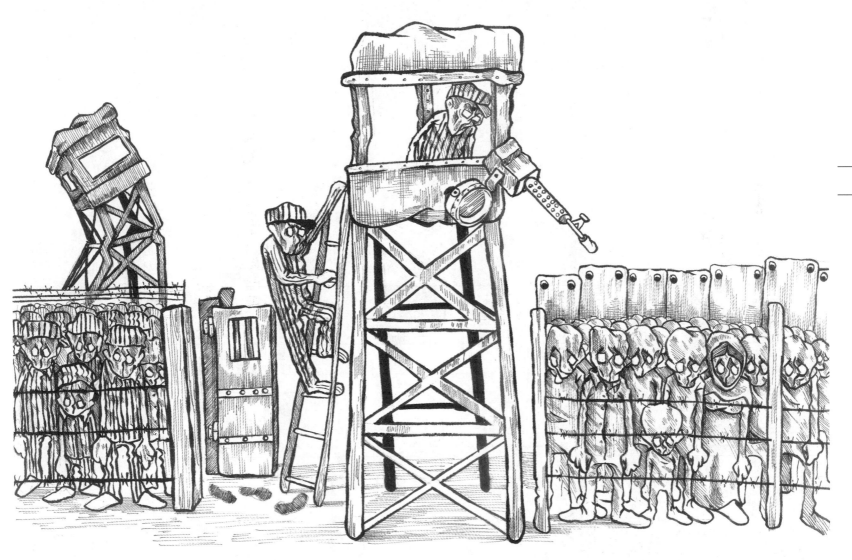

Metamorphosis.

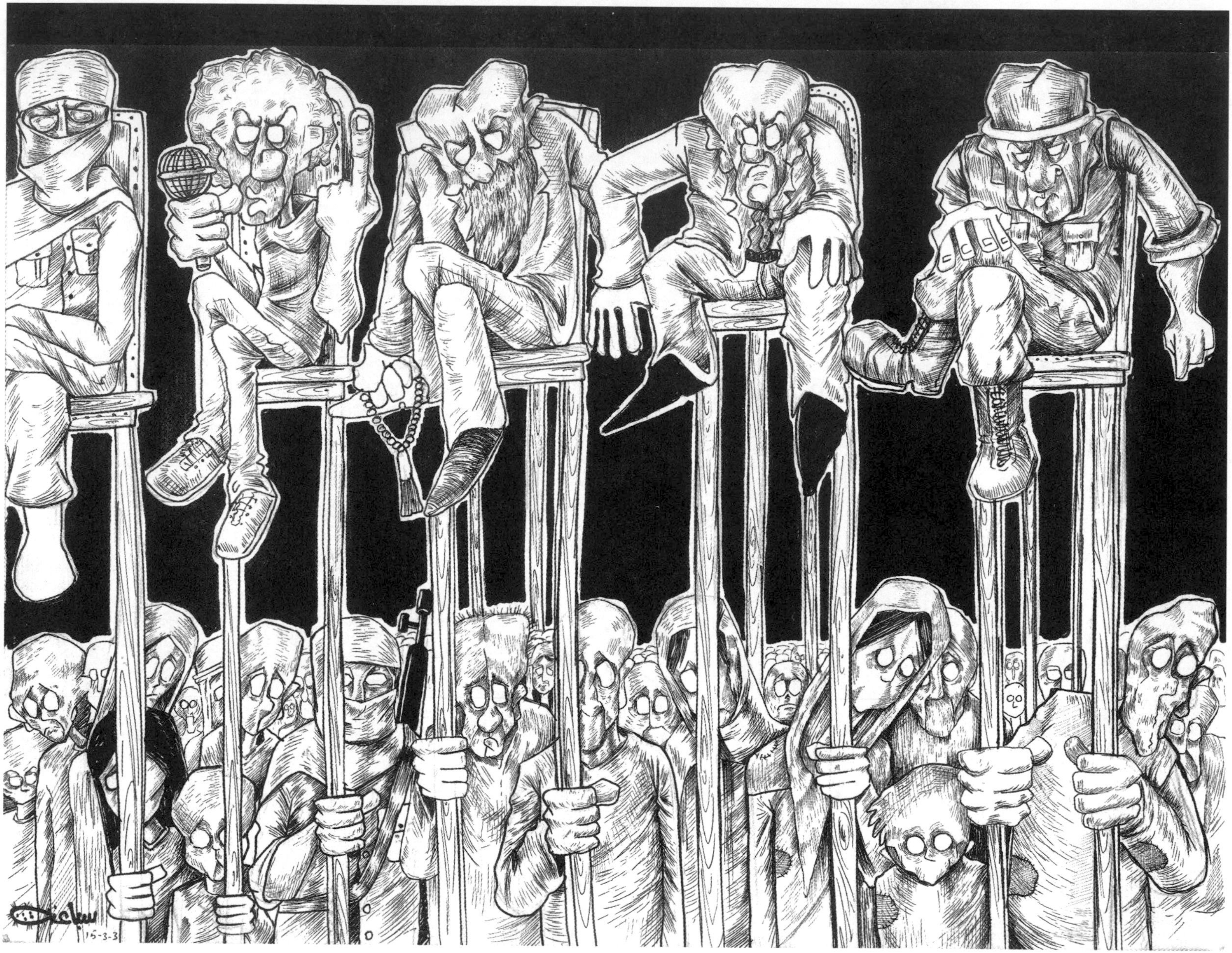

We create all types of oppressors.

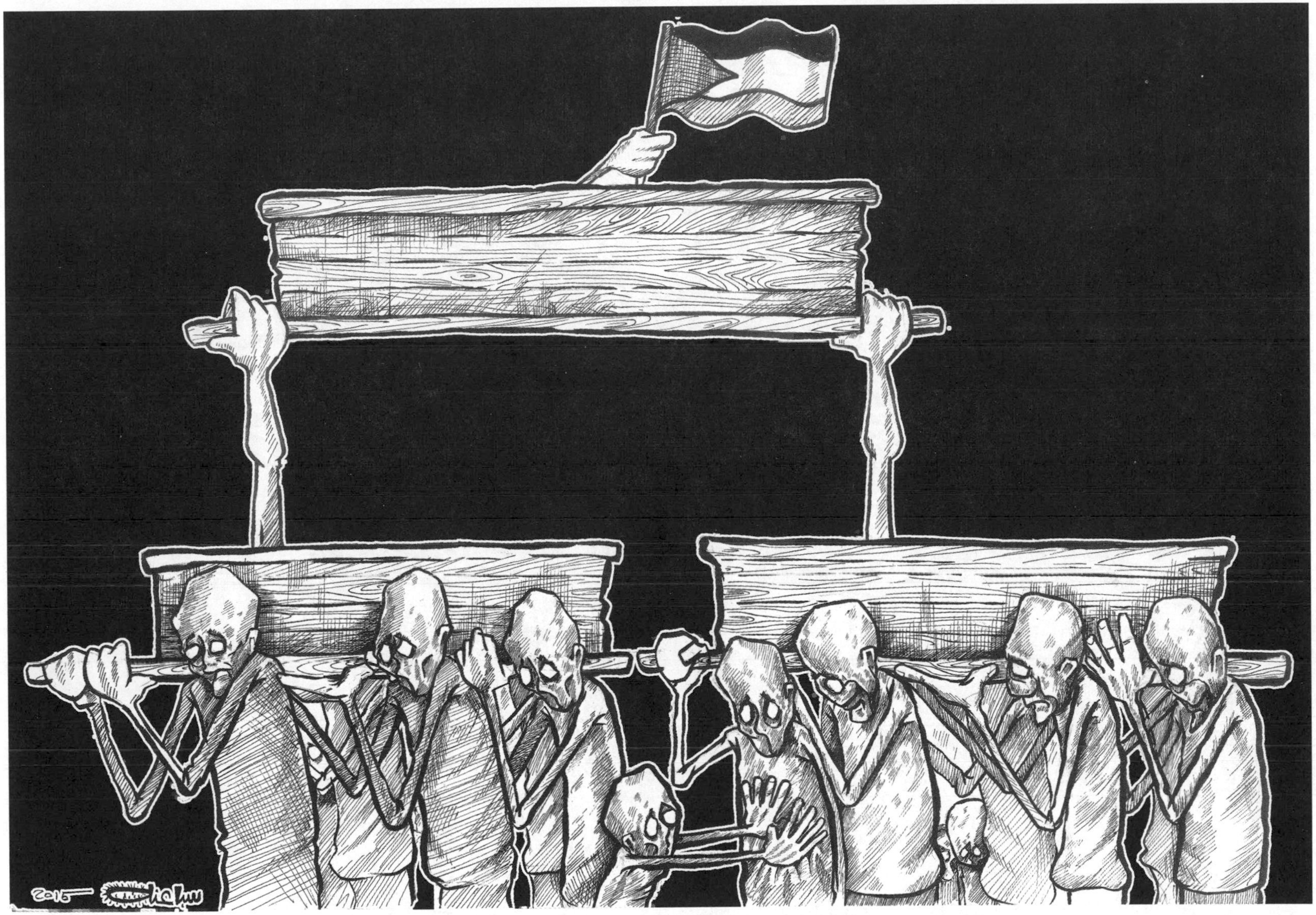

We live and die for a dream.

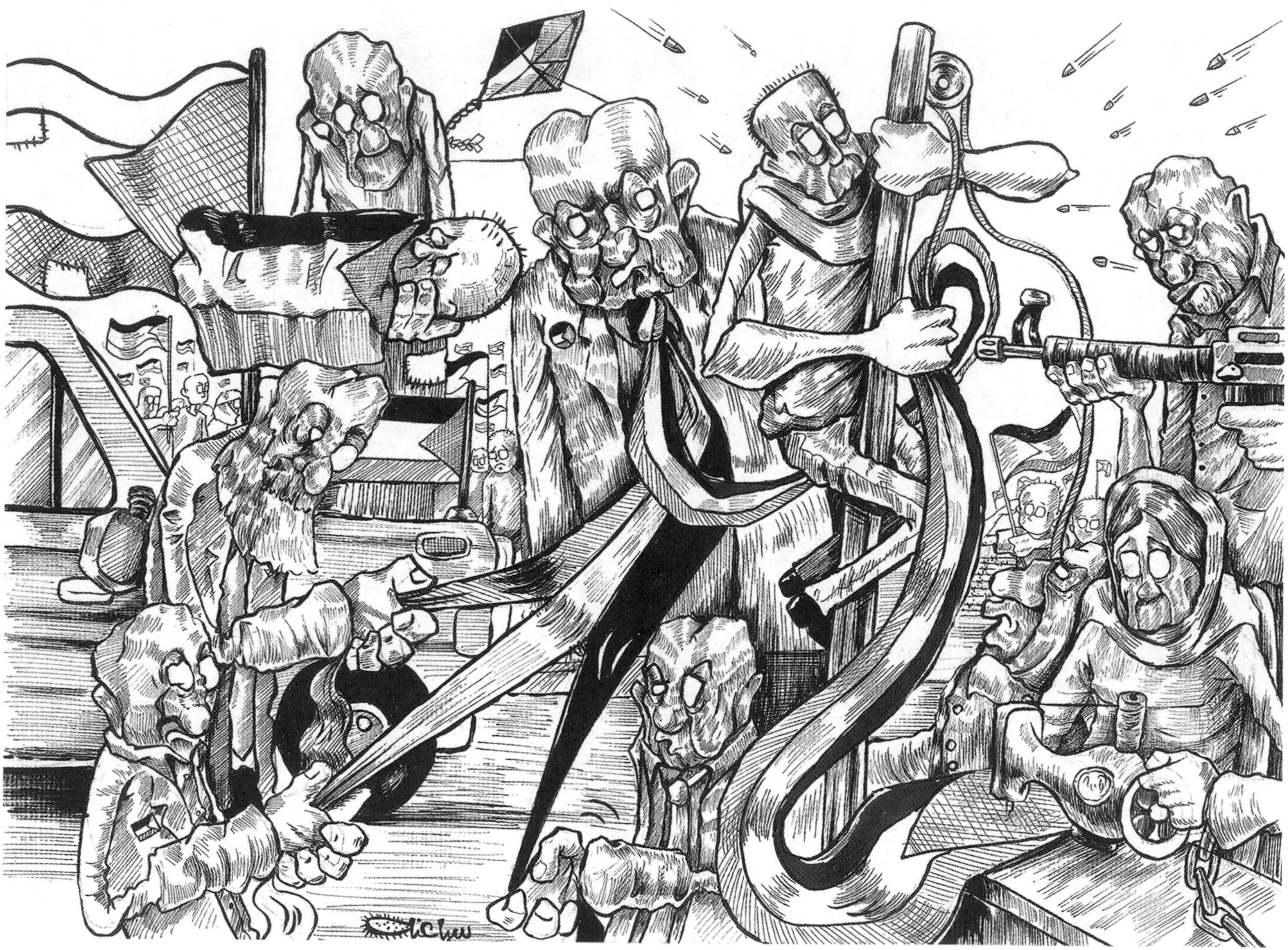

There was a time when raising the flag was an act of defiance.

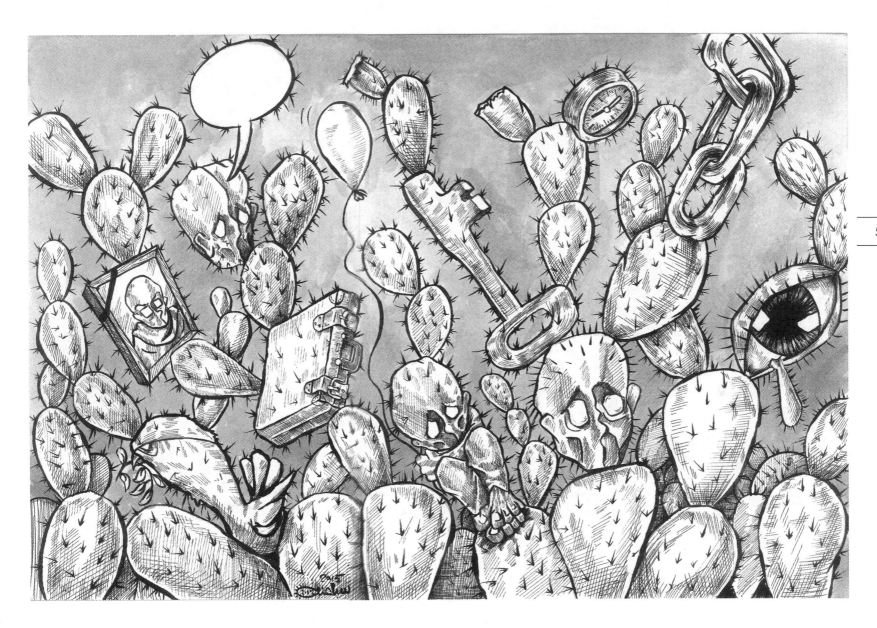

Like cactus, we are tough and patient.

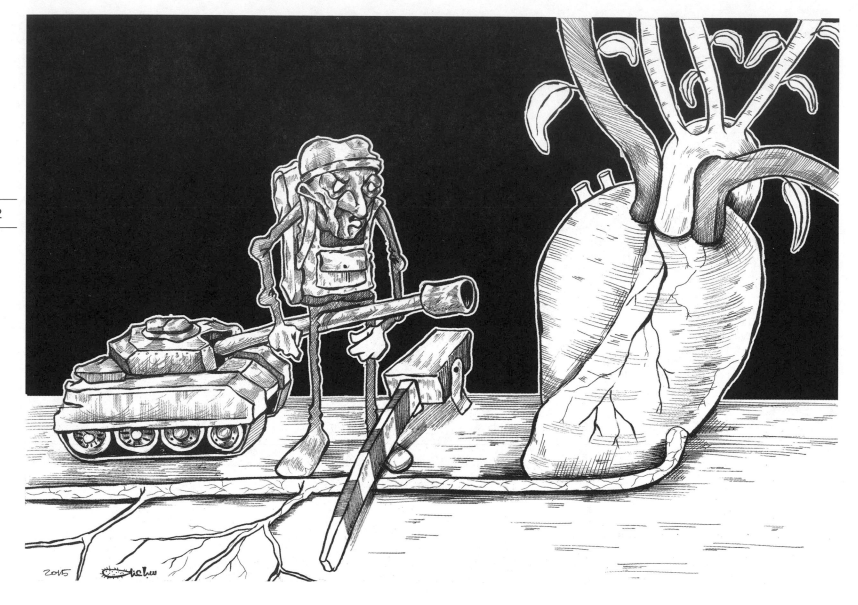

Your firepower doesn't scare me.

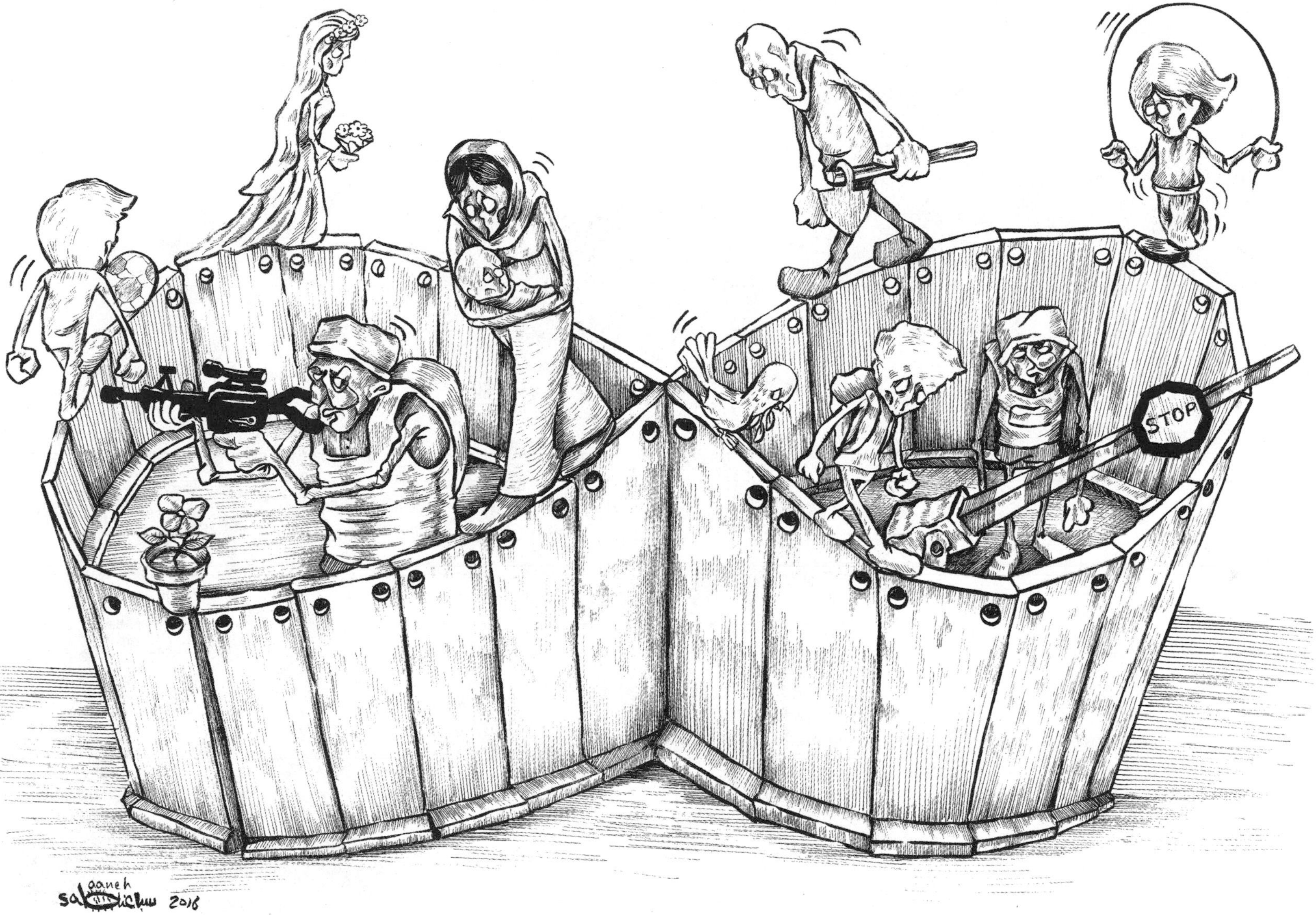
STOP

How much longer?

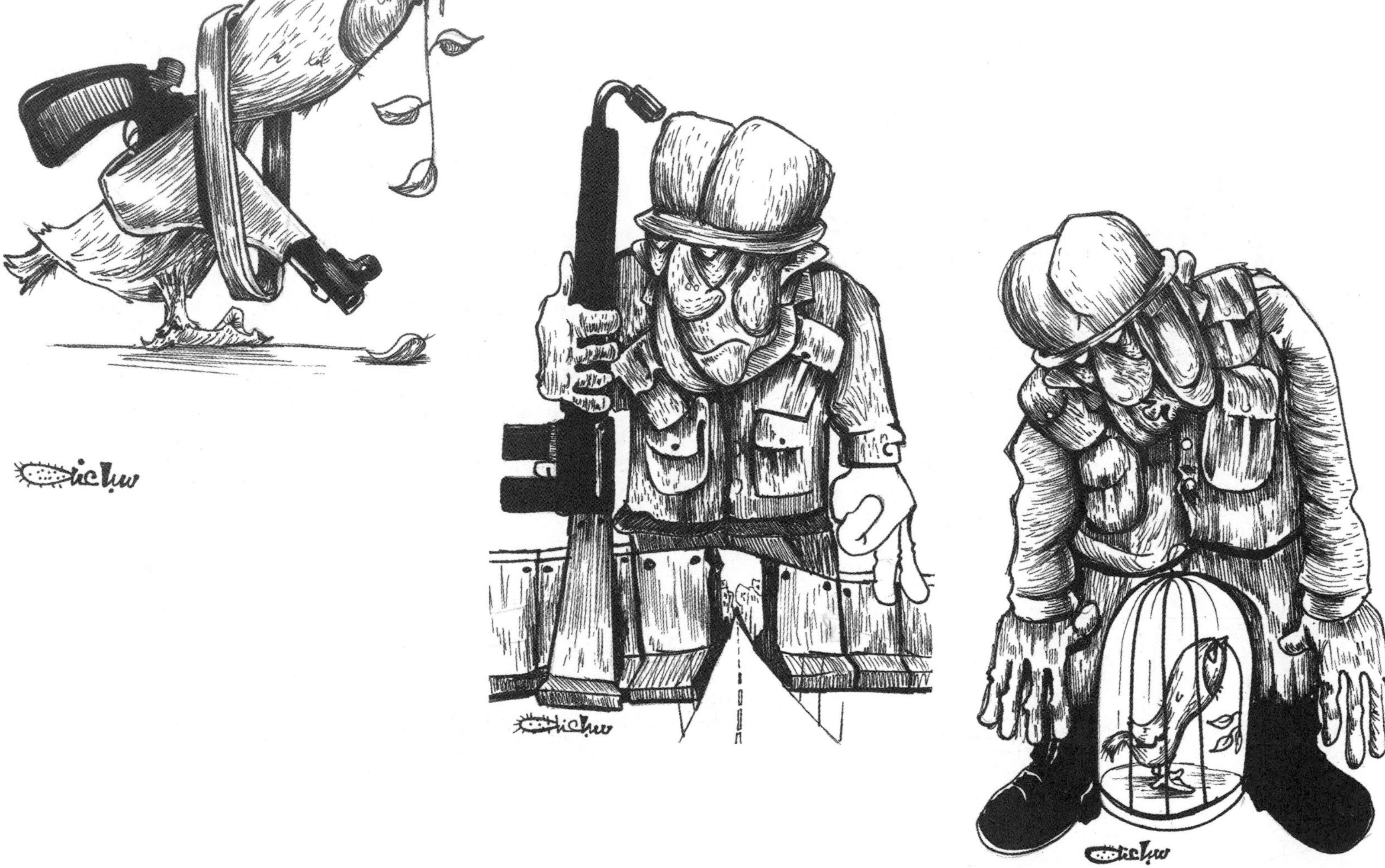

Their soldiers.

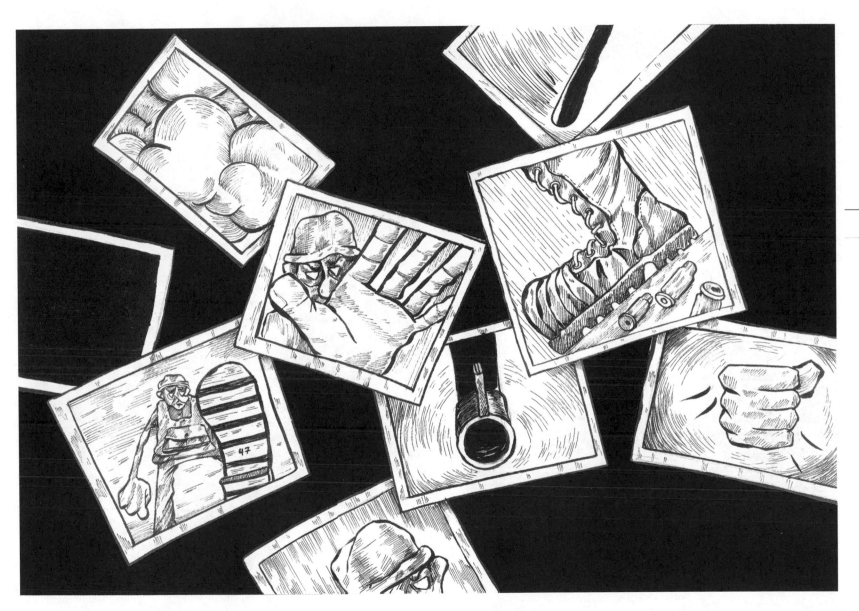

Which is the journalist's last photo?

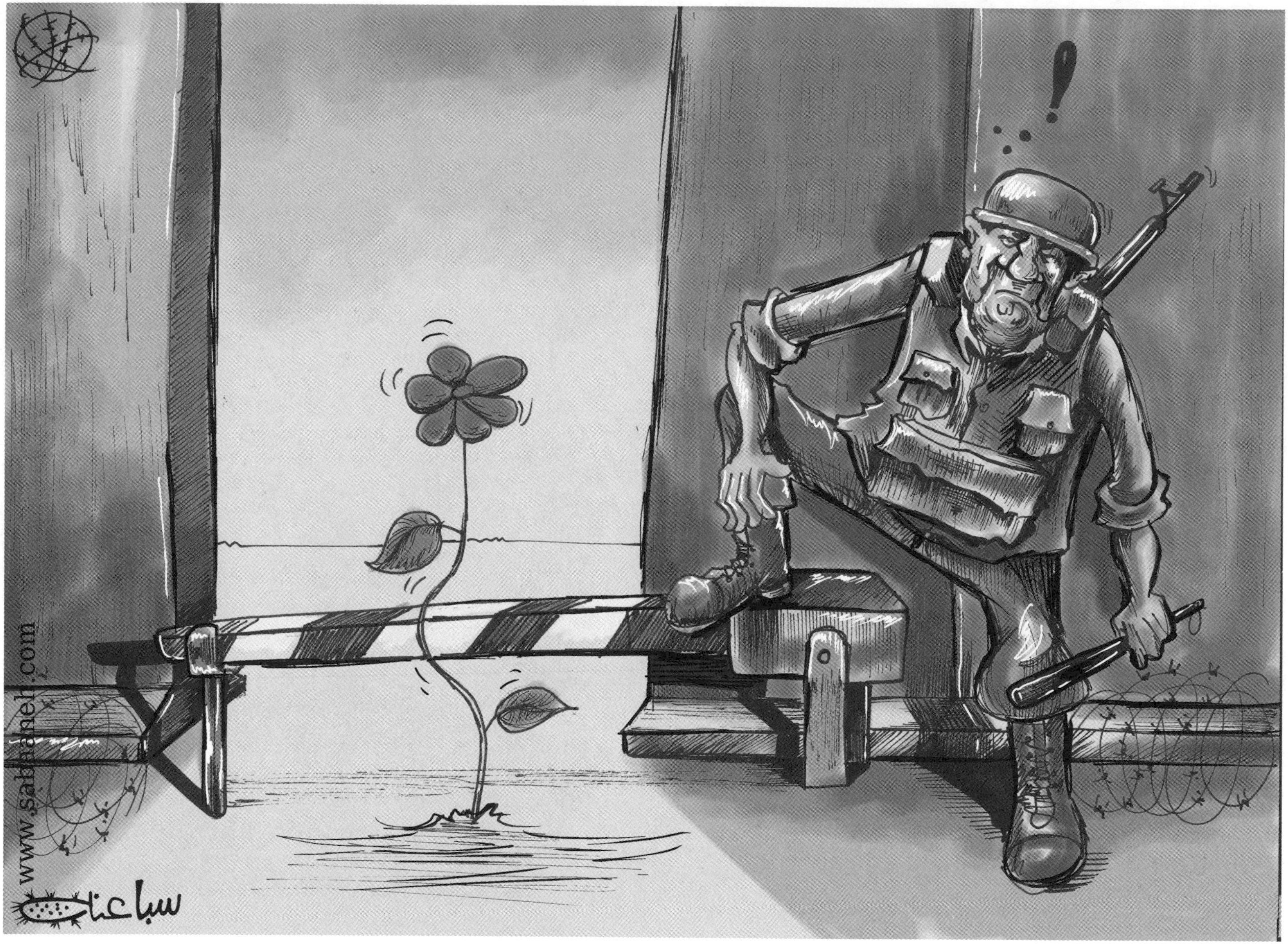

Halt. Everything must halt.

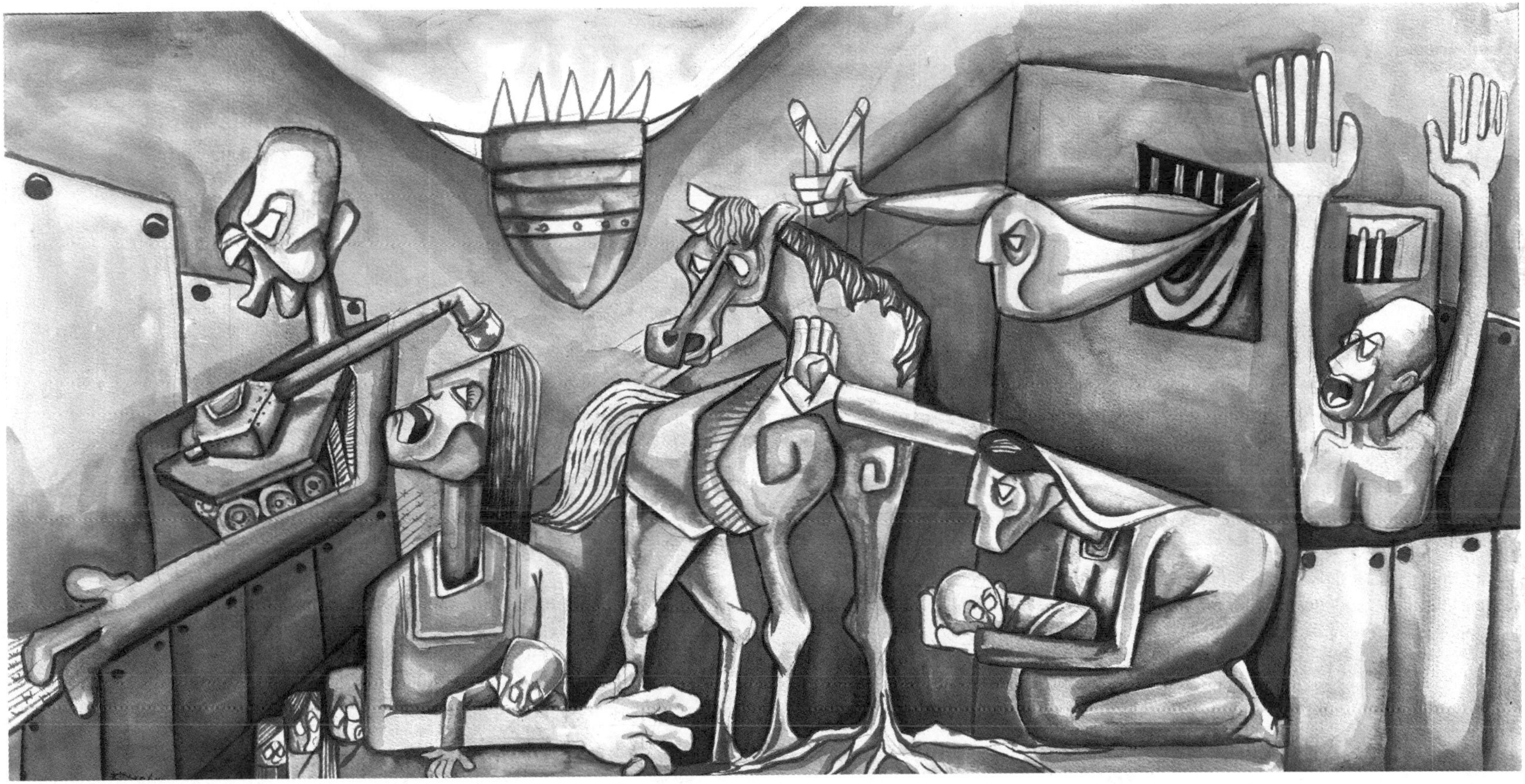

The first intifada was the stuff of legends.

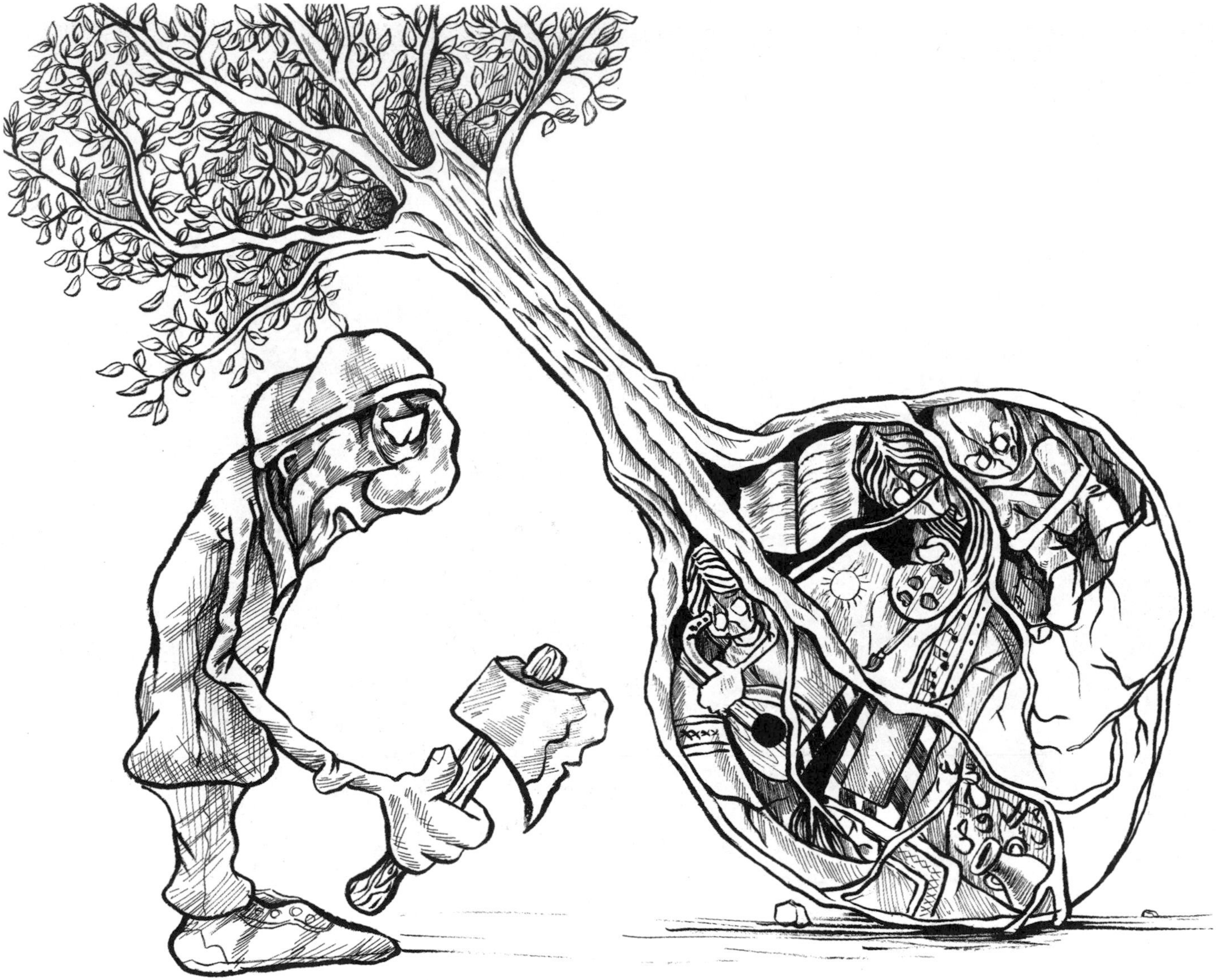

Our culture is our root in the soil.

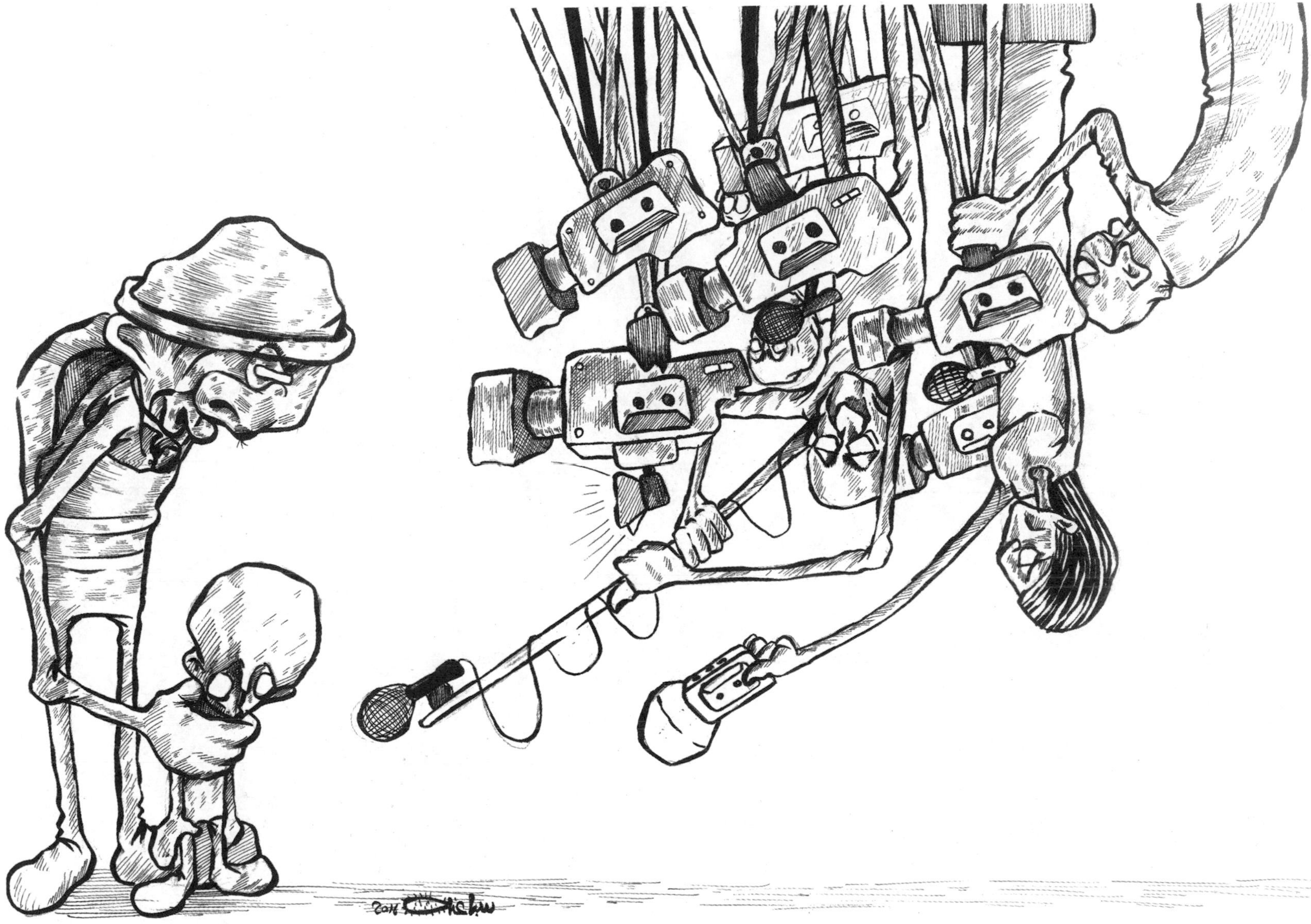

Bringing you the news.

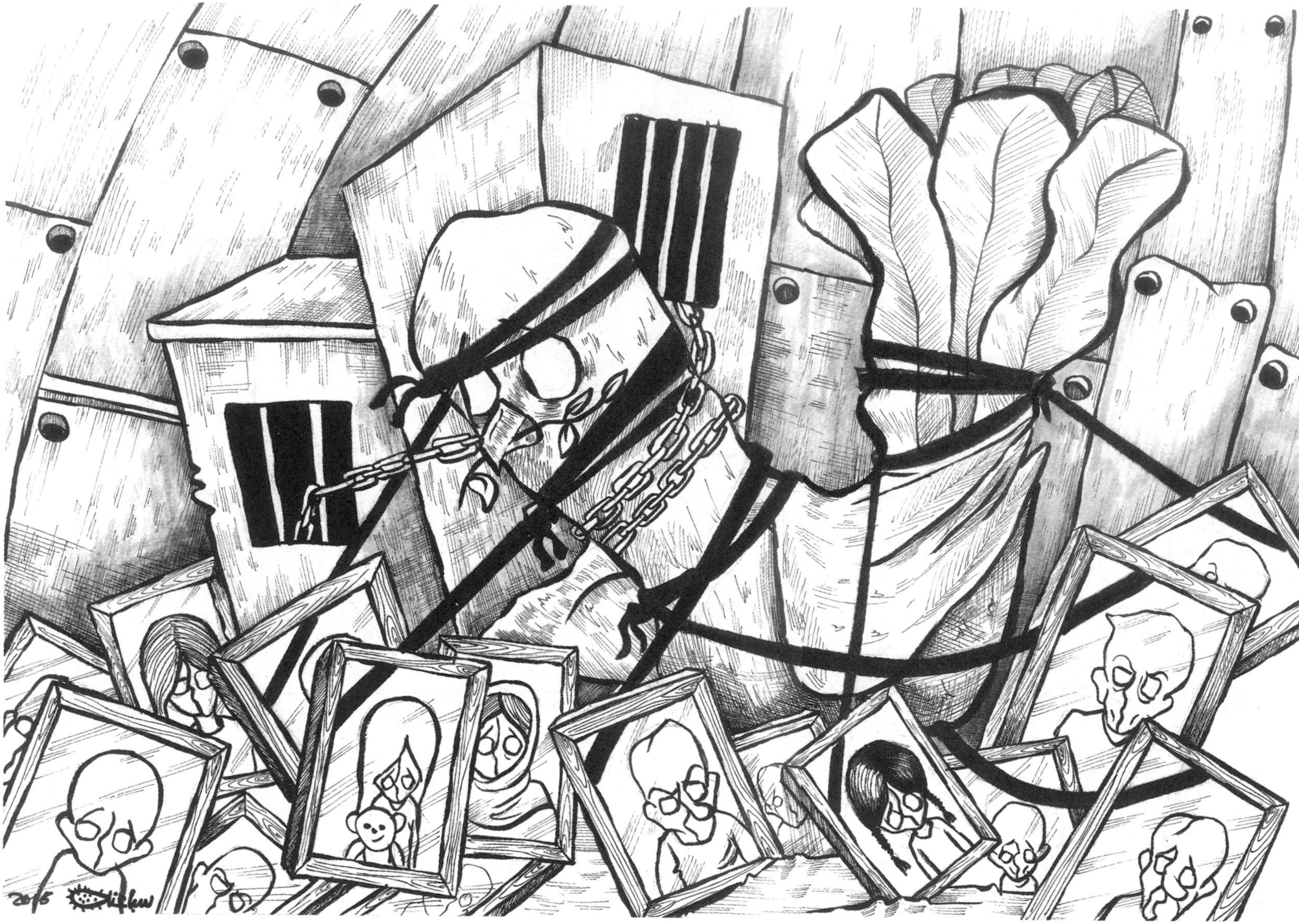

Bonds of peace.

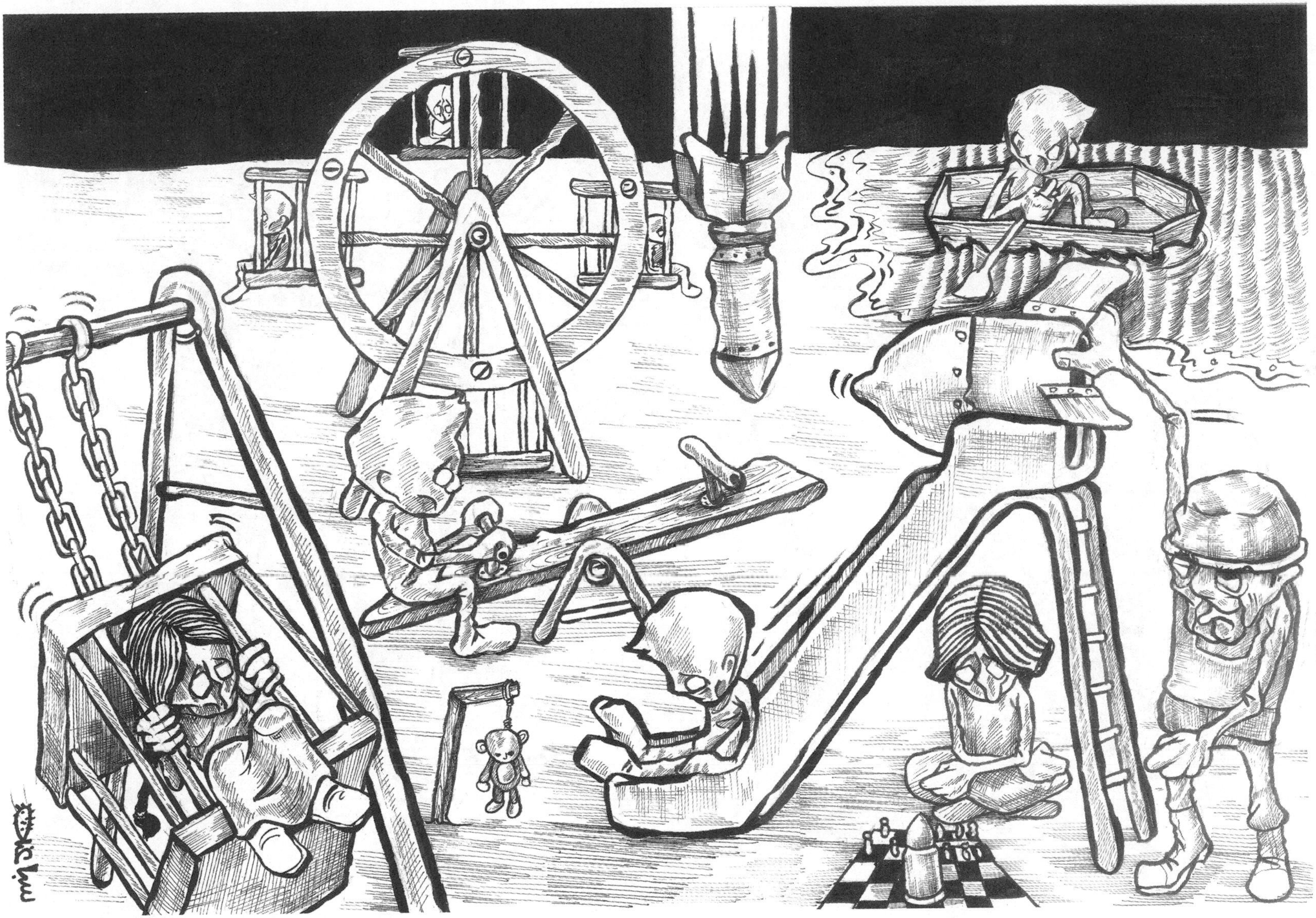

How and where will our children play?

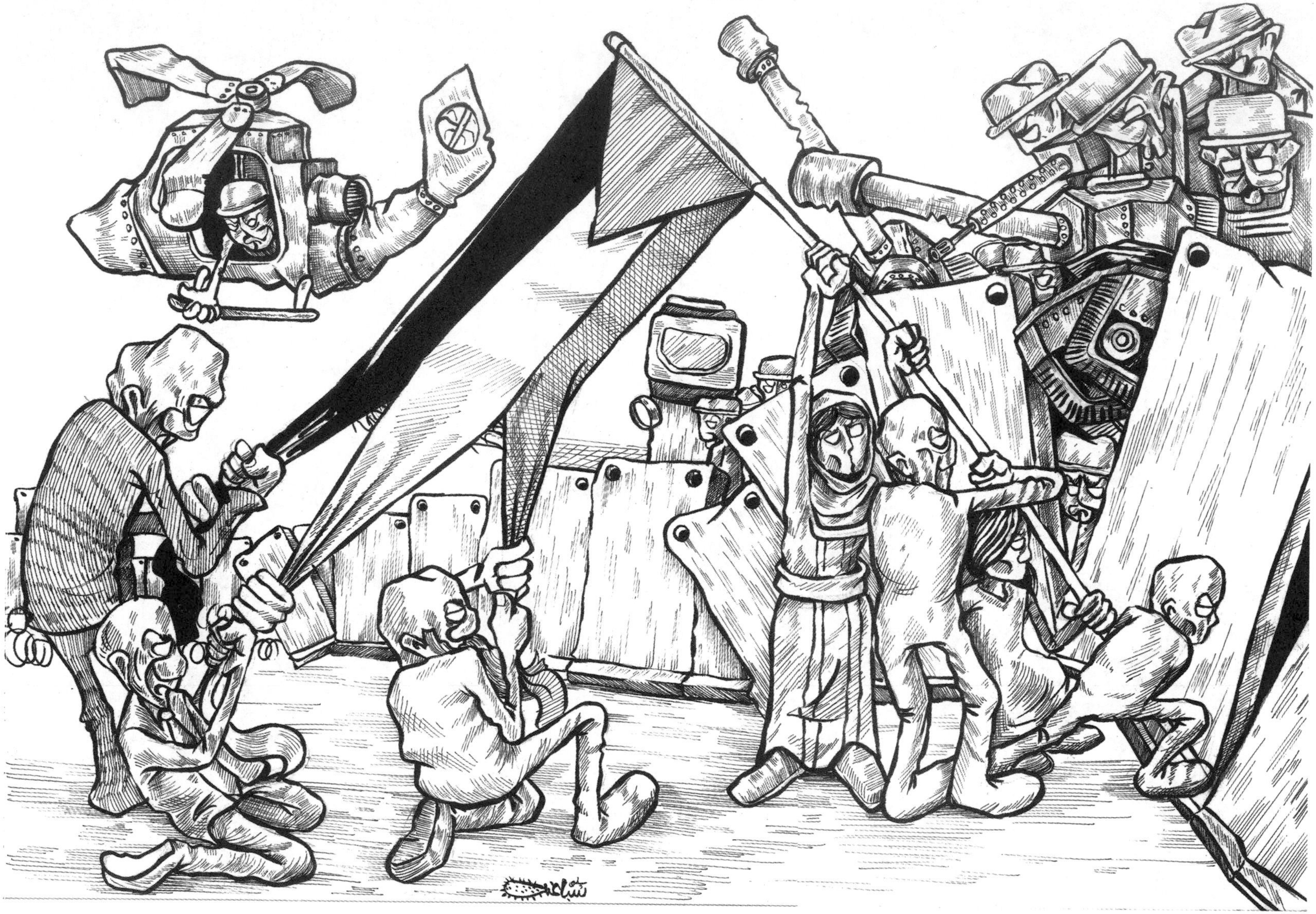

Once upon a time, our flag brought us together.

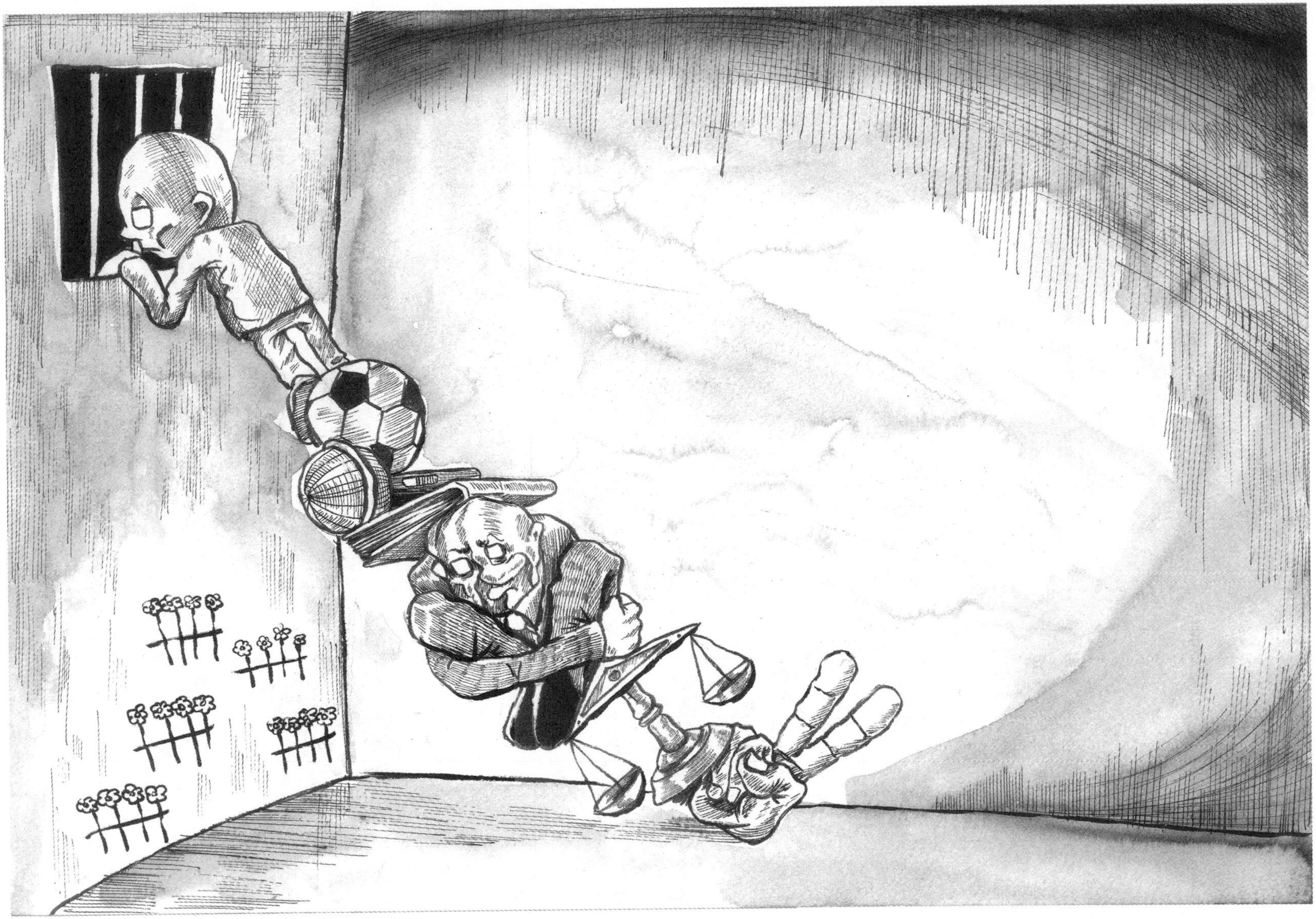

Your victories and your laws are irrelevant to me as long as he is in prison.

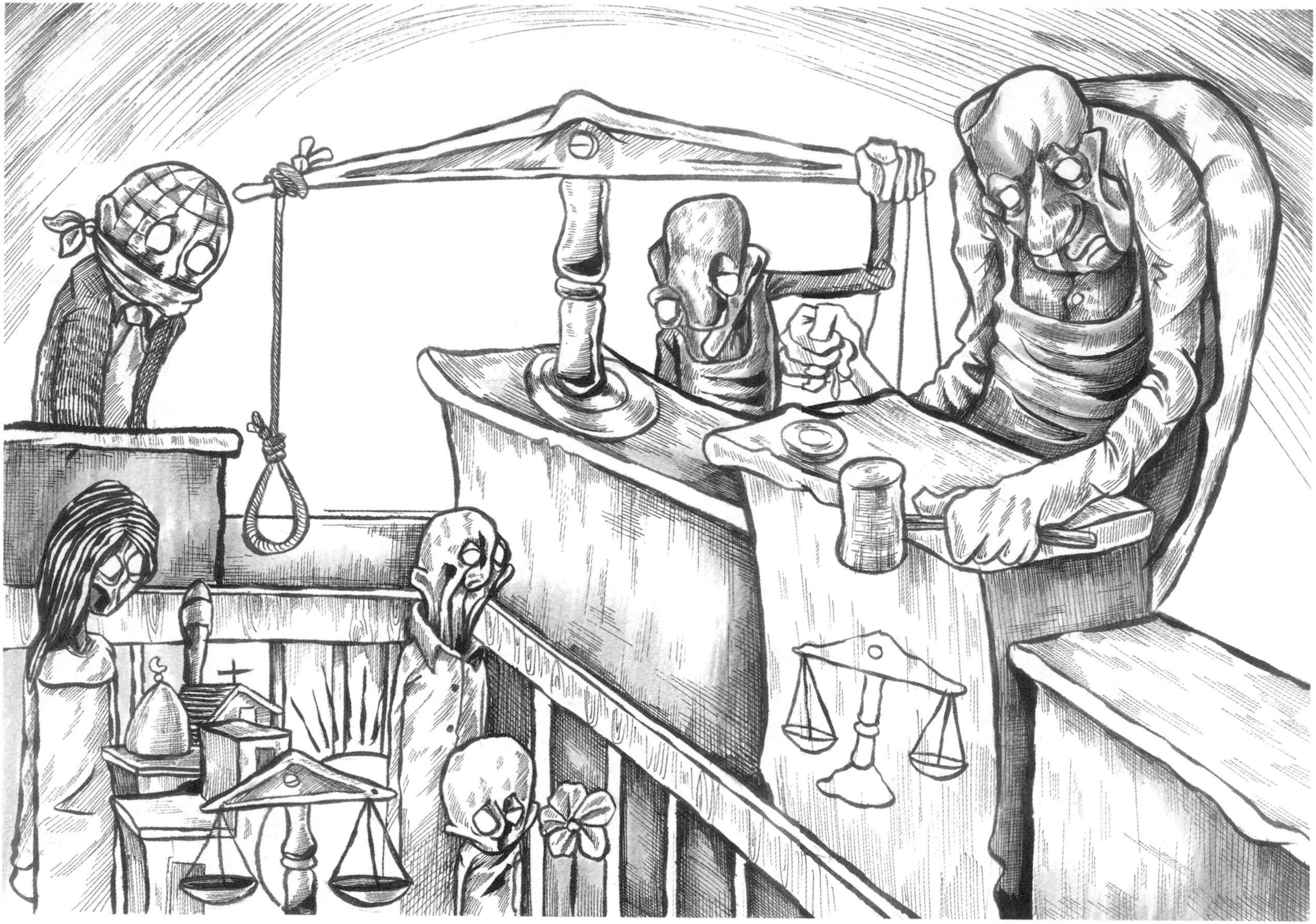

The occupation's courts and laws are a Palestinian's noose.

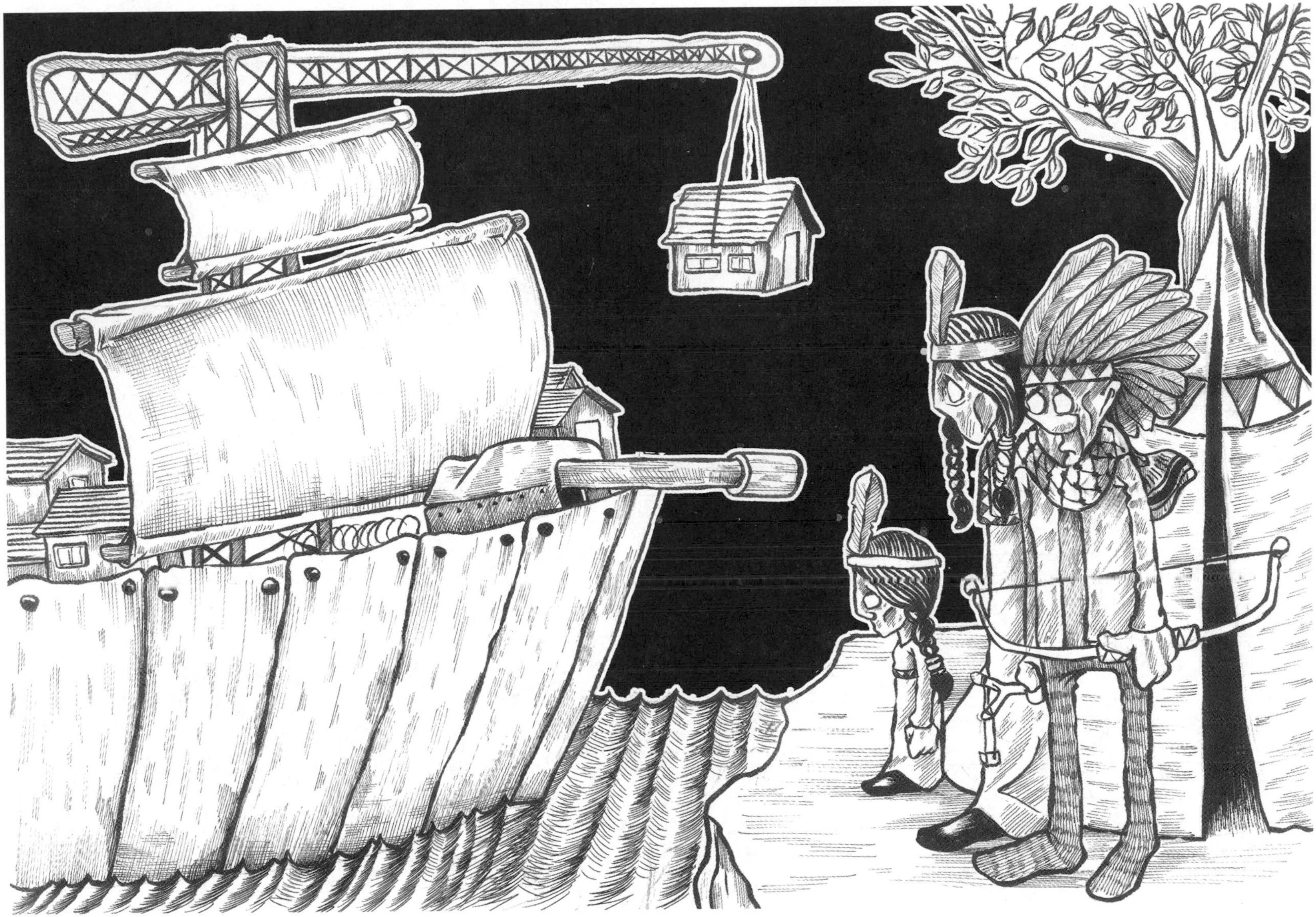

Indigenous people.

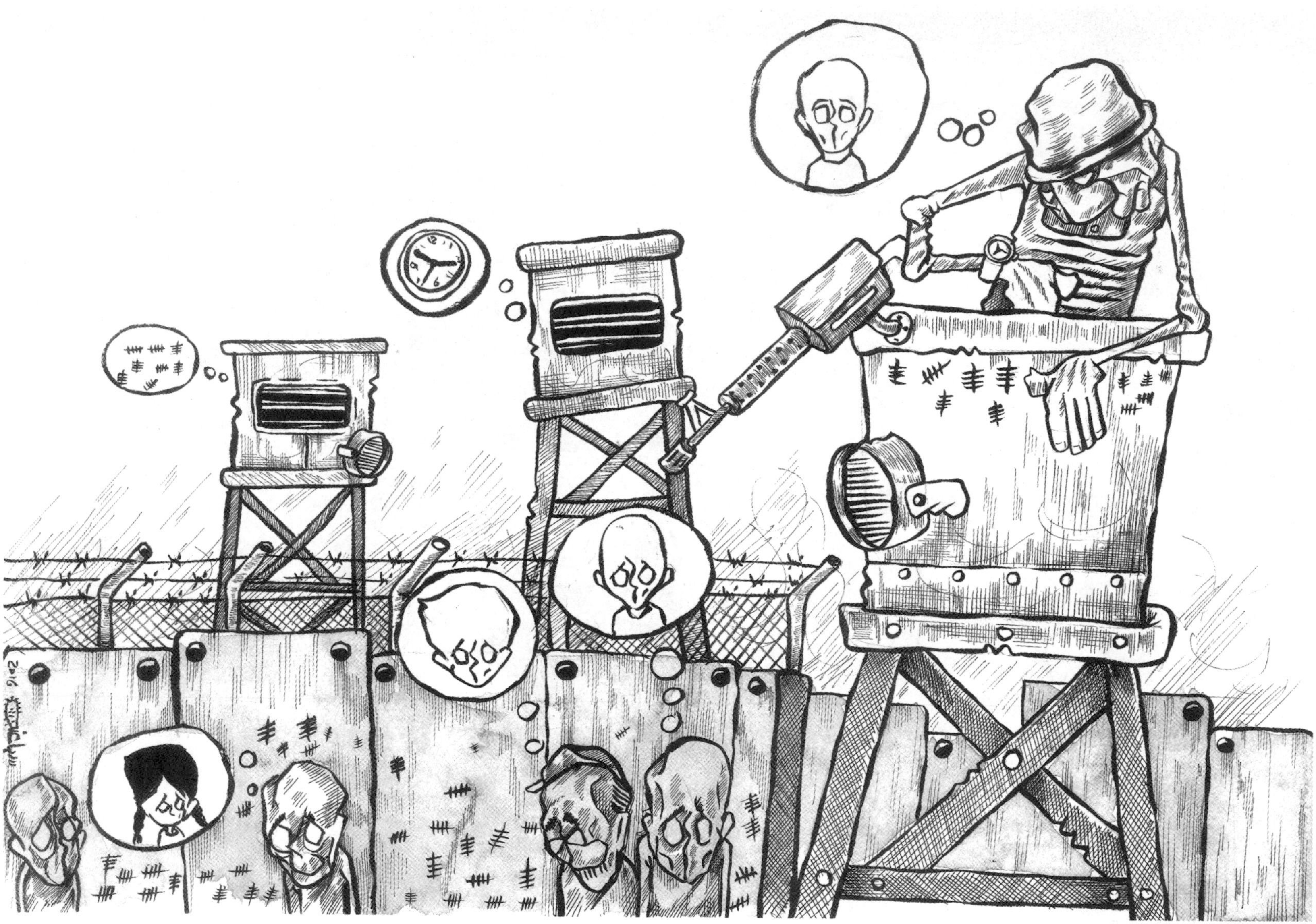

Marking time.

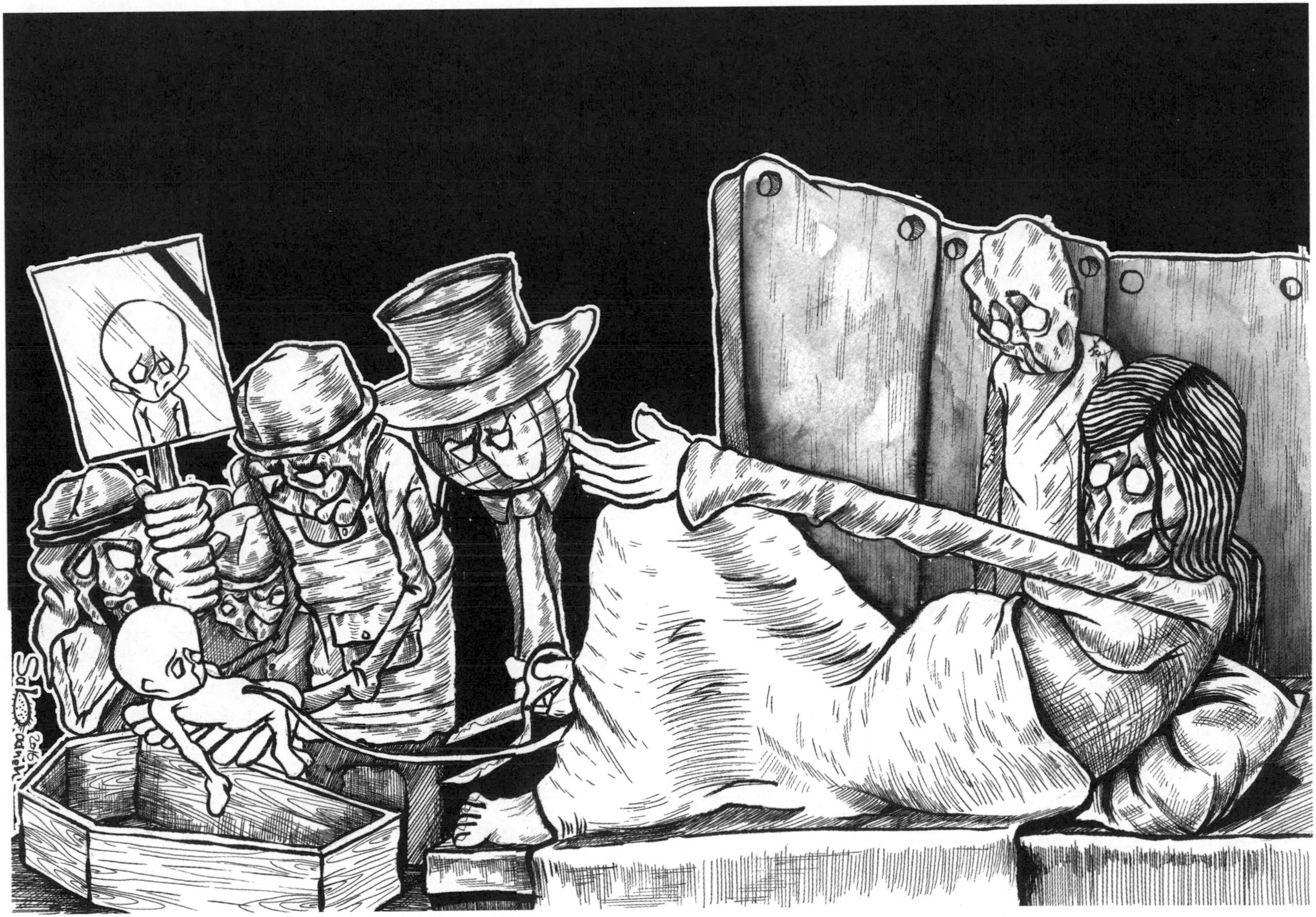

They accuse us of sending our children to death.

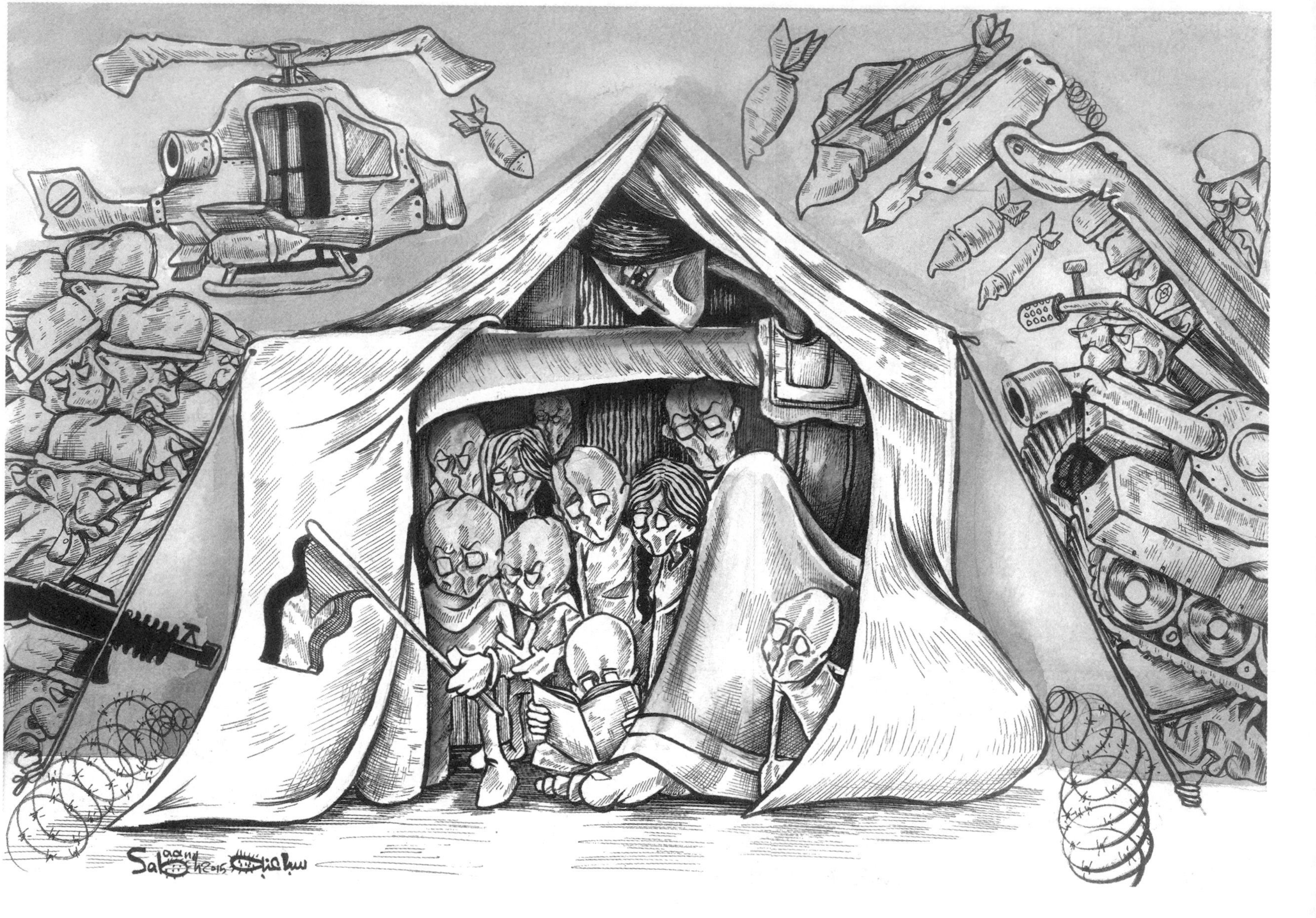

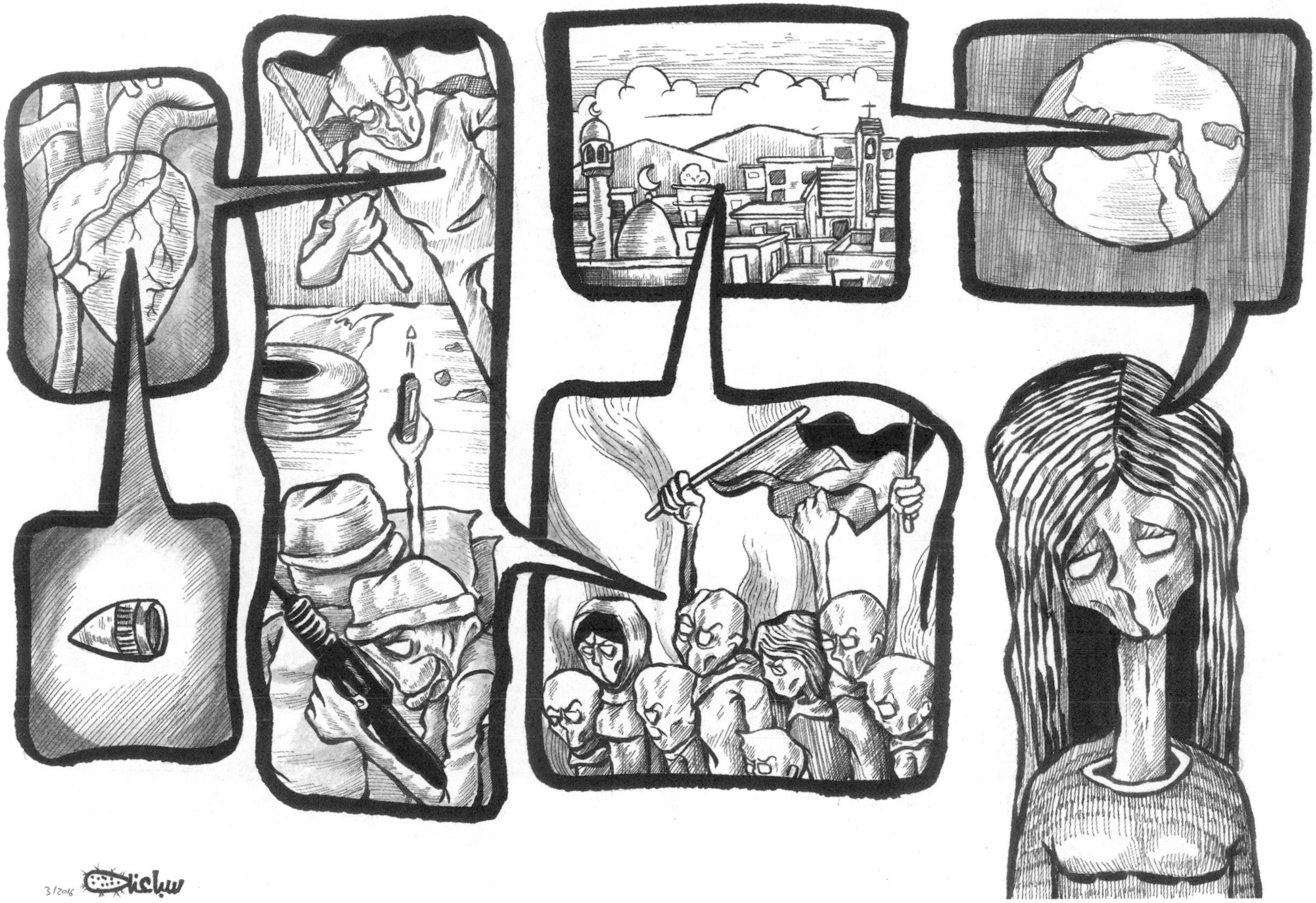
3/2016

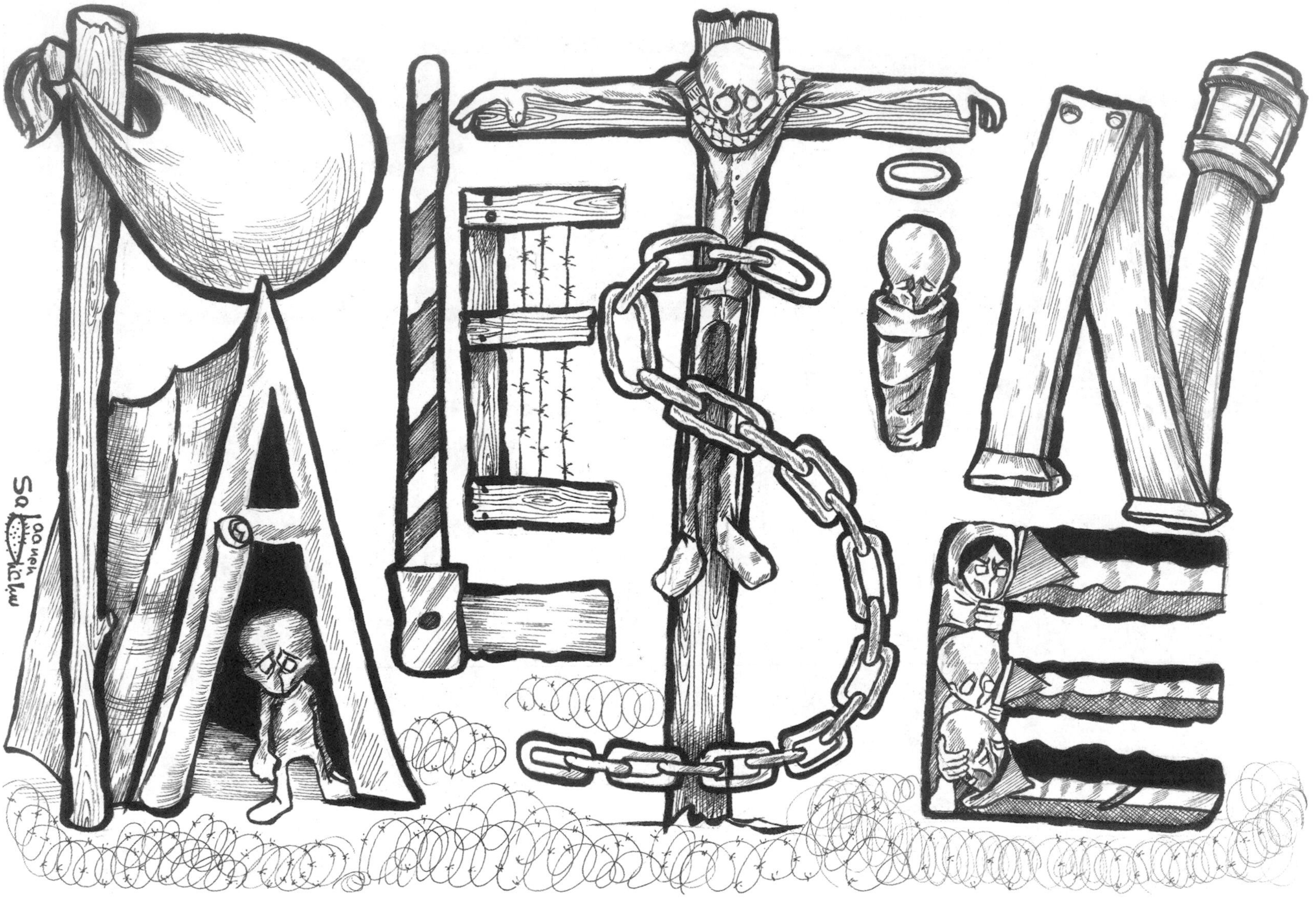

Spell it out.

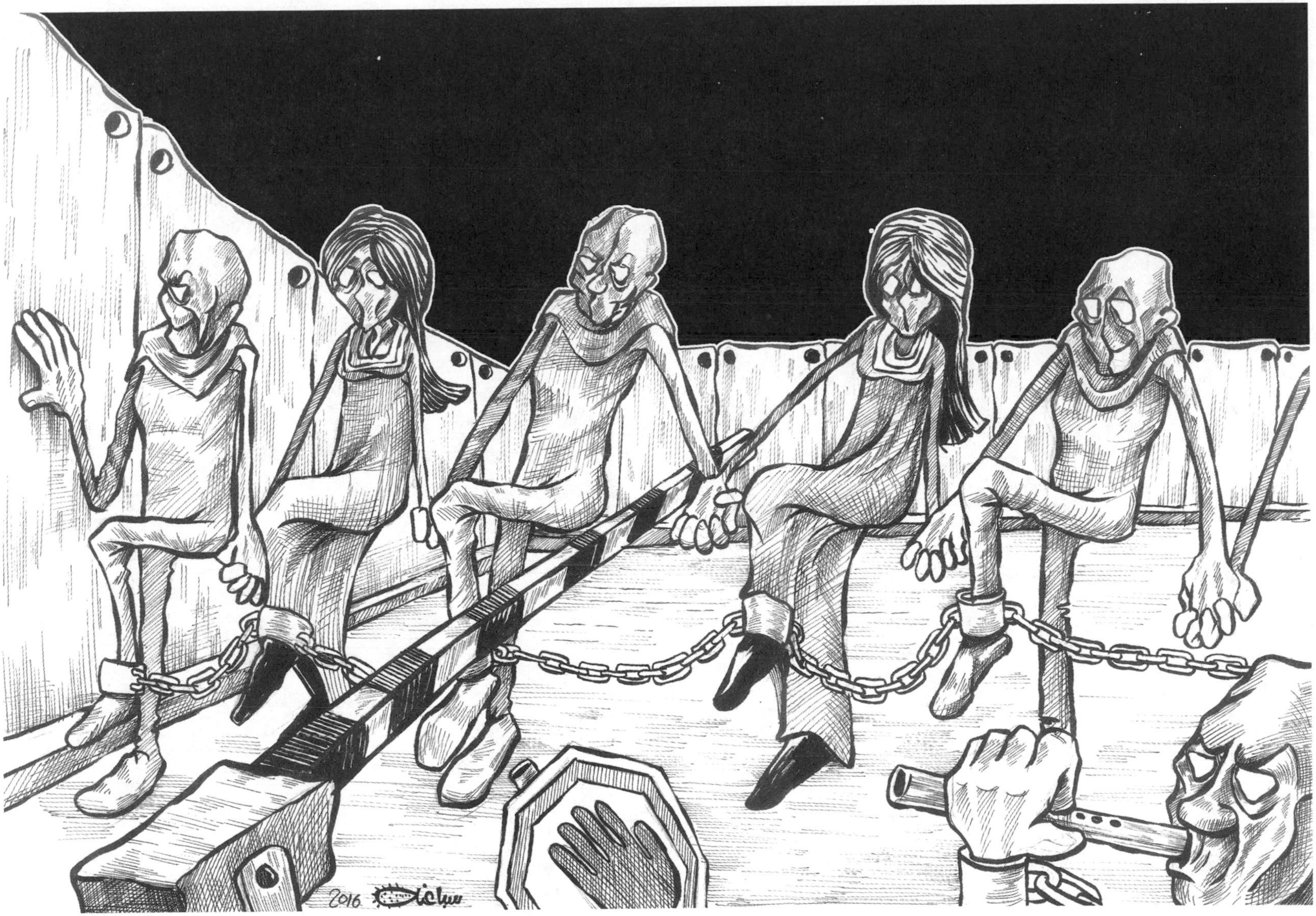
2016

Who prevents joy? Who kills it?

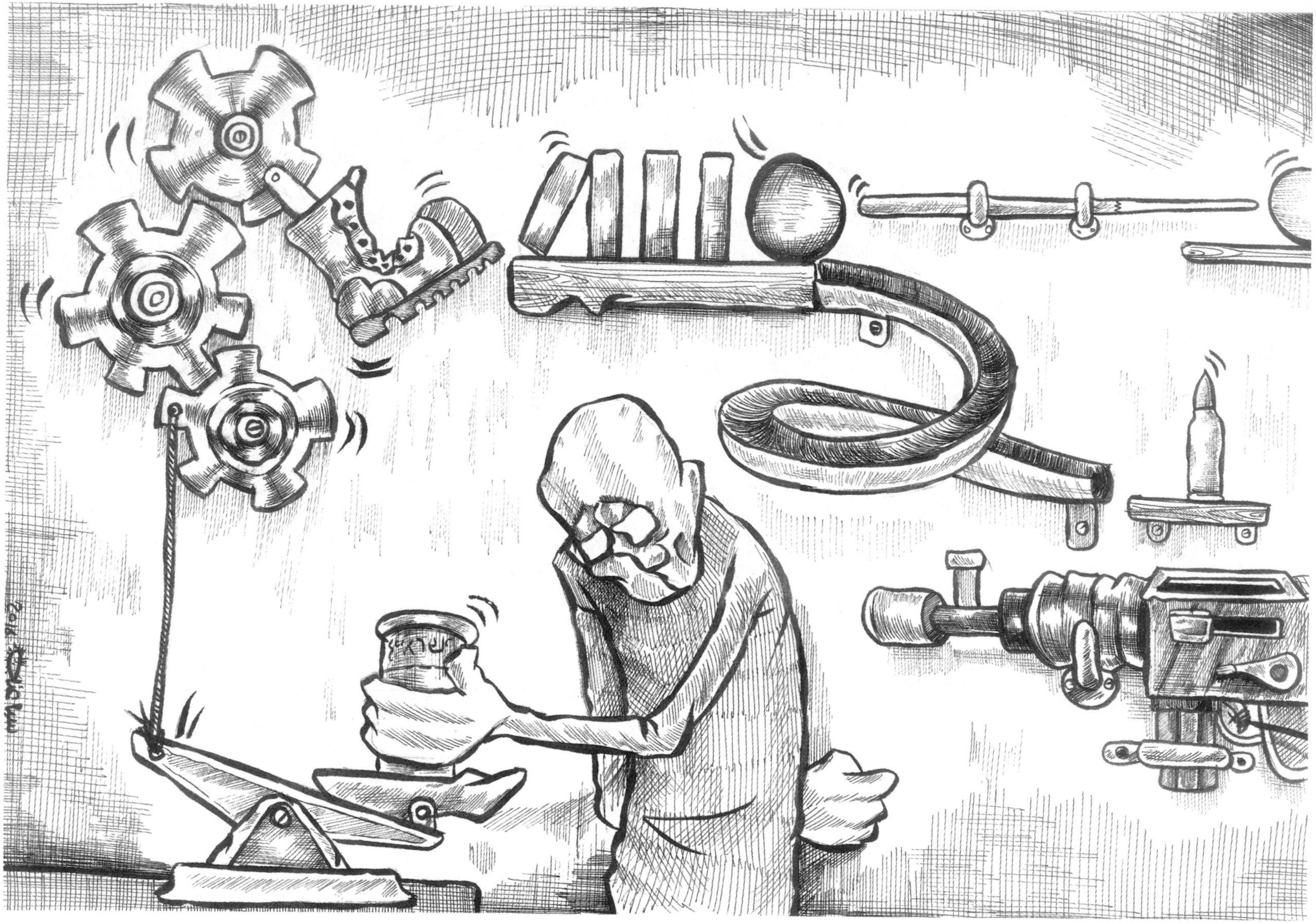

Made in Israel.

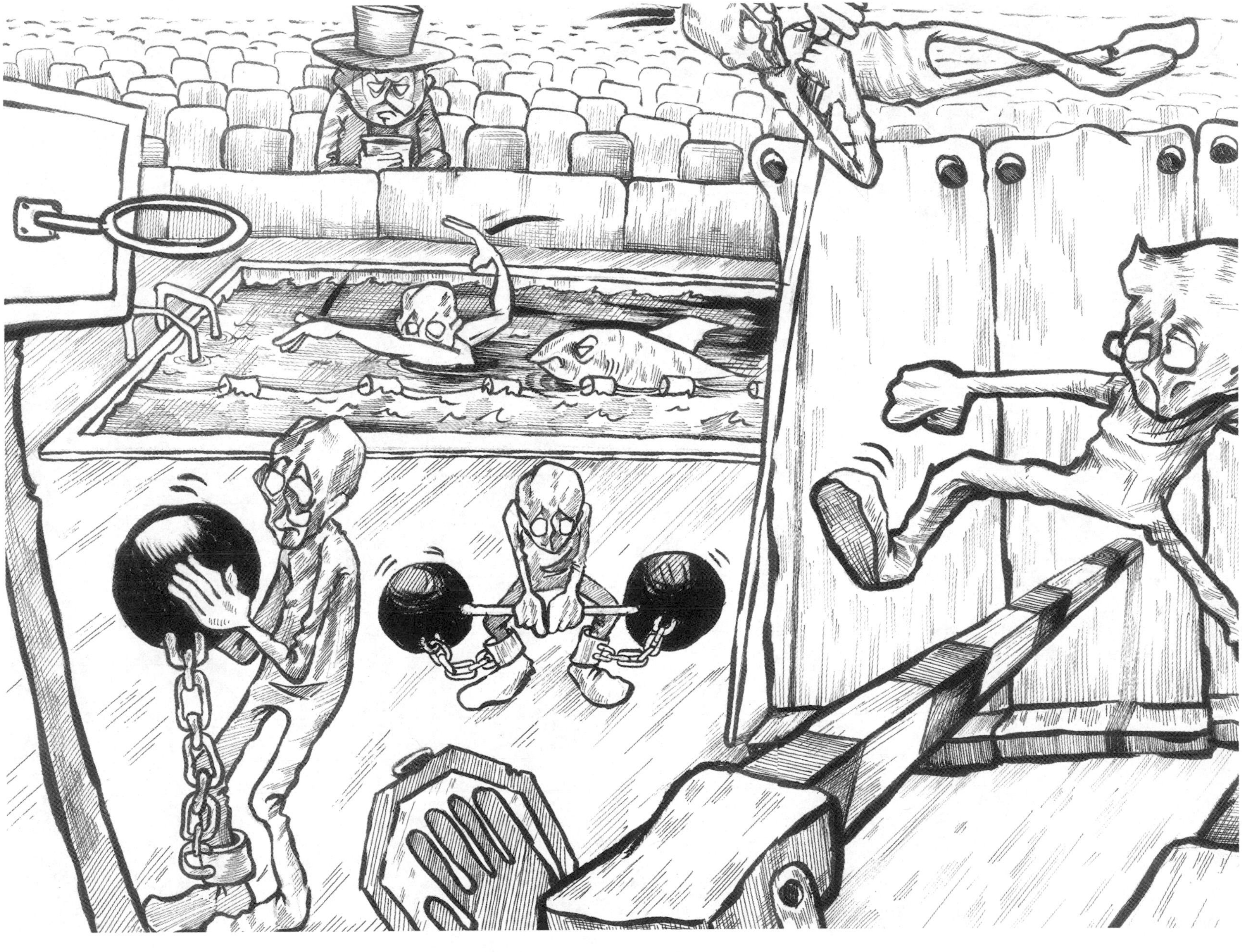

Getting a workout.

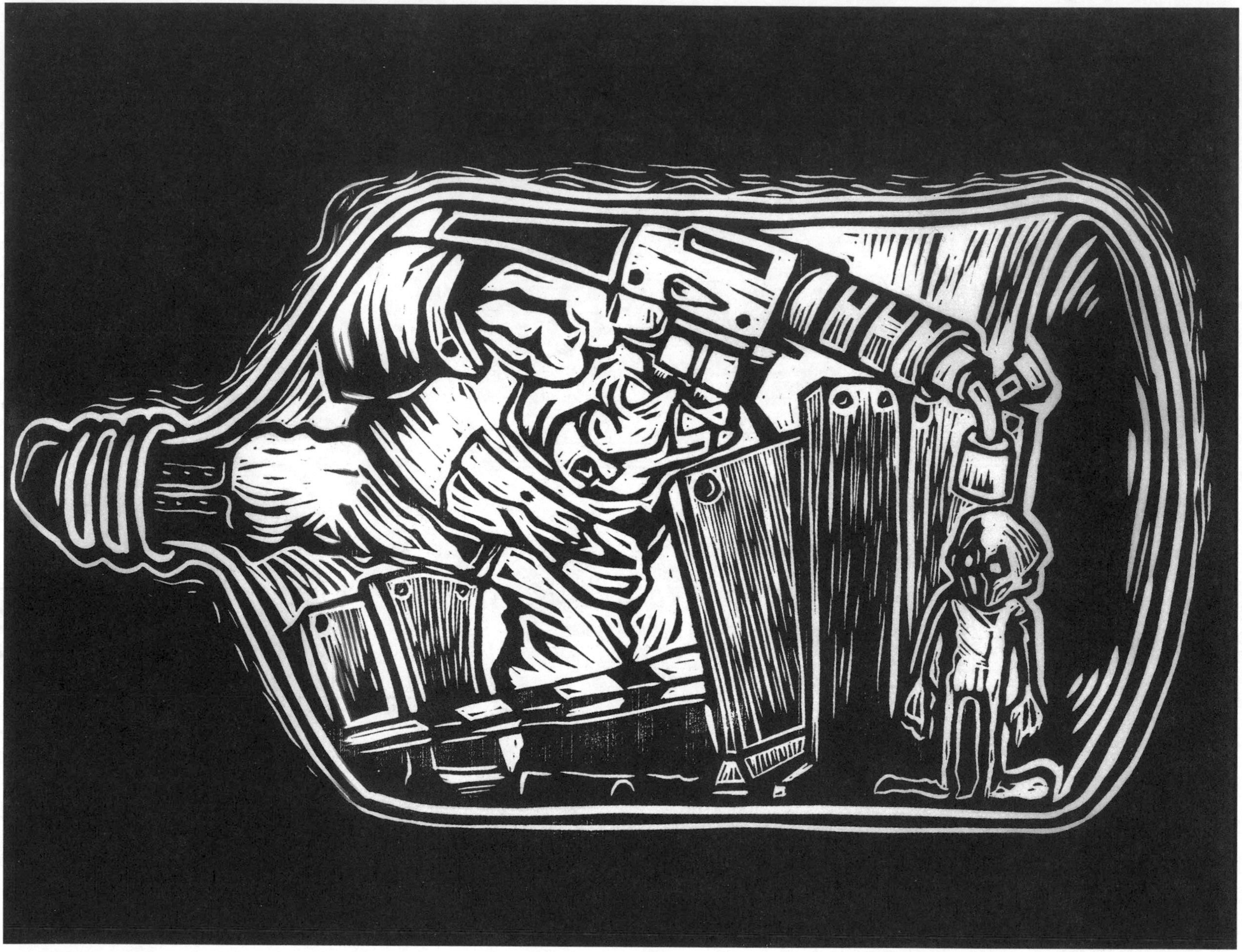

All of us are hostages of the place.

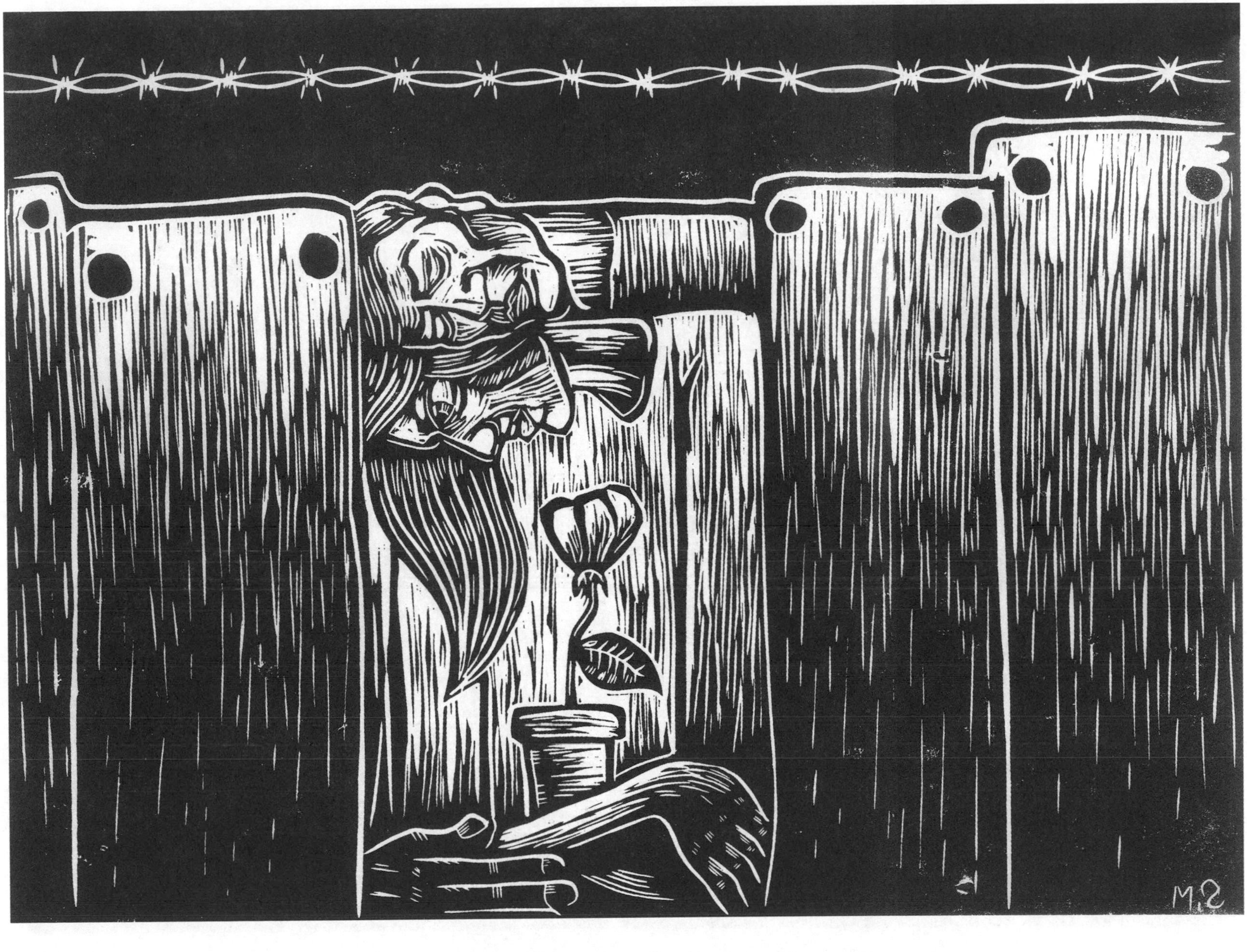
M.S

We will live despite the siege.

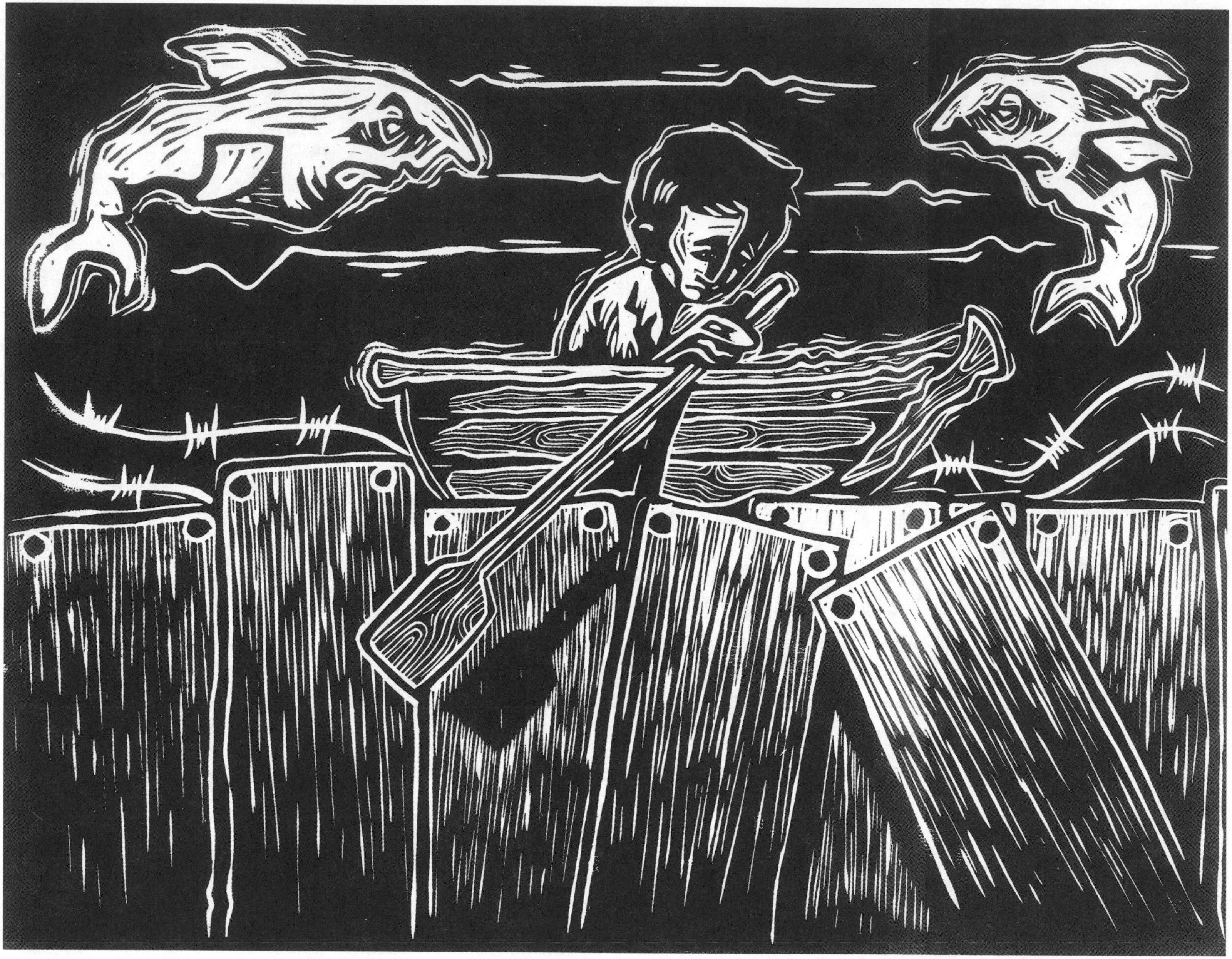

I am a Palestinian—refugee, murdered, besieged, robbed.

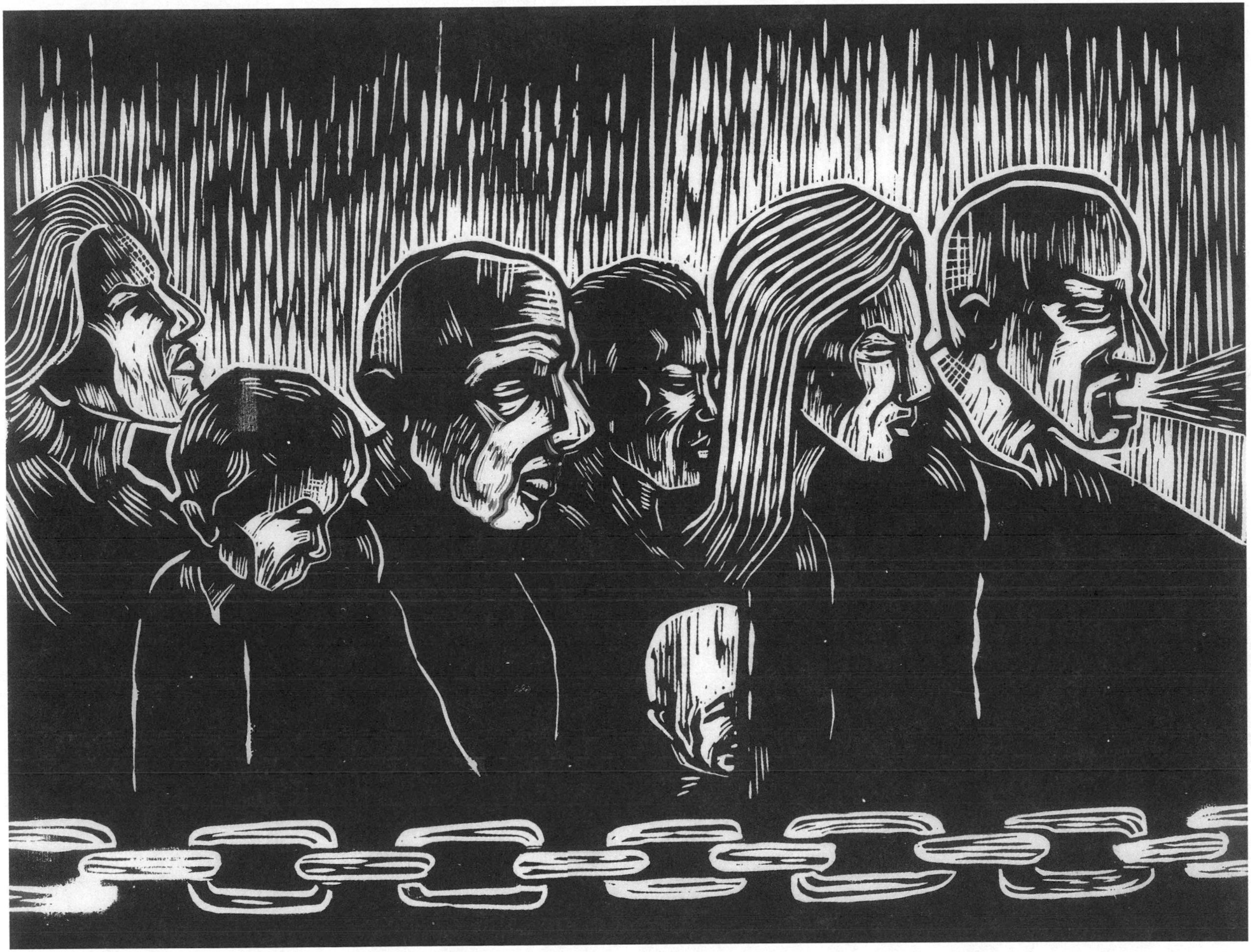

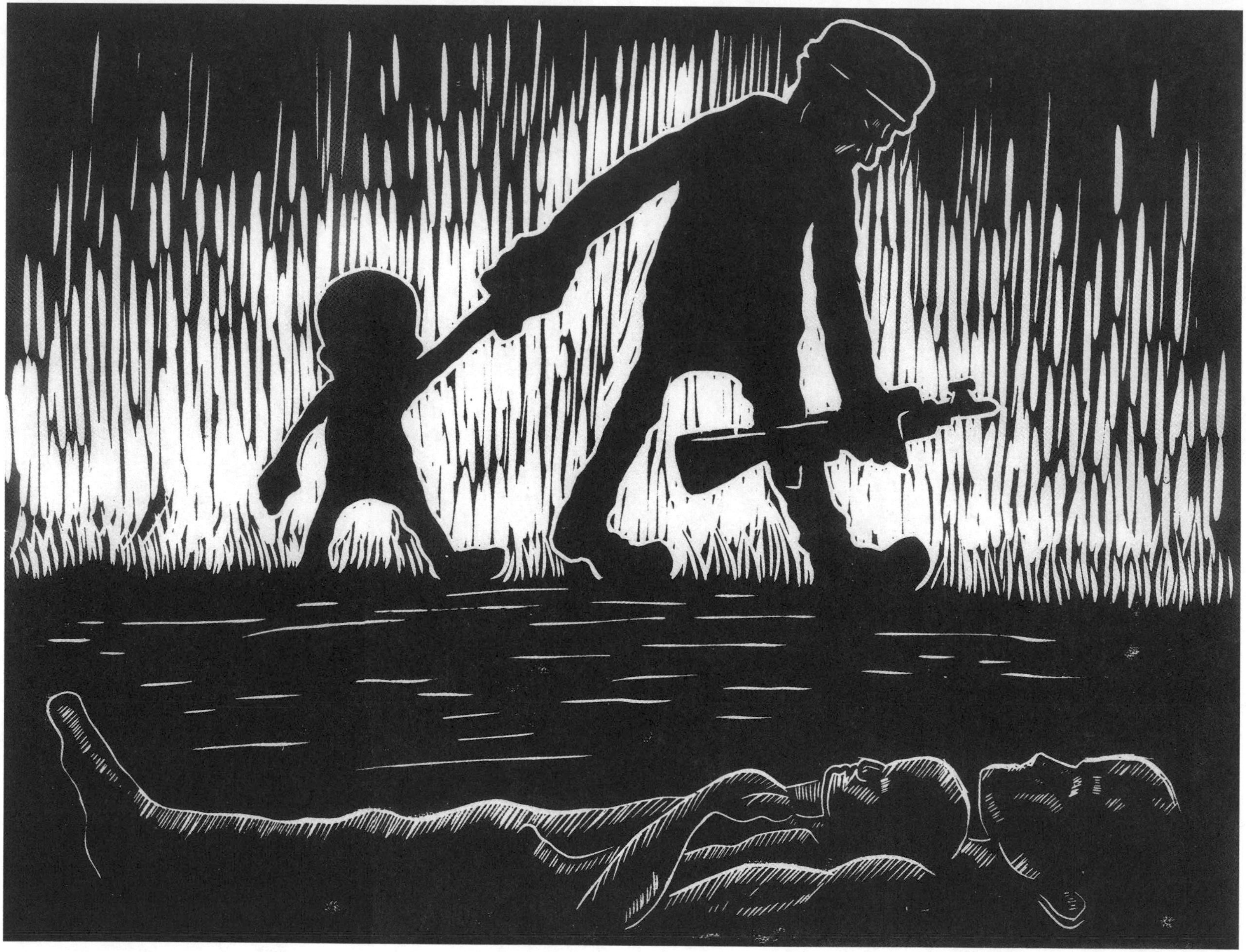

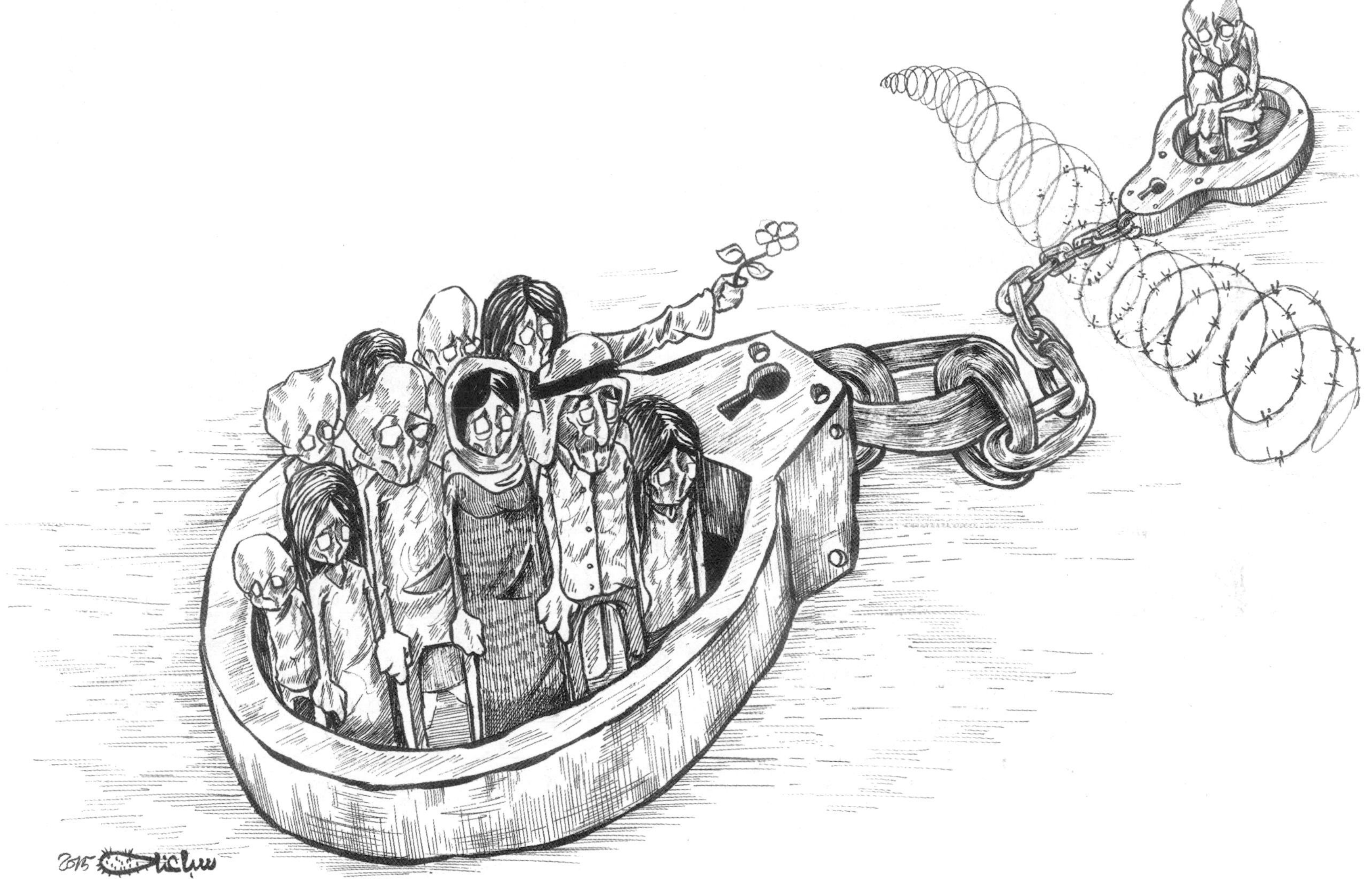

Families of political prisoners are prisoners too.

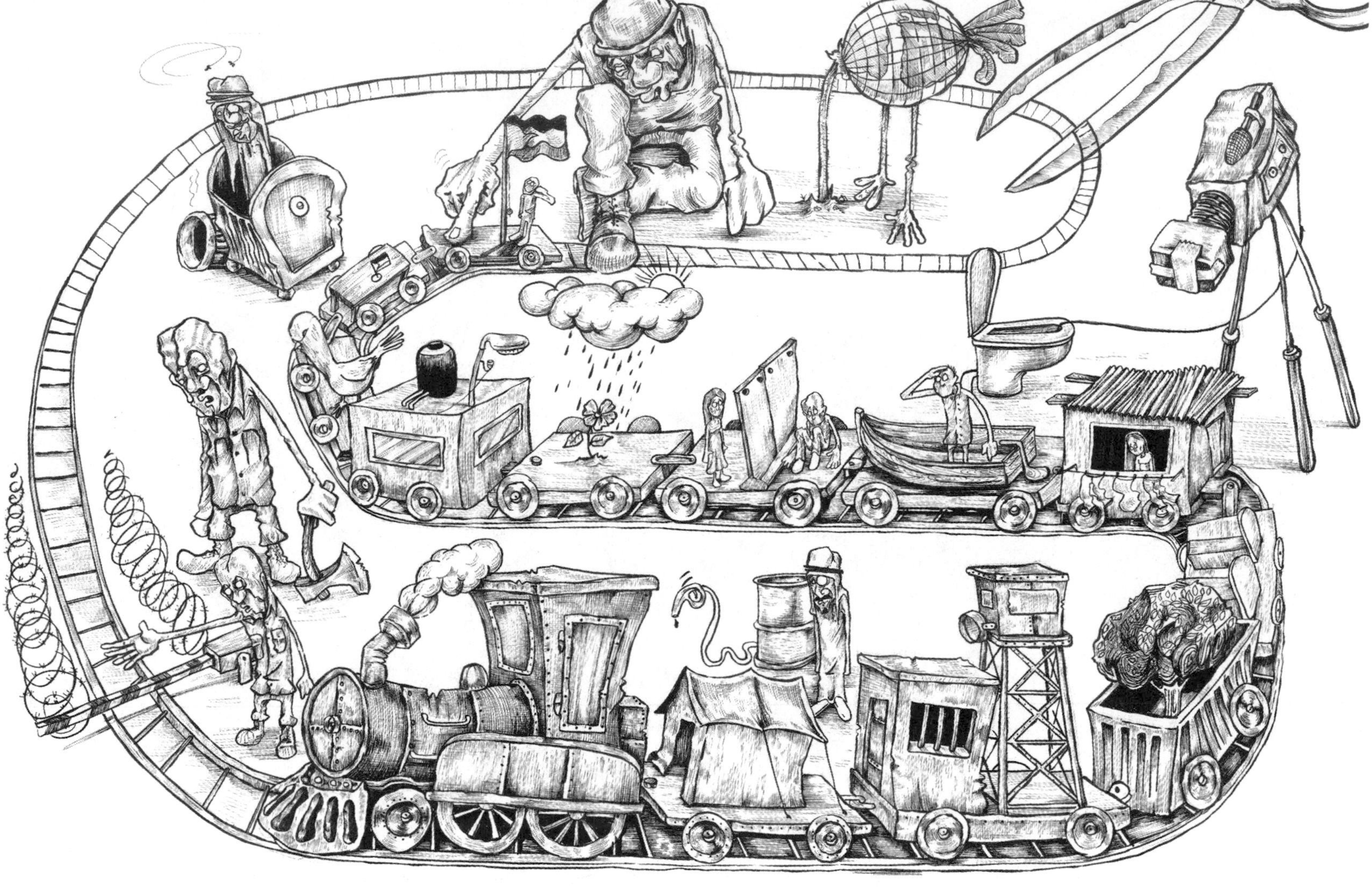

A Palestinian life.

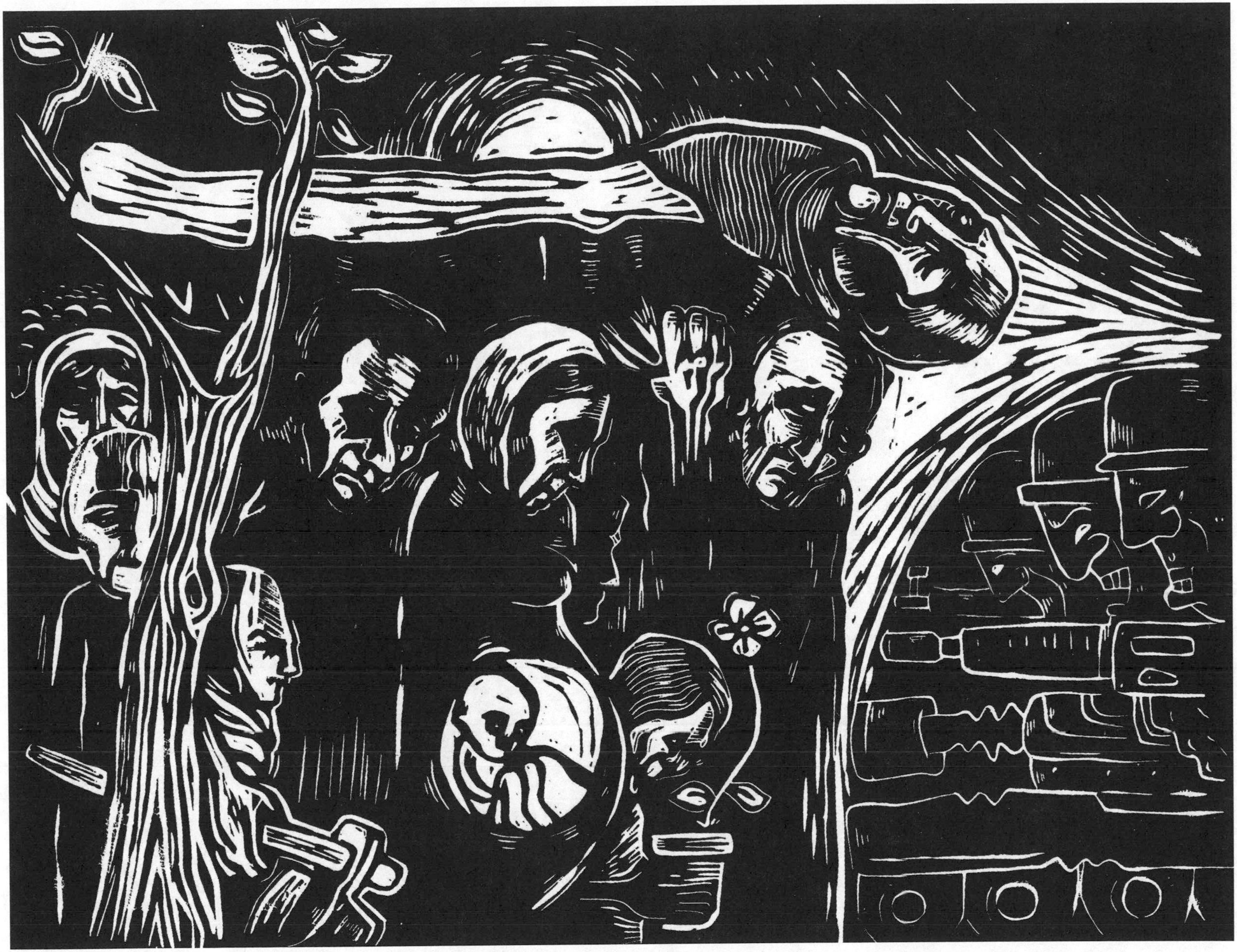

Life goes on.

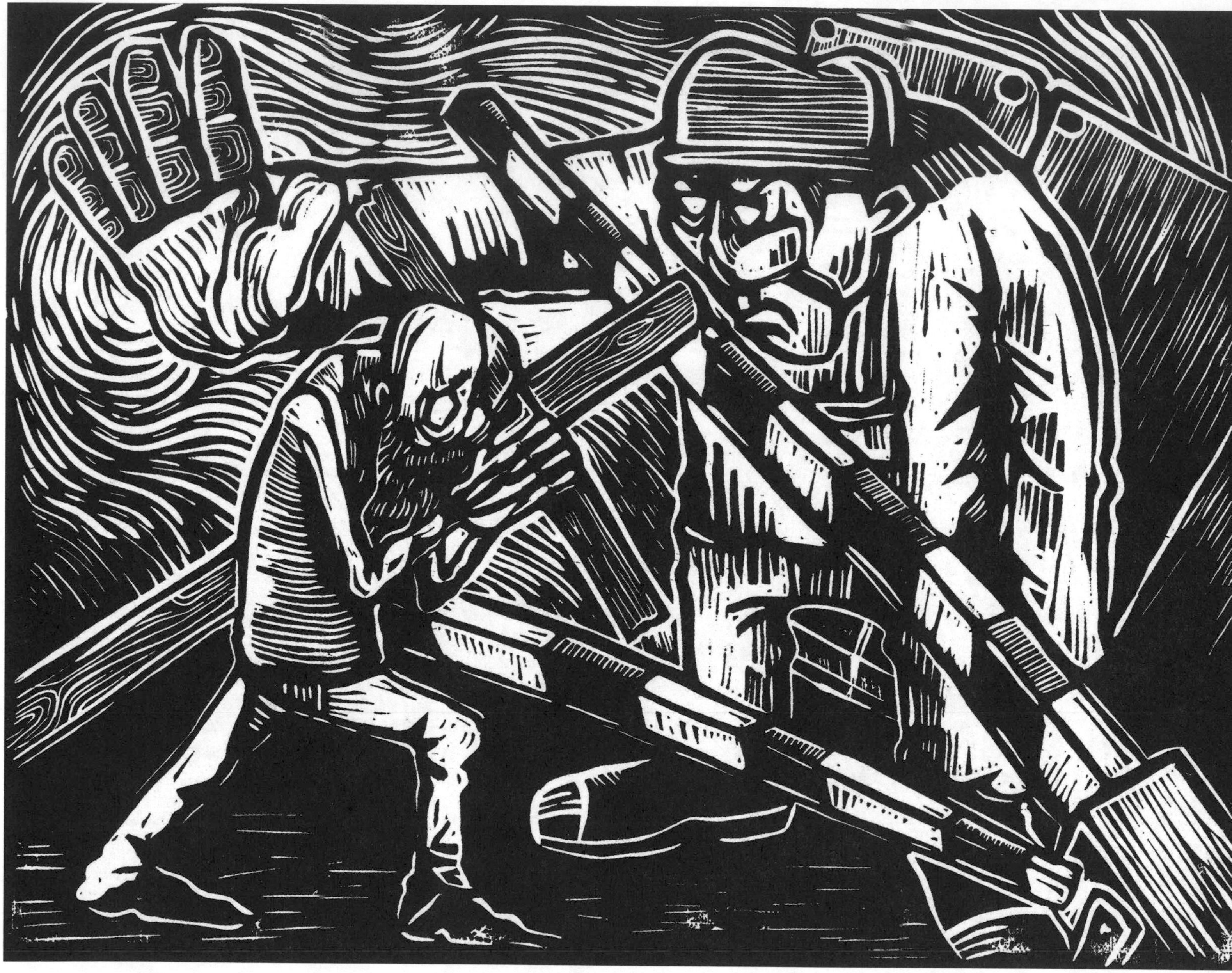

Via Dolorosa.

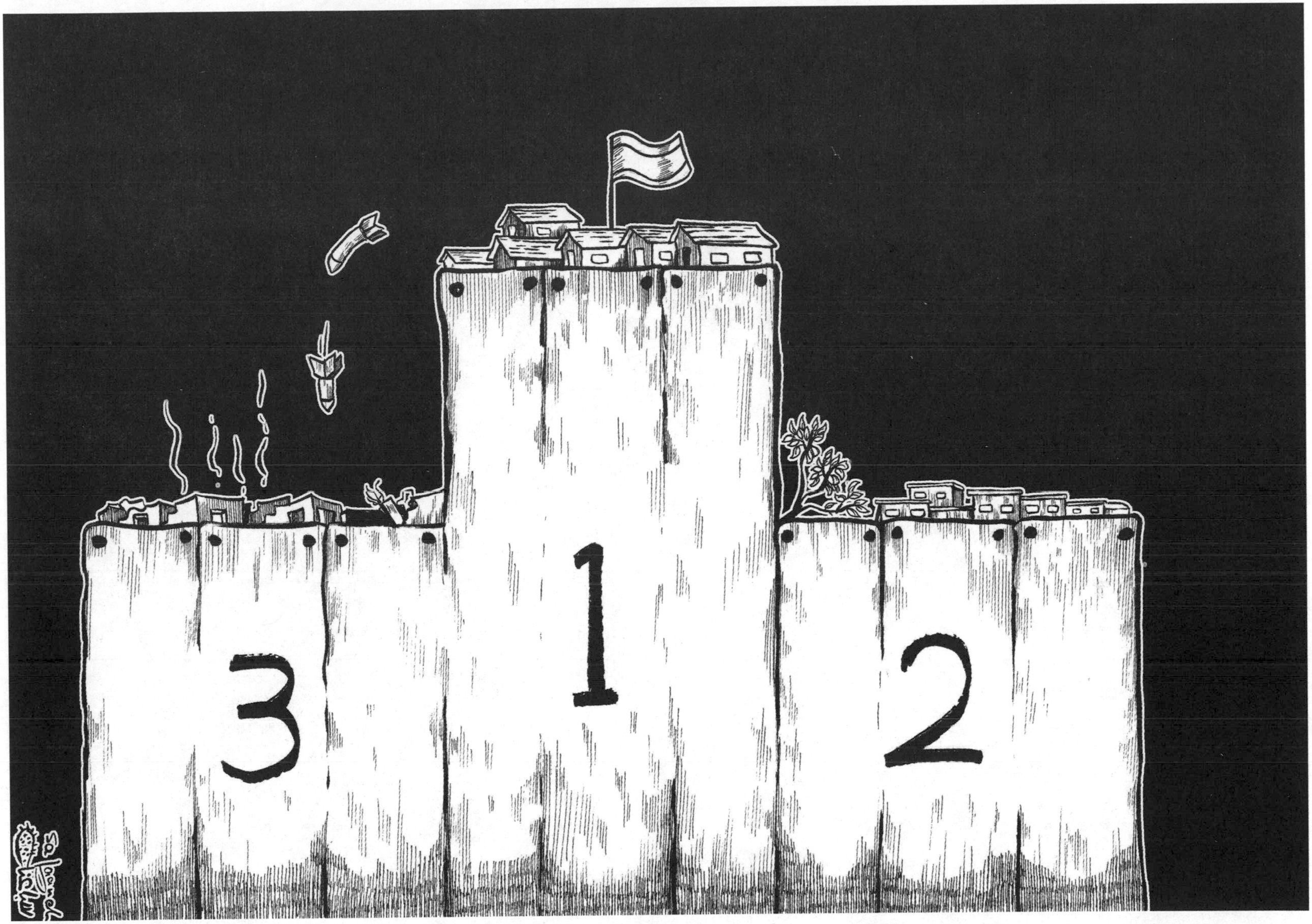
3
1
2

And the winners are Israel, the West Bank, and Gaza.

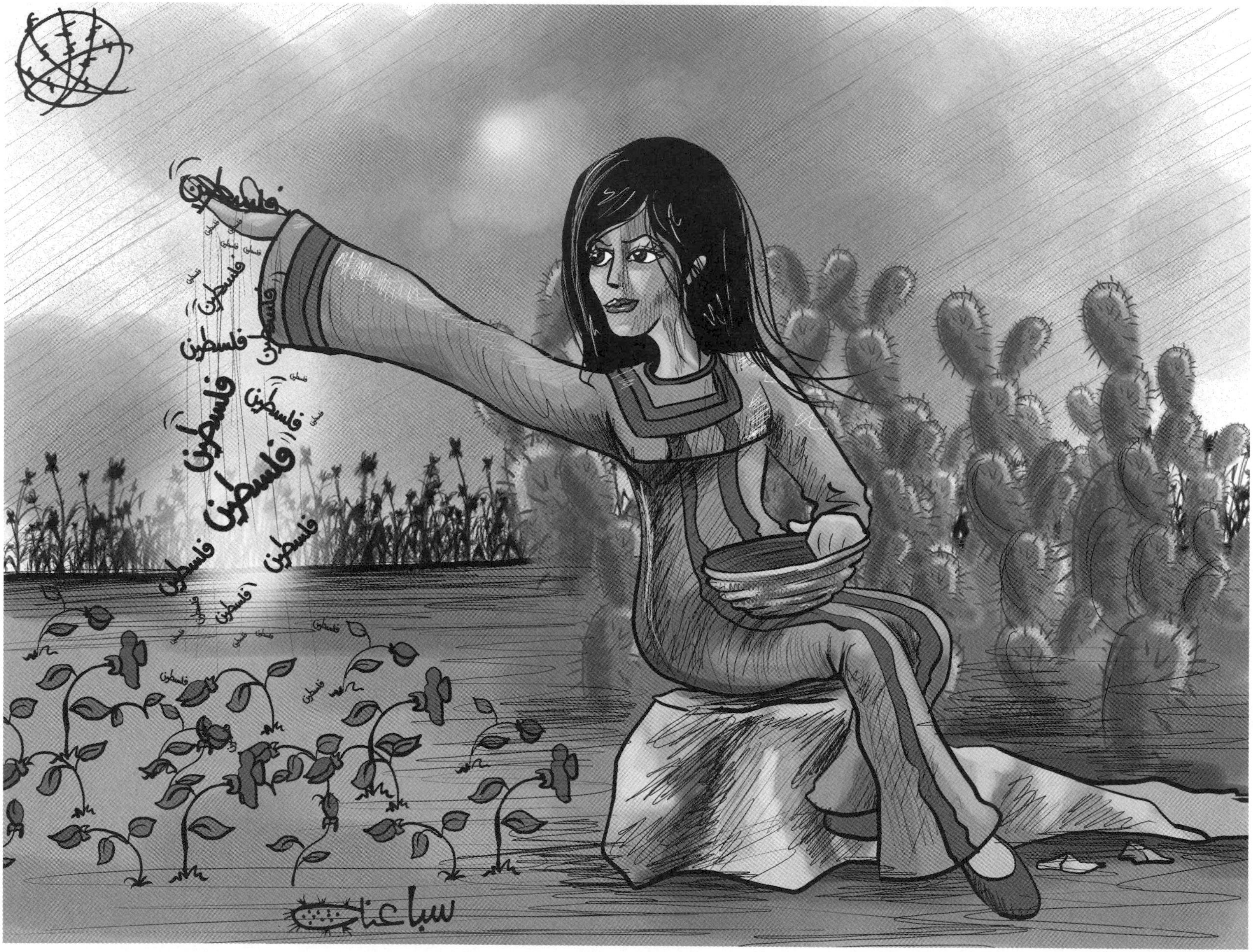
فلسطين
سباعنة

We carry within us the seeds of the homeland.

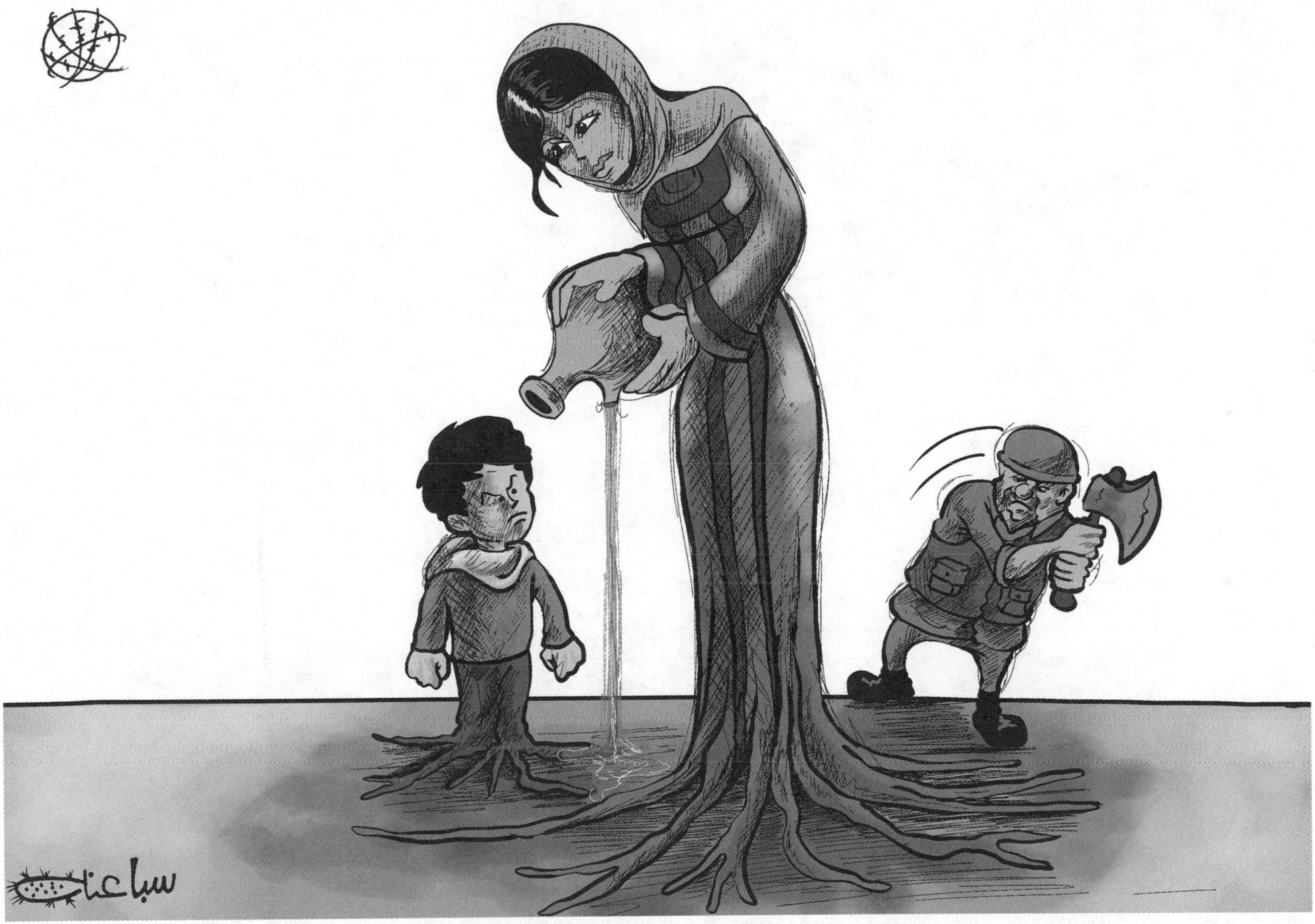

We will remain.

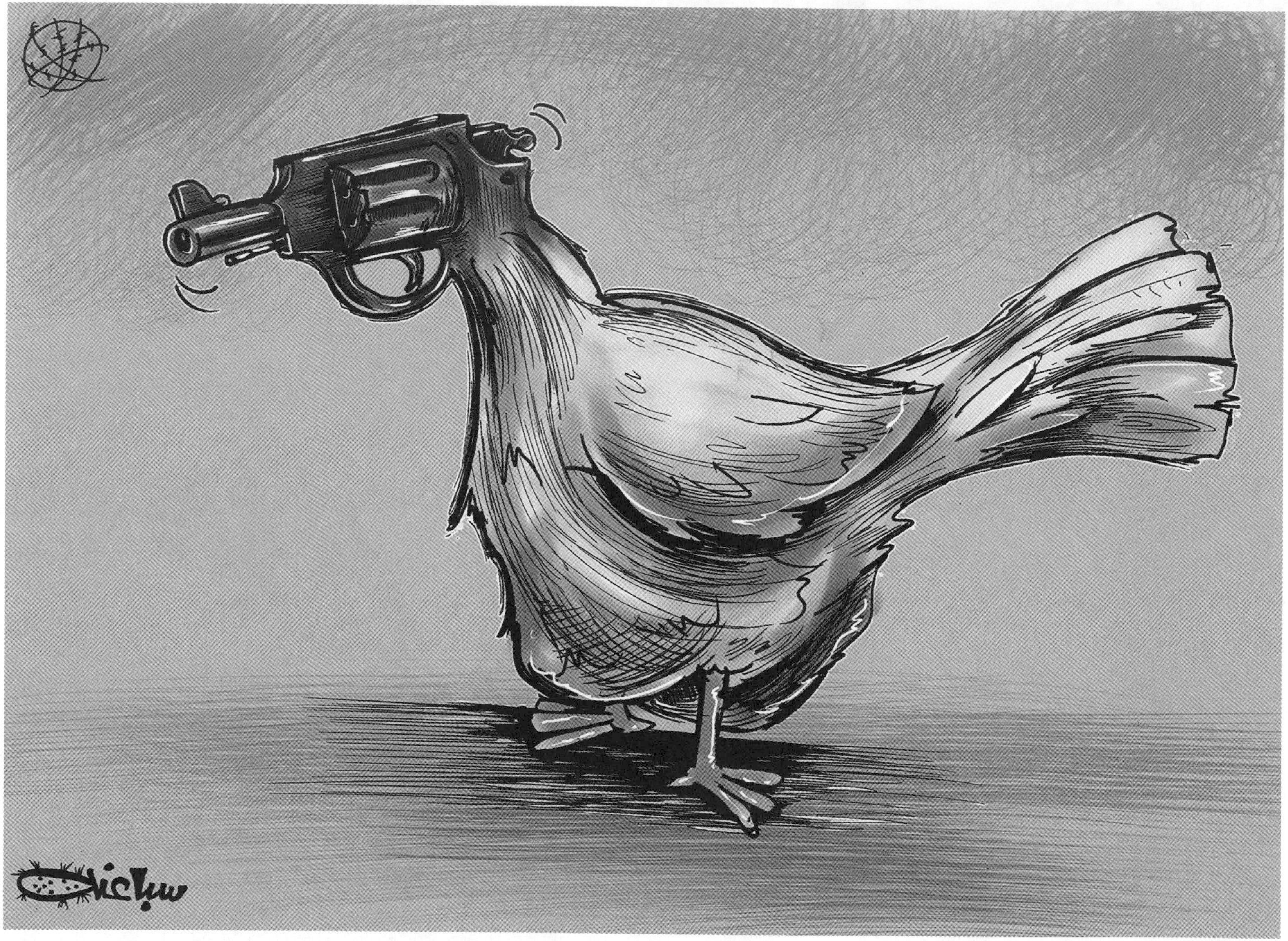

A symbol of peace.

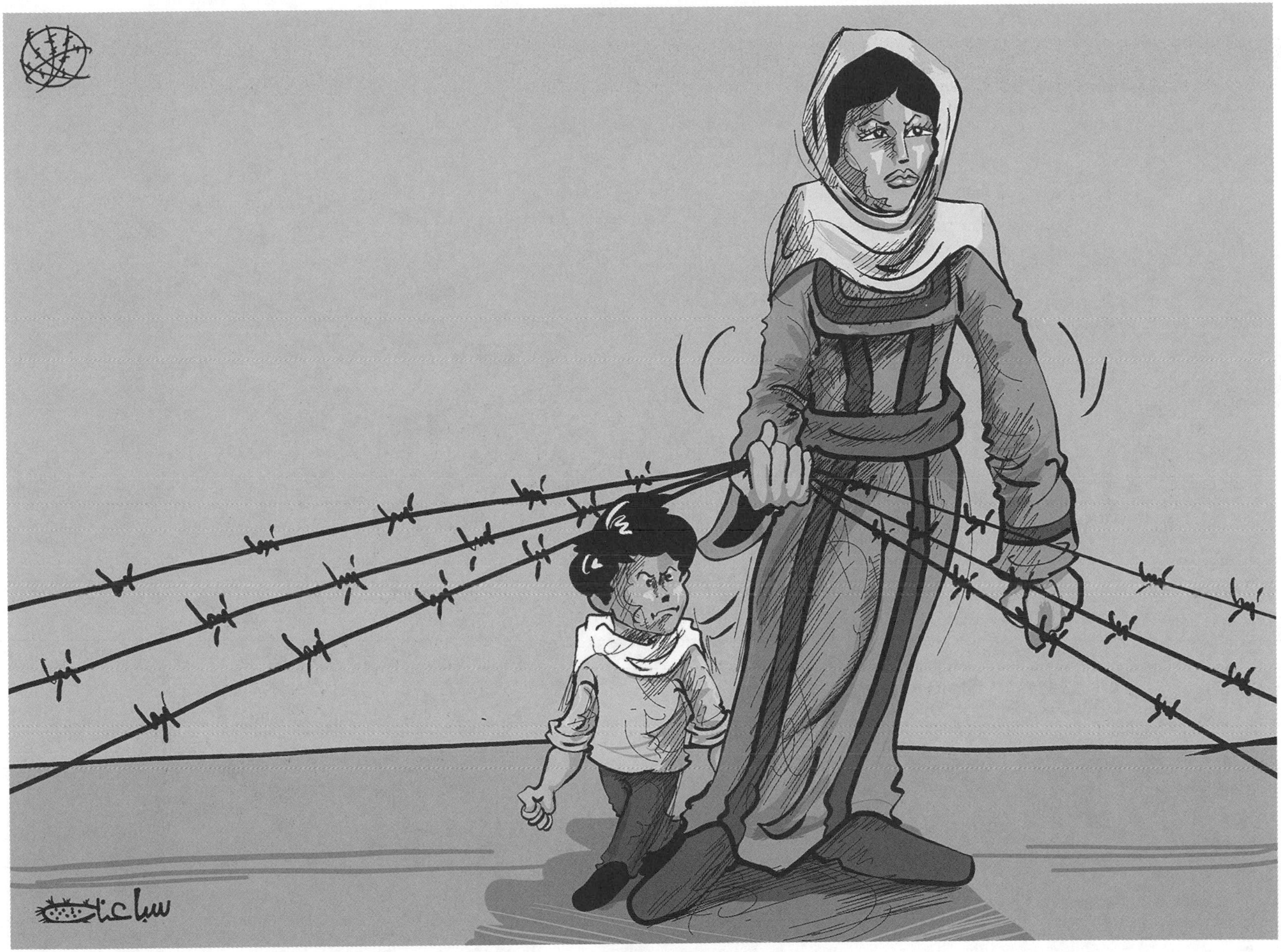

Determination.

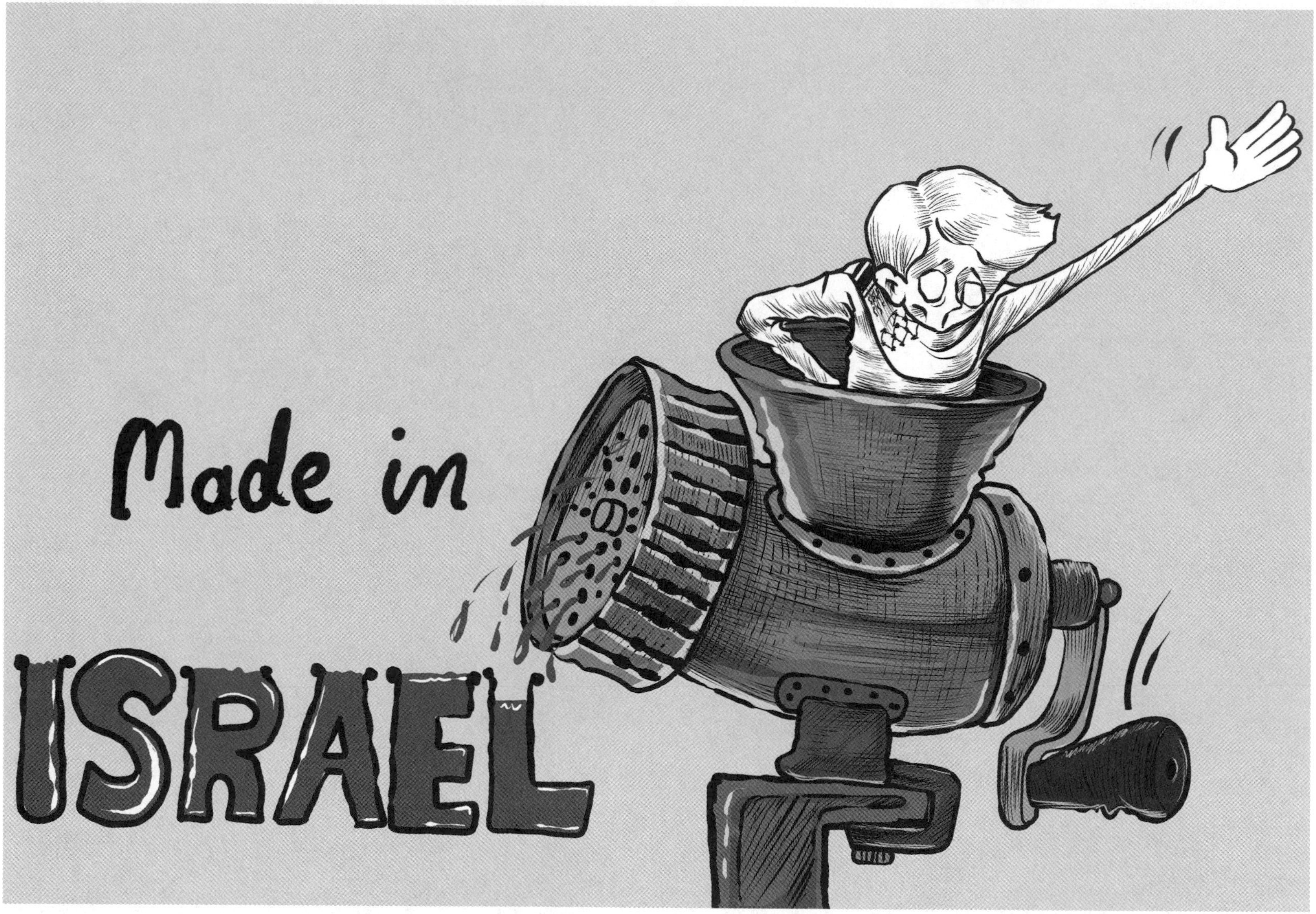
Made in
ISRAEL

Their products are killing us.

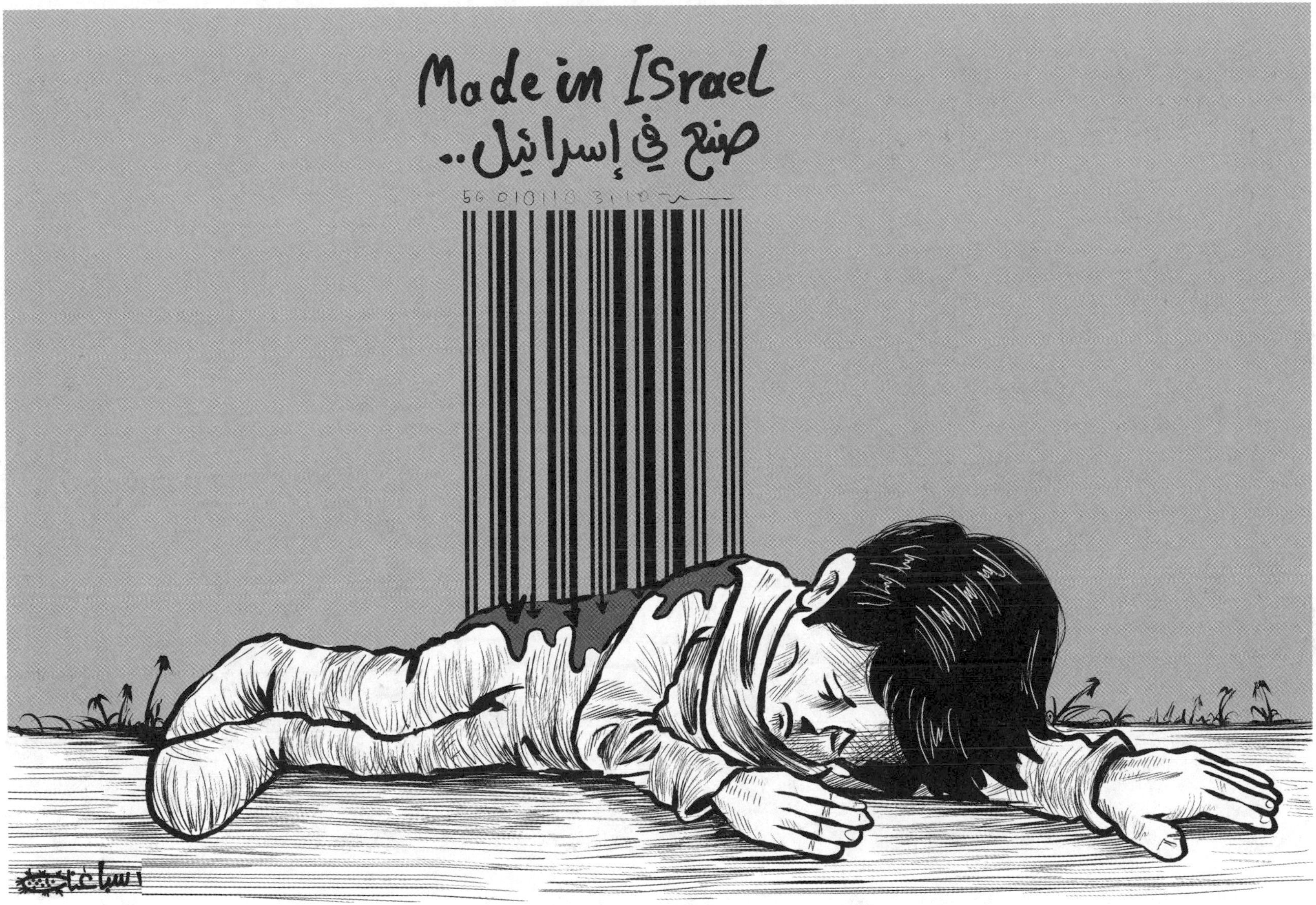
Made in Israel
صنع في إسرائيل..

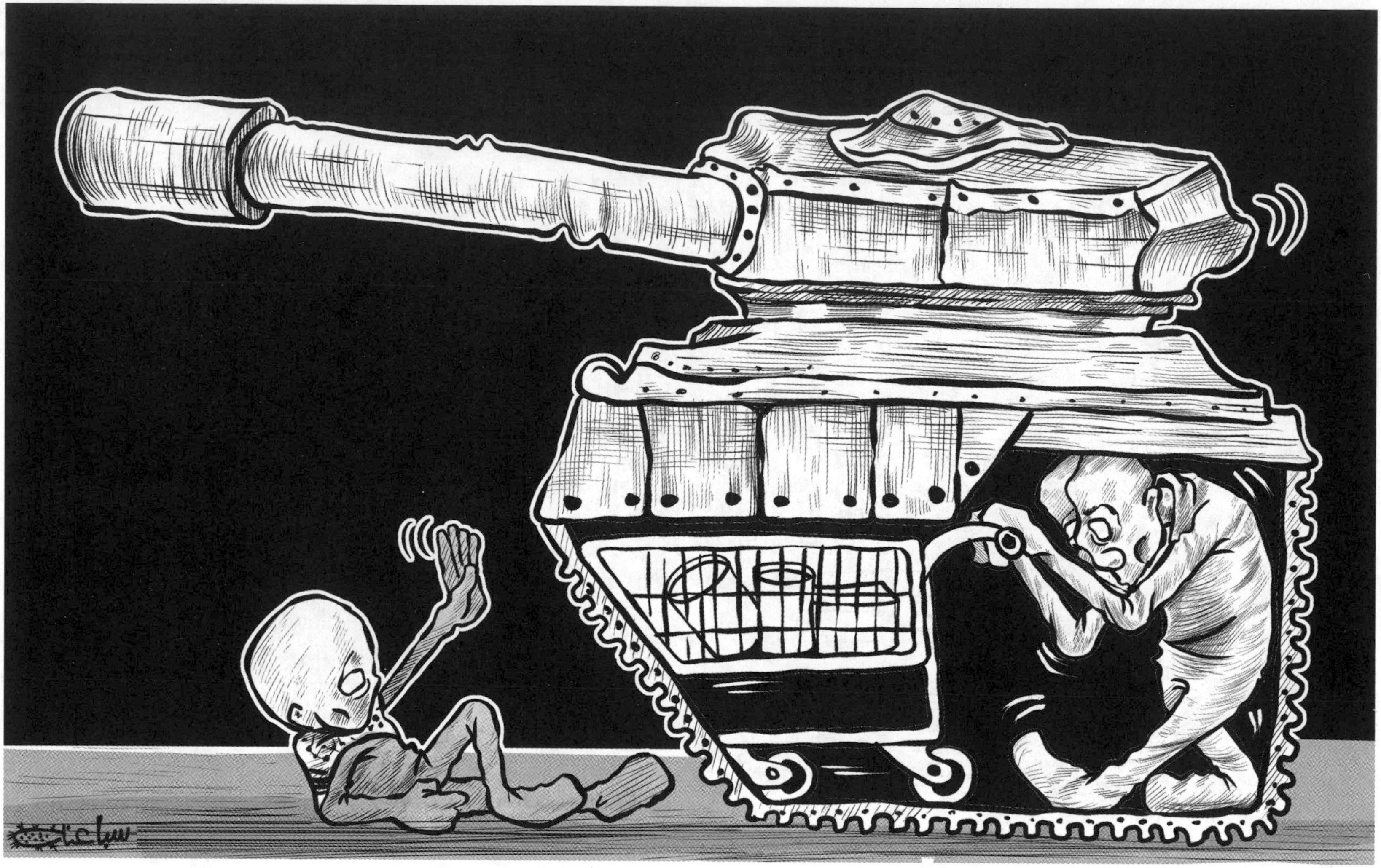

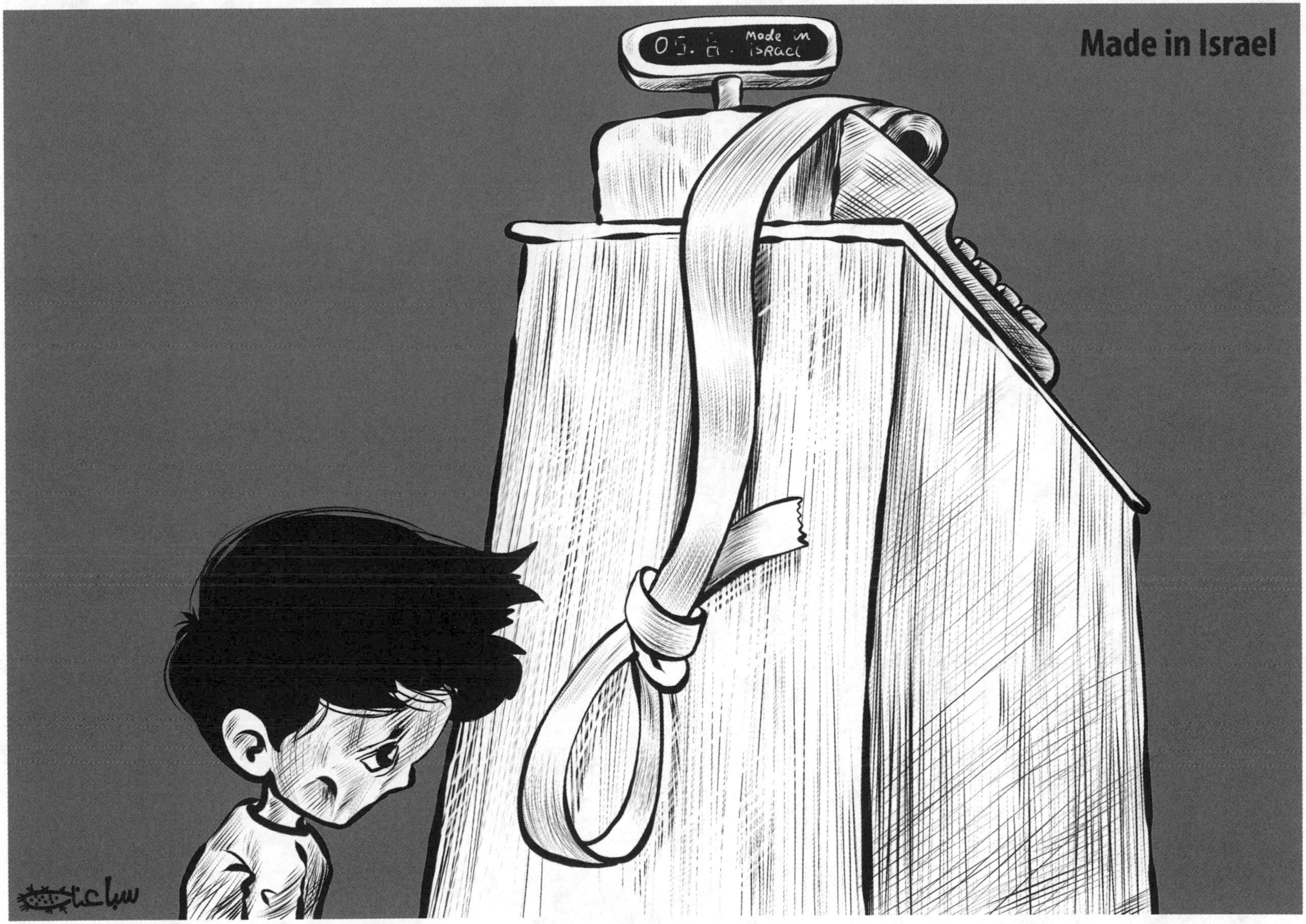
Made in Israel
05.
Made in Israel
سباعنة

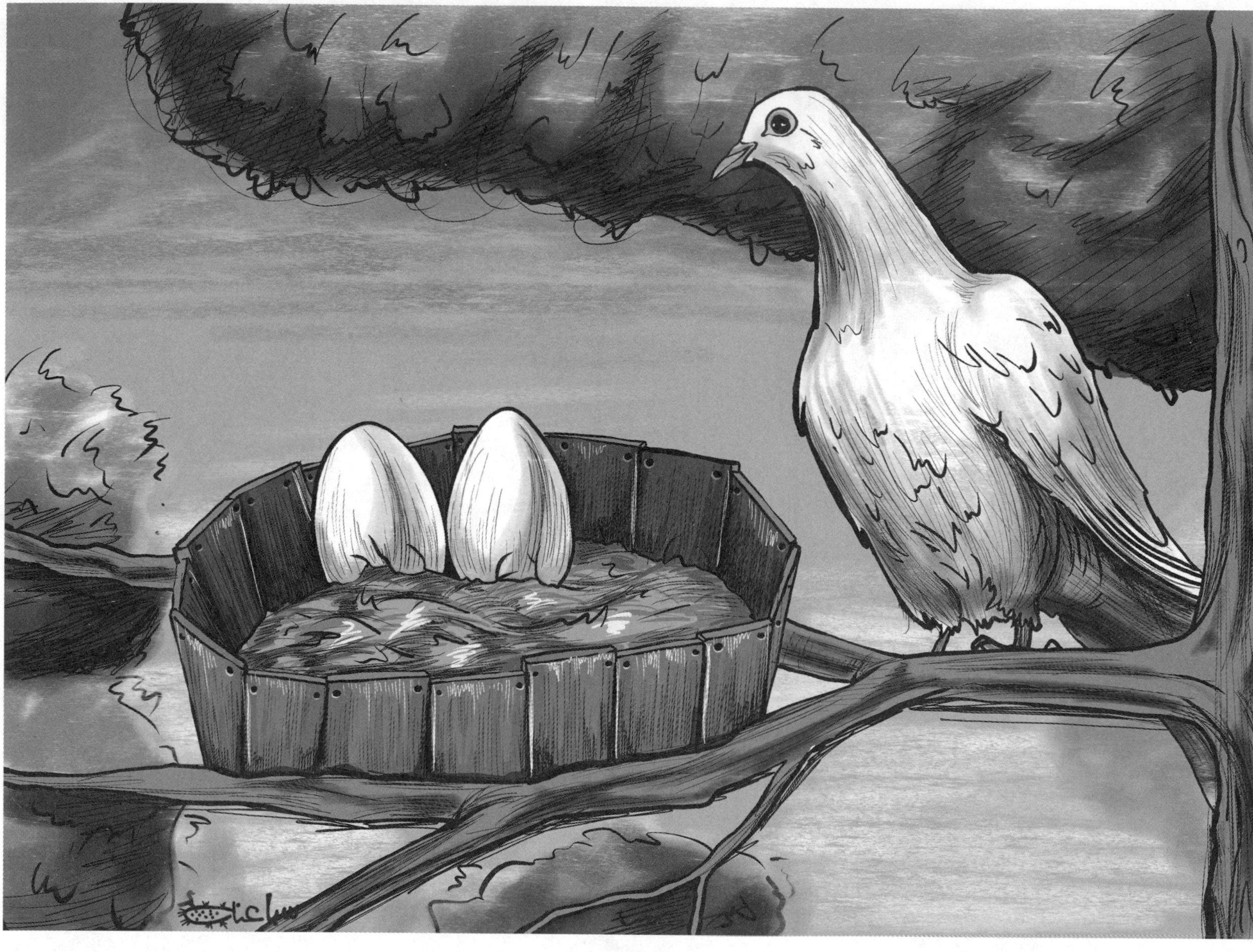

Peace under siege.

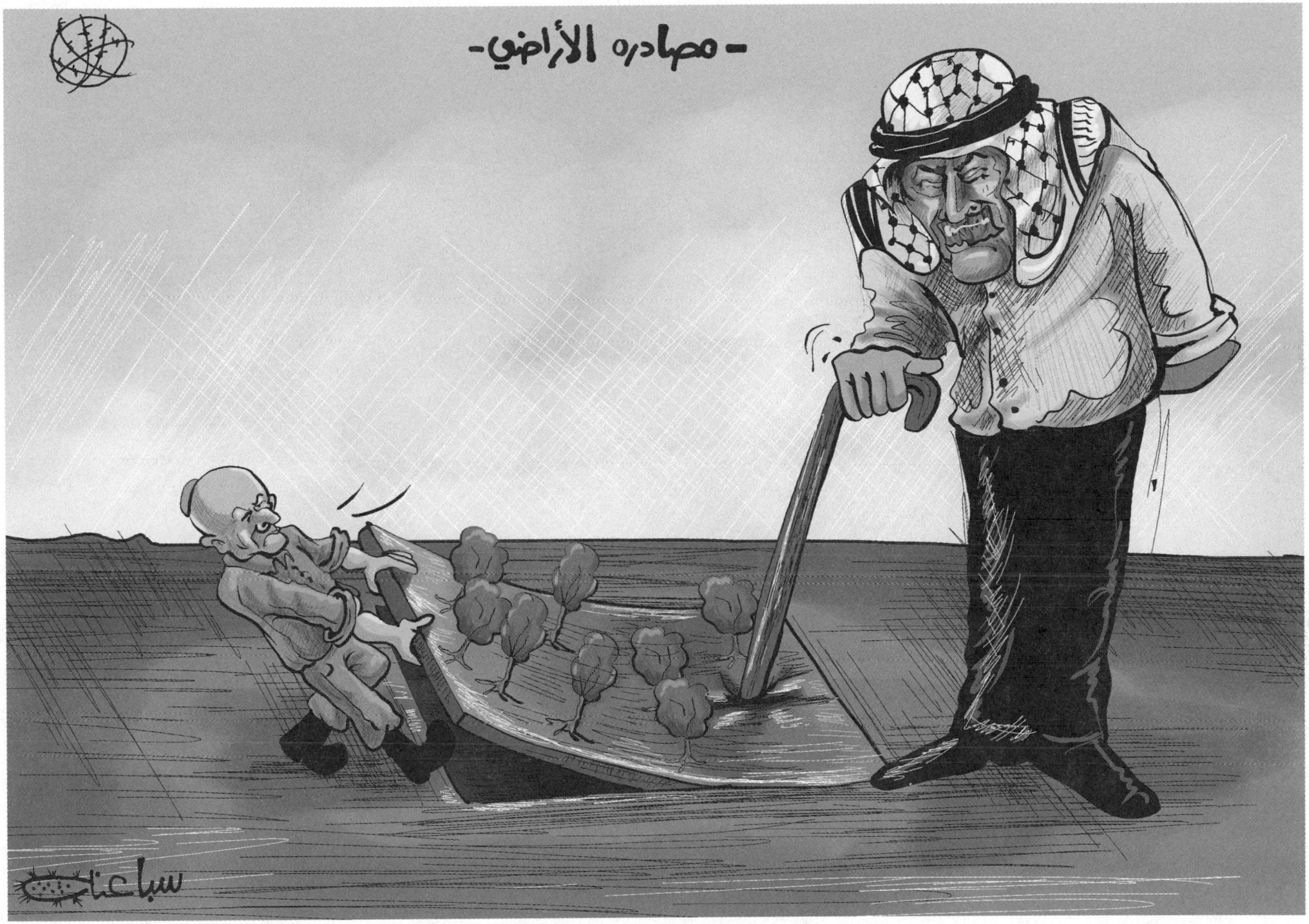
-مصادرة الأراضي-
سباعنة

It's not yours to claim.

CHAPTER 3

PALESTINE AND THE WORLD

I used to think that we Palestinians were the only ones suffering ongoing disaster until I learned that other people in other places, who speak other languages and whose features and complexions do not resemble mine, also suffer and bleed just as we do, and often in silence. They too prematurely bury their loved ones, or cannot live together as a family, or find themselves at the mercy of powerful greed, or are forced to wait until their circumstances change. They wait.

To be a Palestinian is to feel a kinship with people around the world who suffer. Over the years, when I have found it difficult to explain the hard conditions in which we Palestinians live, I have drawn comparisons with what people know in their own communities, and I say: I am like your unarmed black neighbor who was shot dead last year; I am like indigenous people everywhere whose presence is inconvenient to those in power.

96

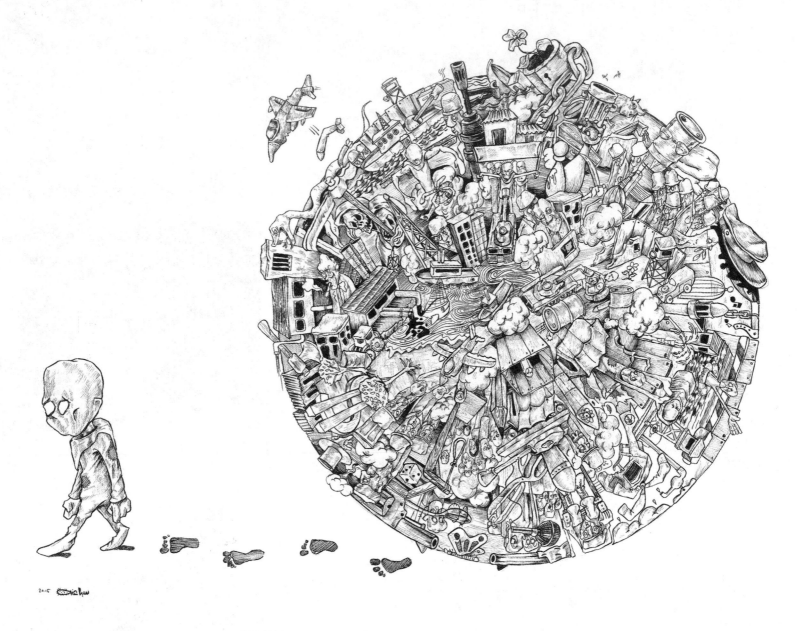

Walking away from the sadness of it all.

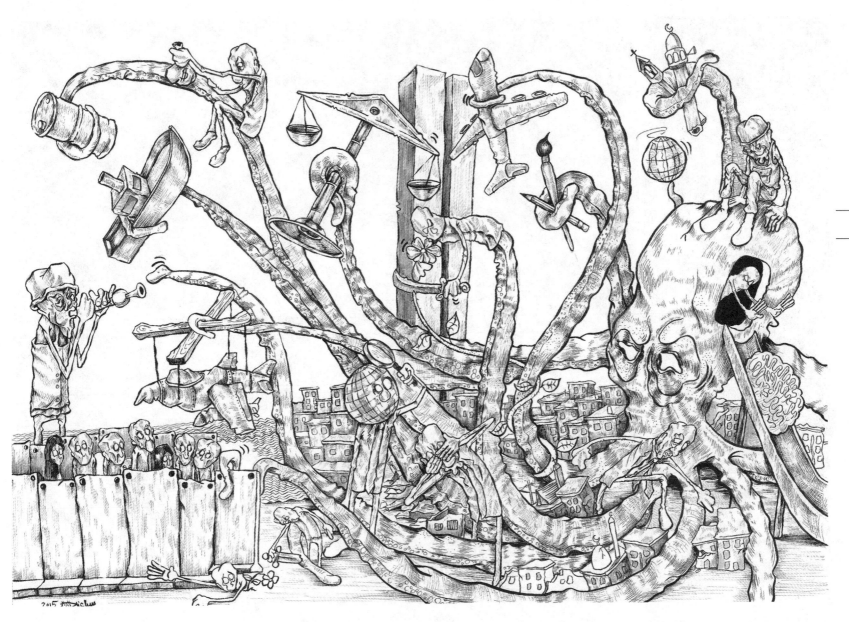

The iron grip of global forces.

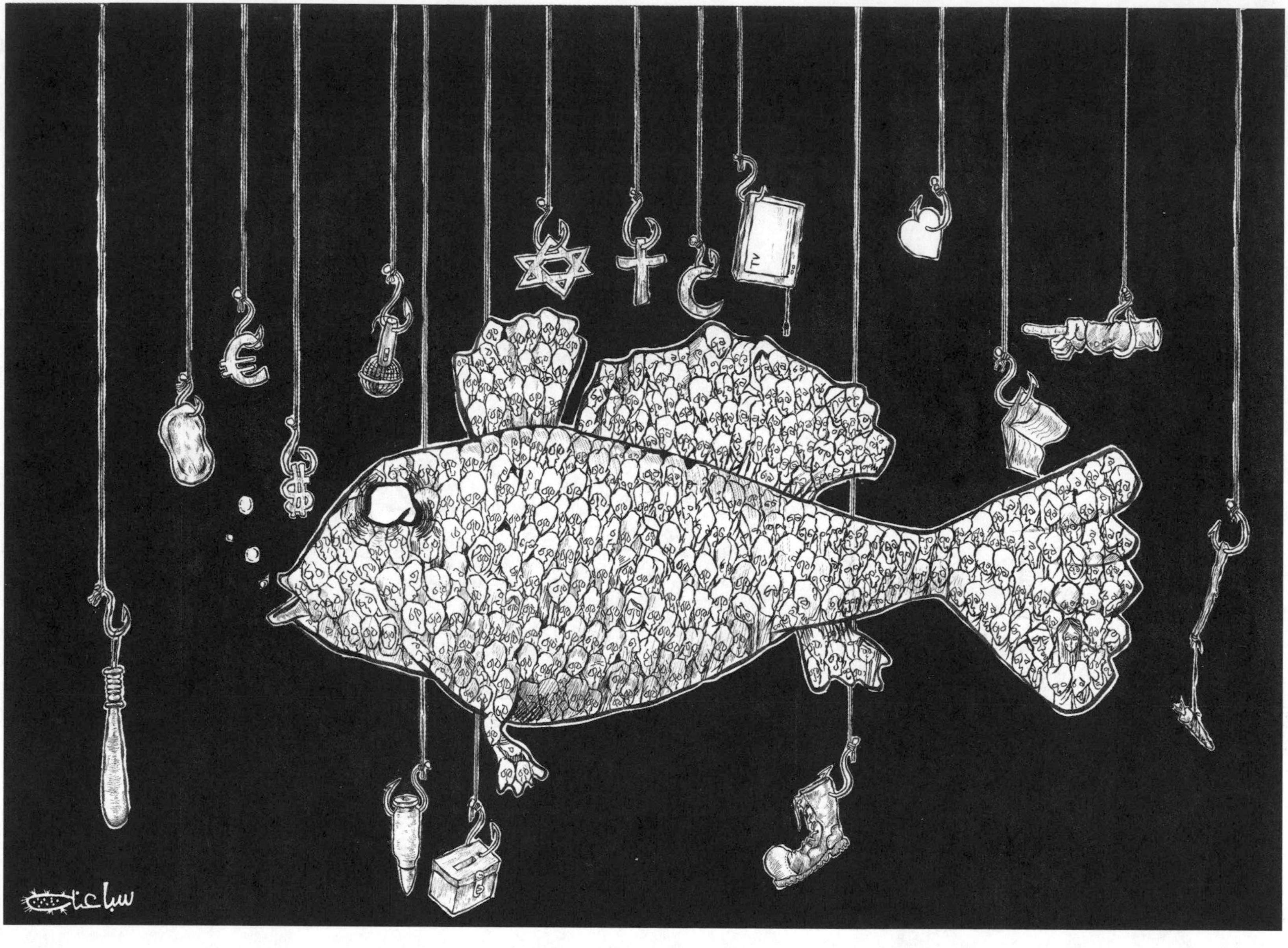

How are nations led, and who leads them?

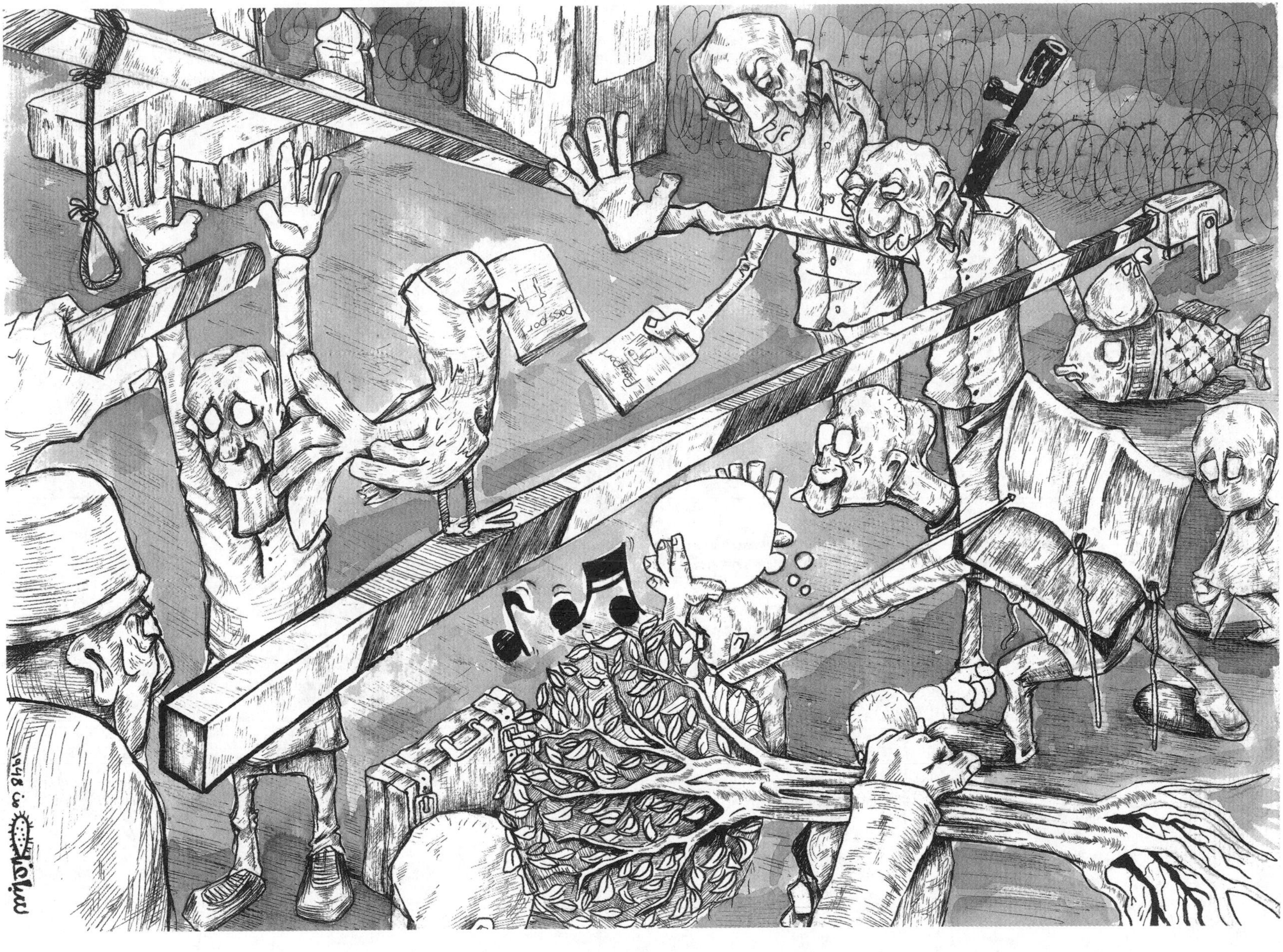
passport

When people leave their homelands.

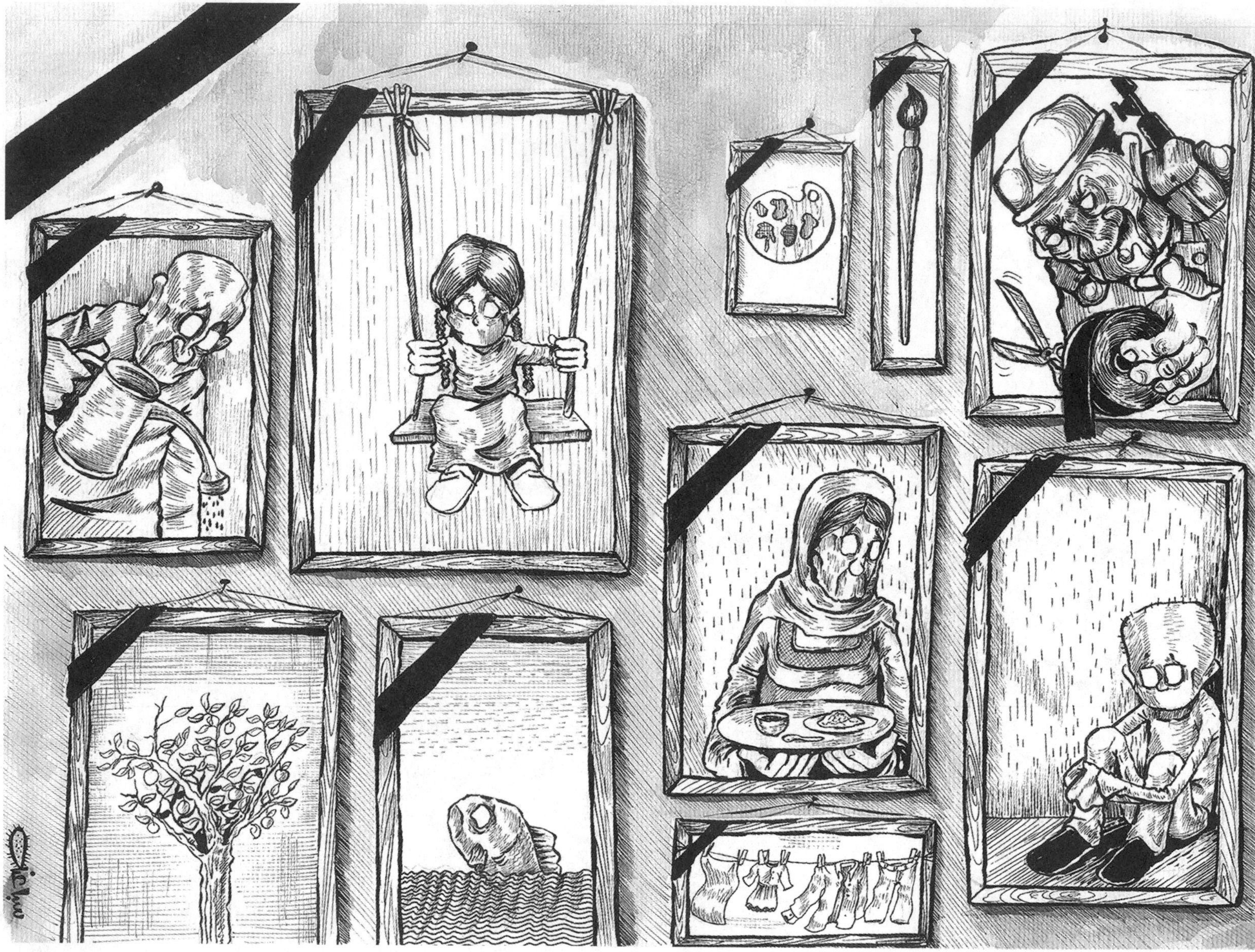

Family photos.

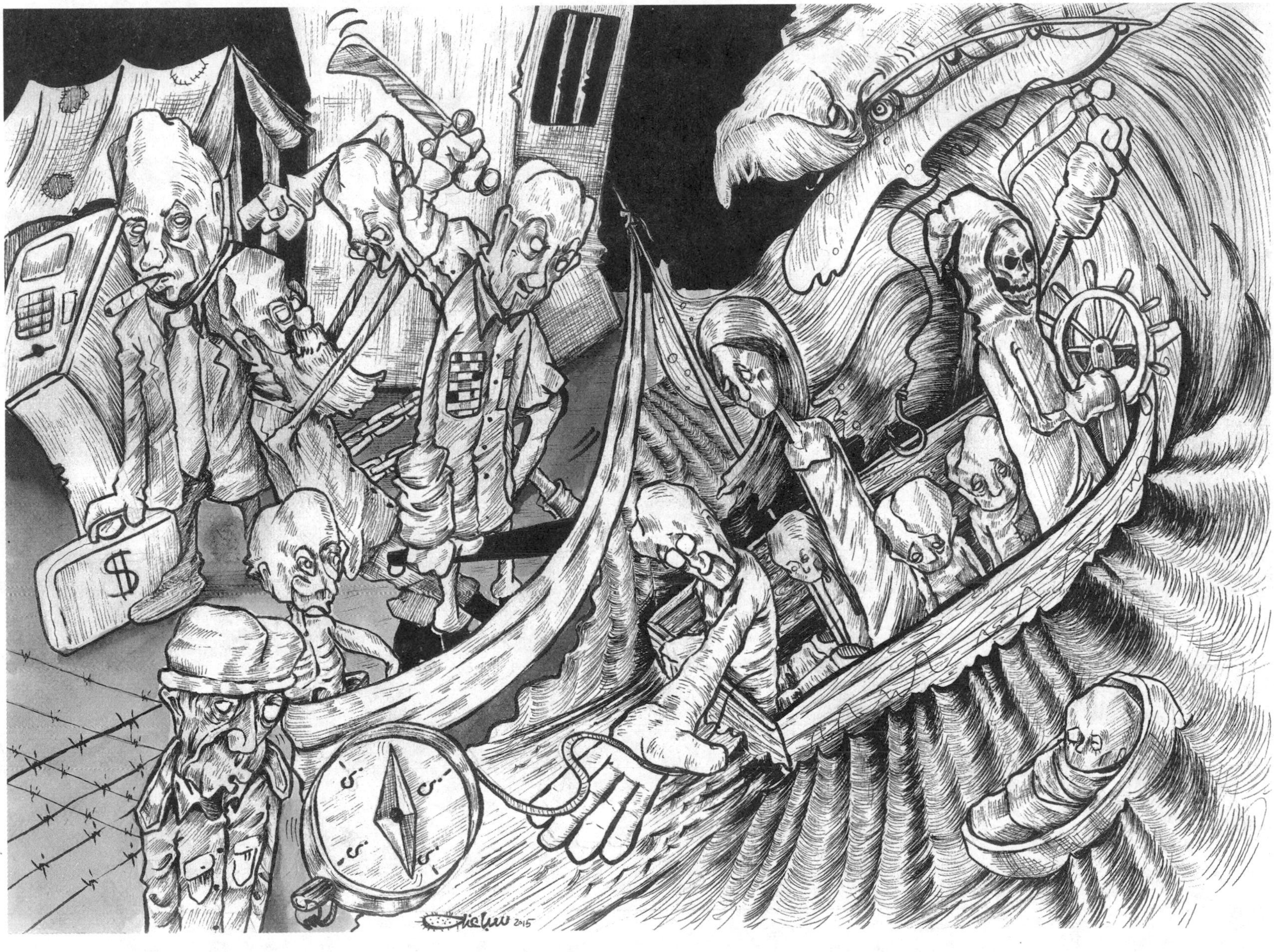

How desperate do people have to be to take such awful risks, and who is responsible?

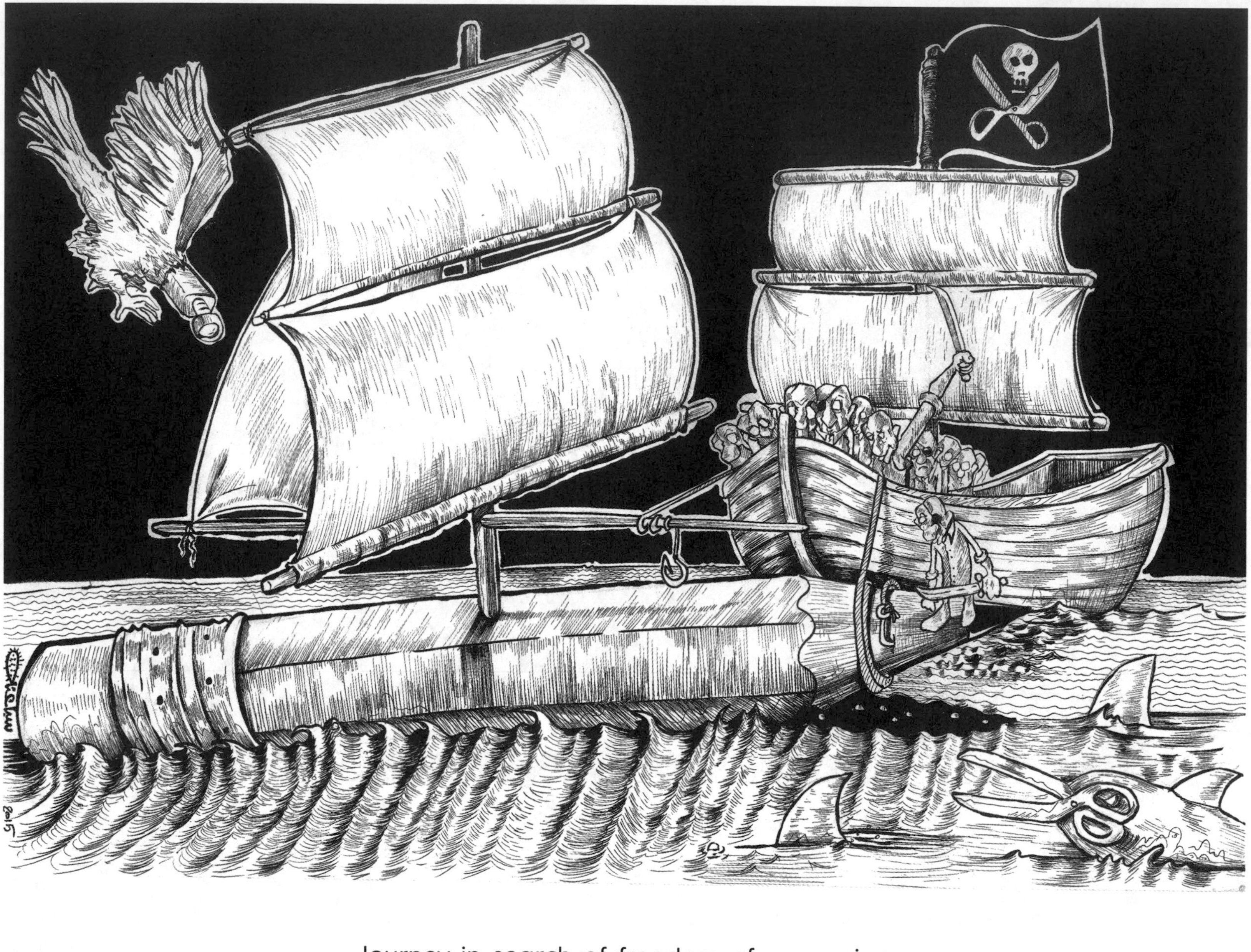

Journey in search of freedom of expression.

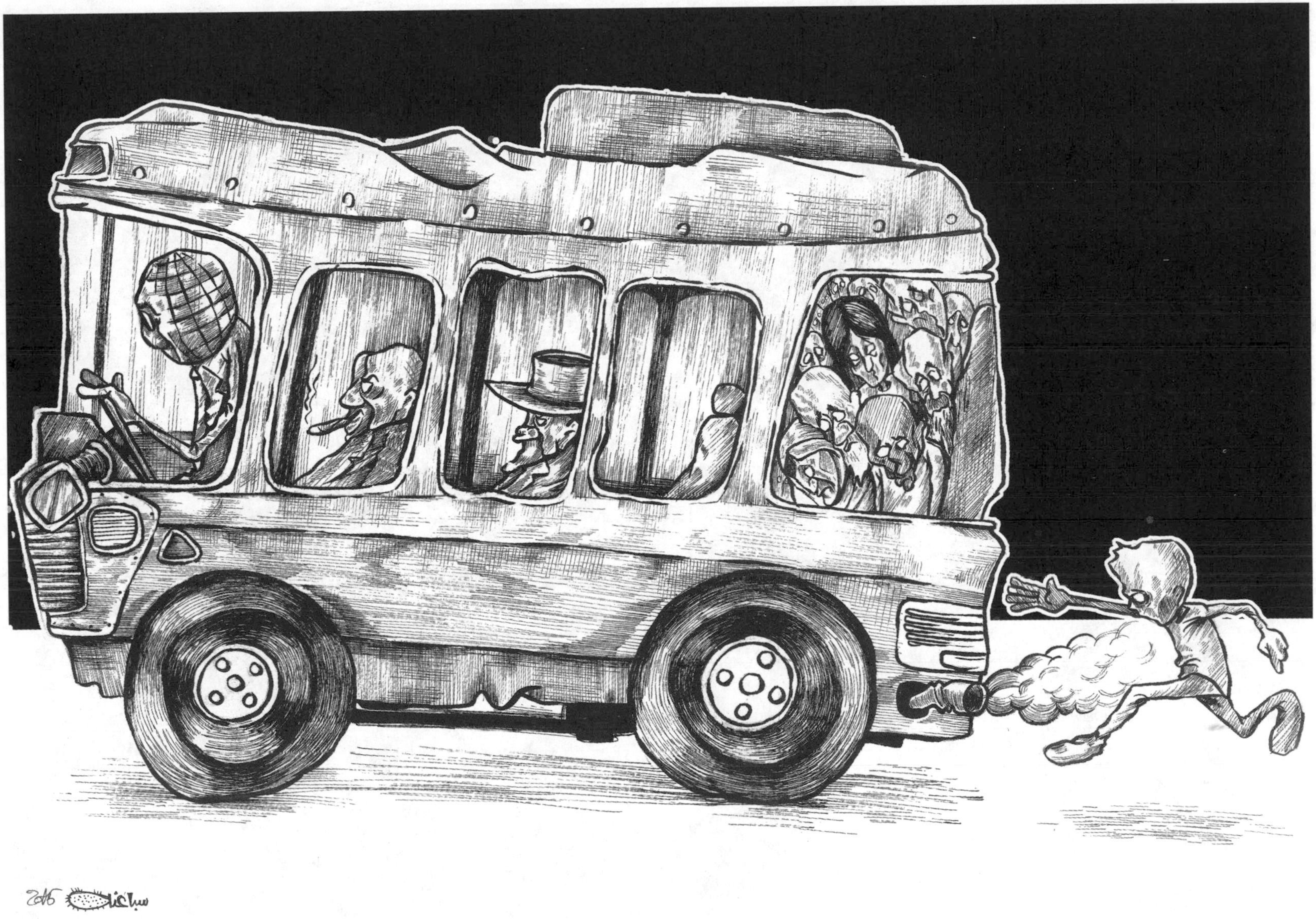

Apartheid is global.

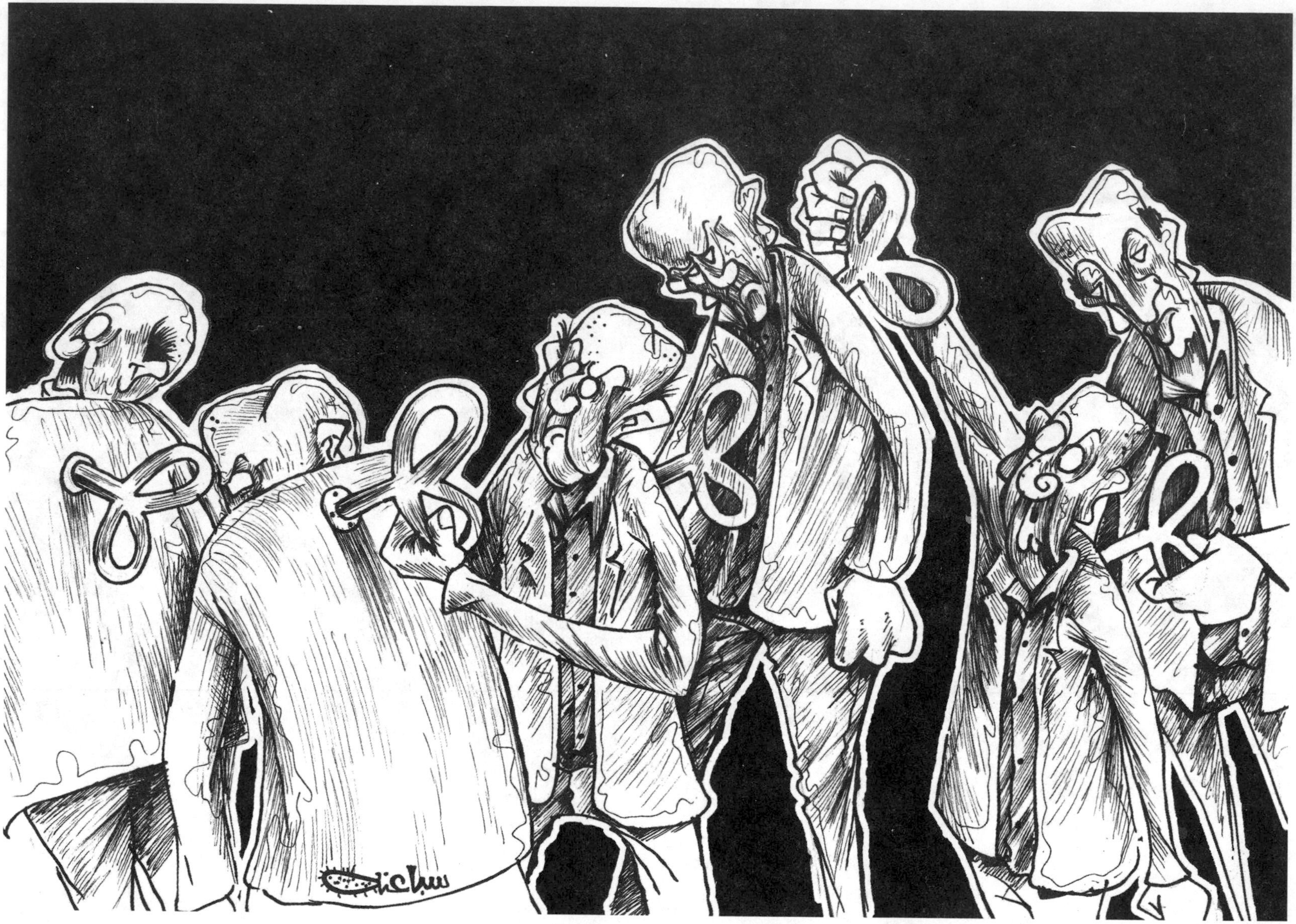

Interrelated interests and functional politics.

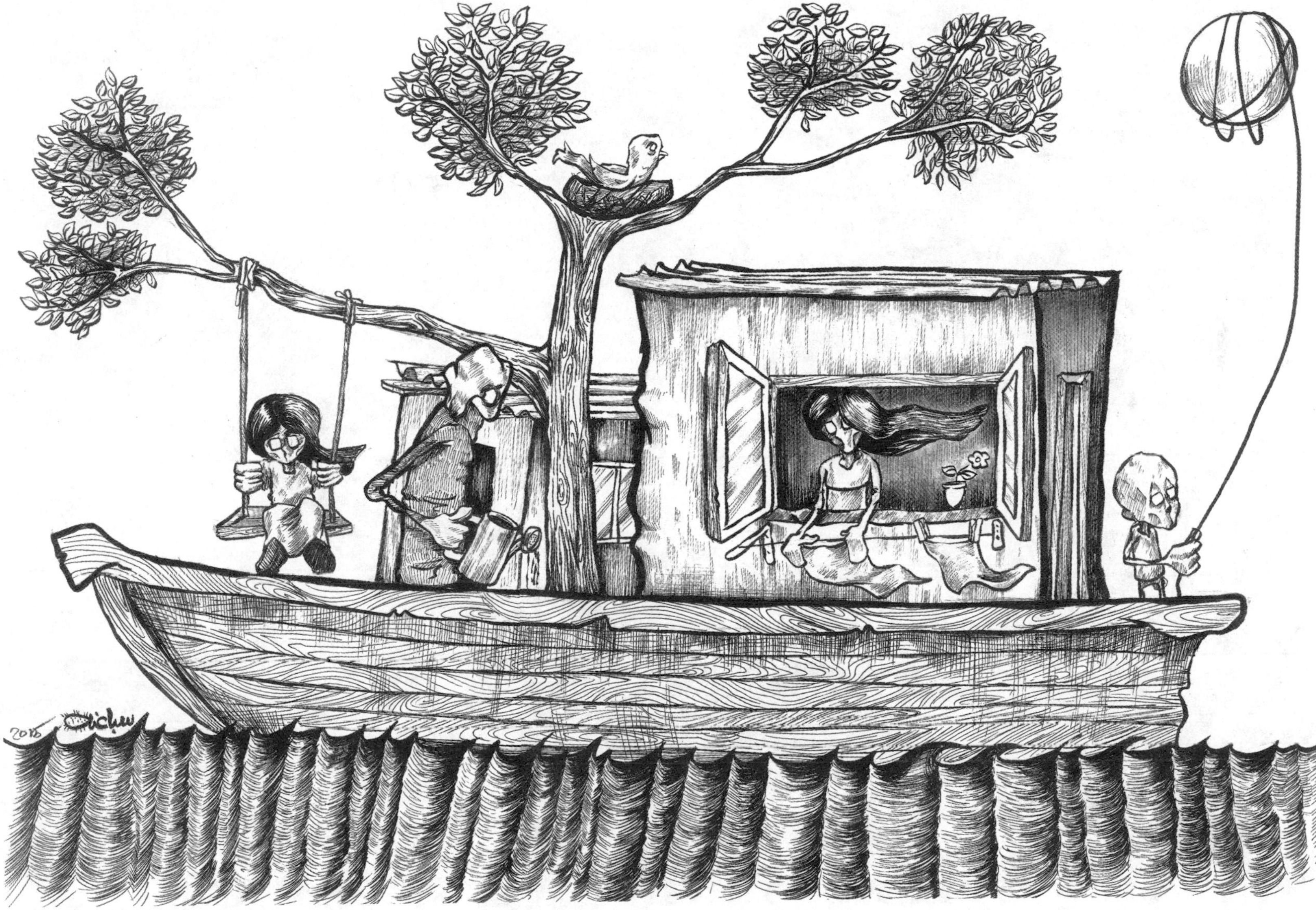

In search of a normal life.

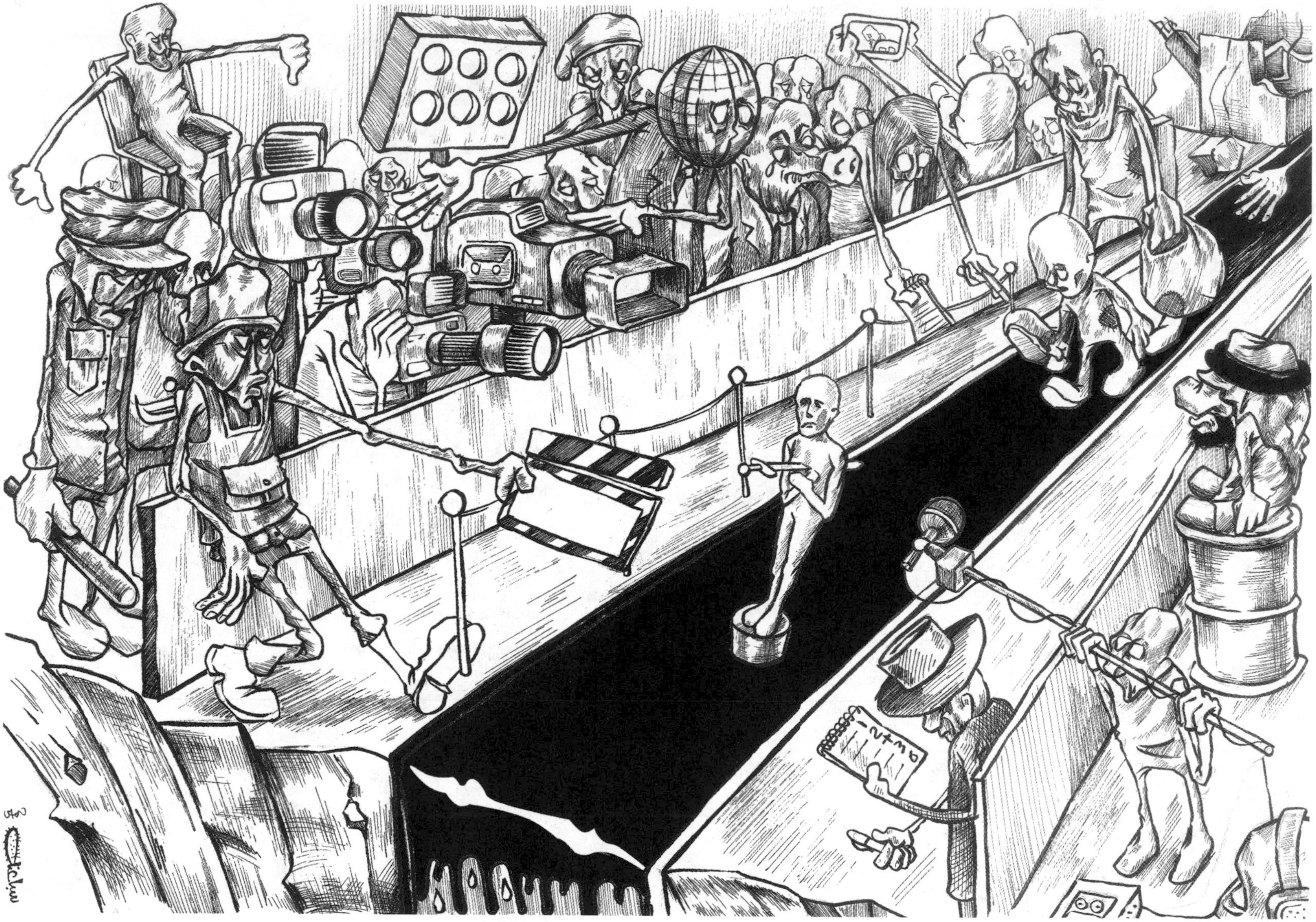

In this race there are no winners.

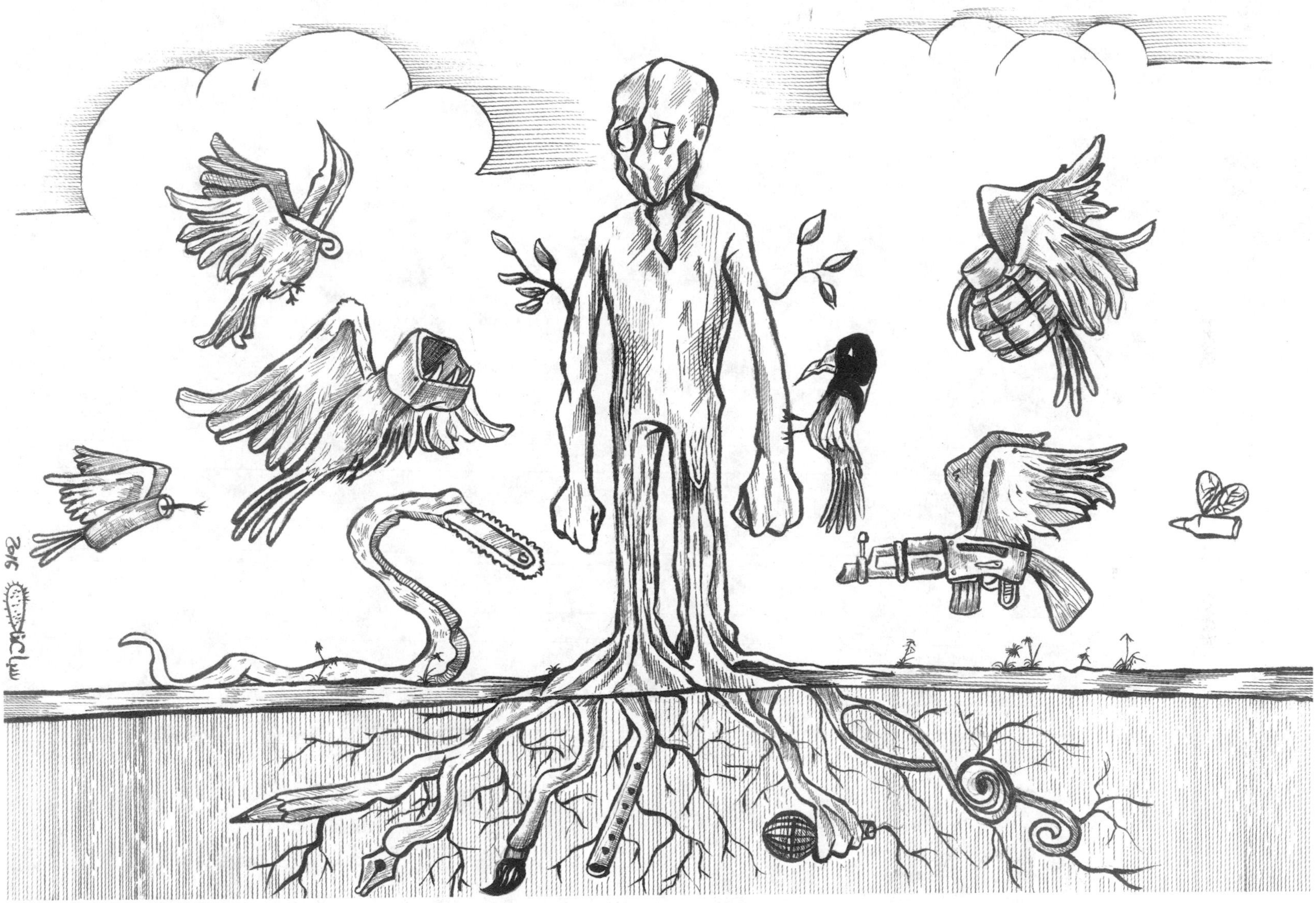

Various forms of cultural roots.

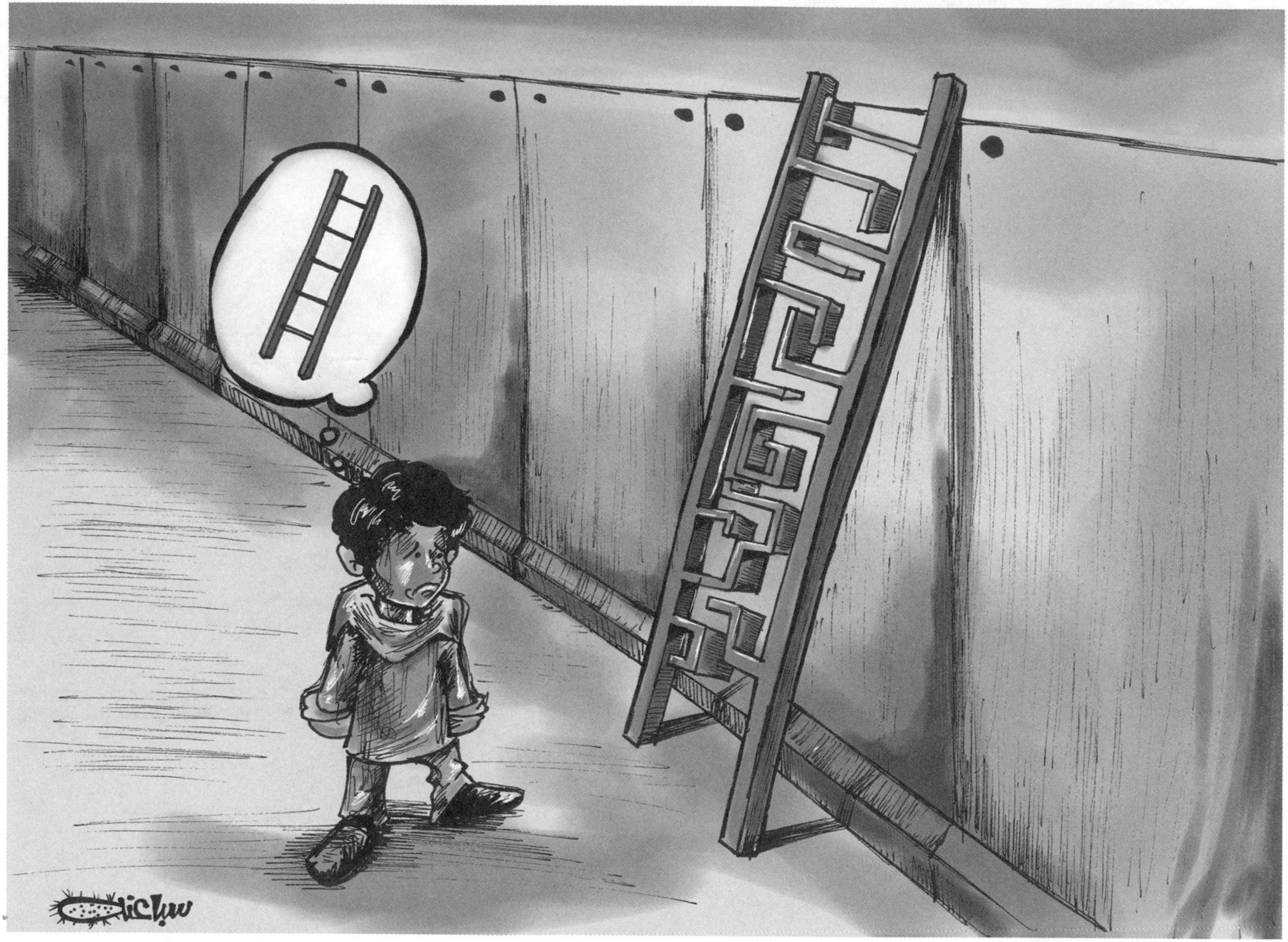

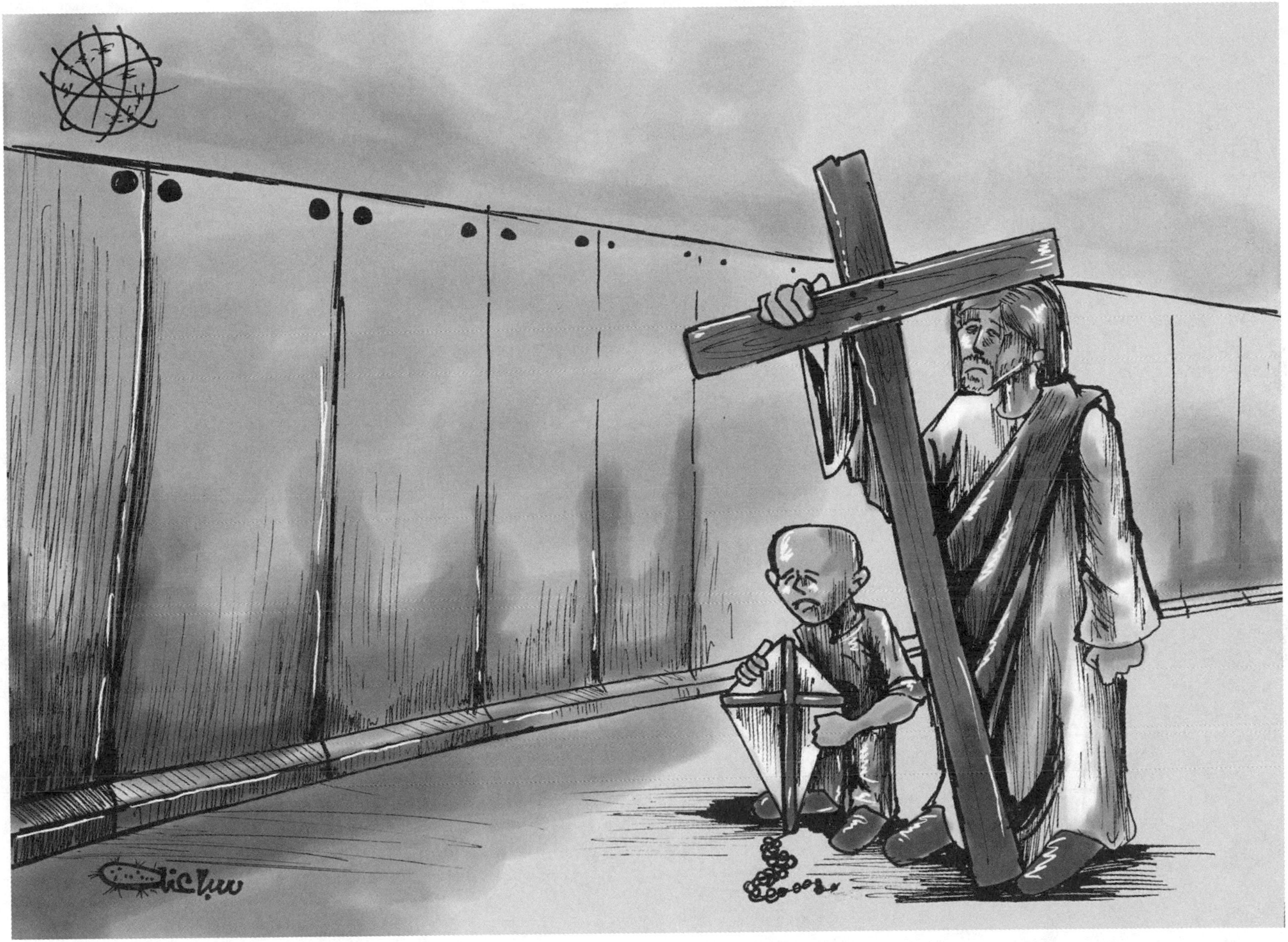

Every age has a prophet.

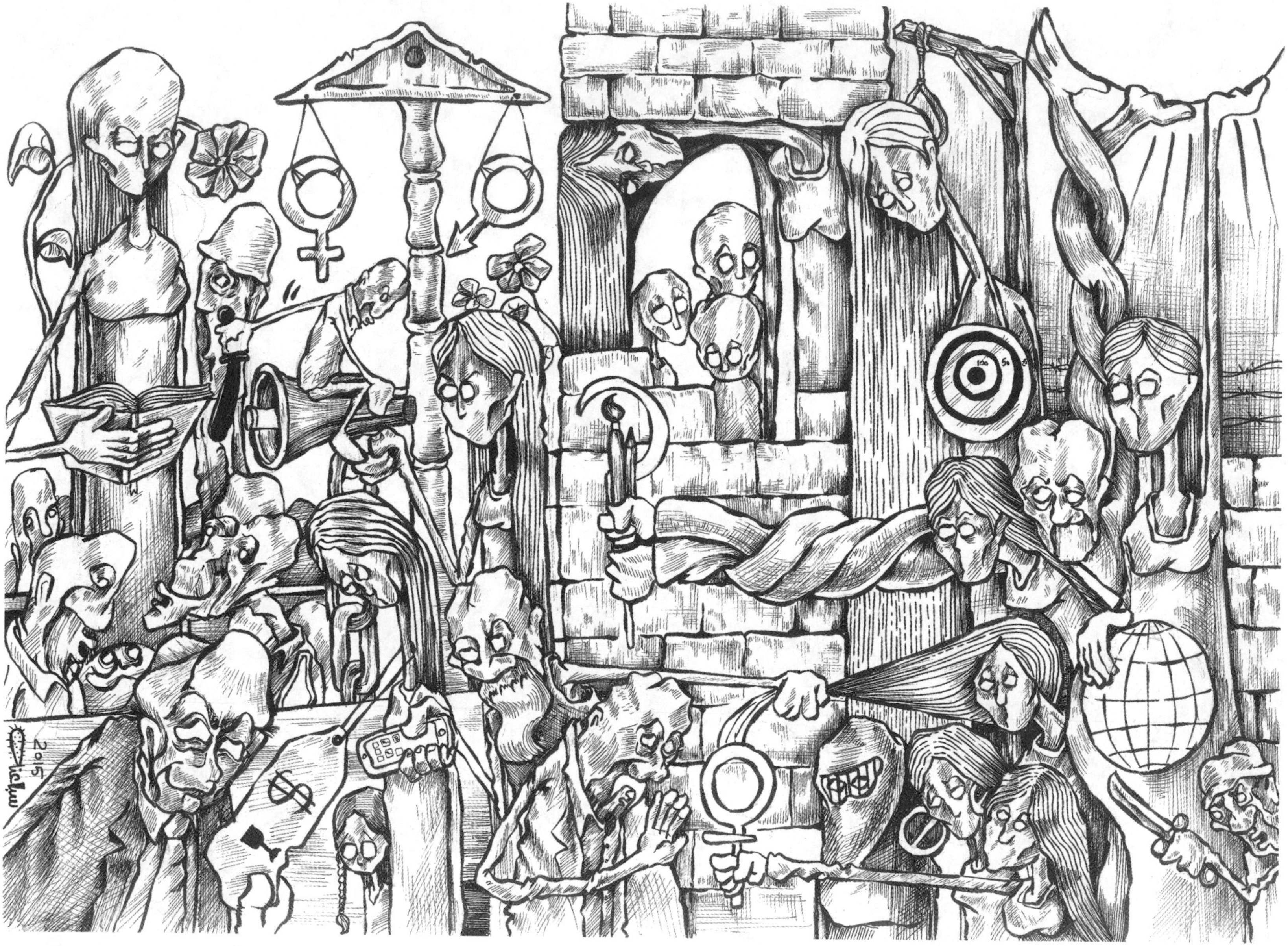

Status of women globally.

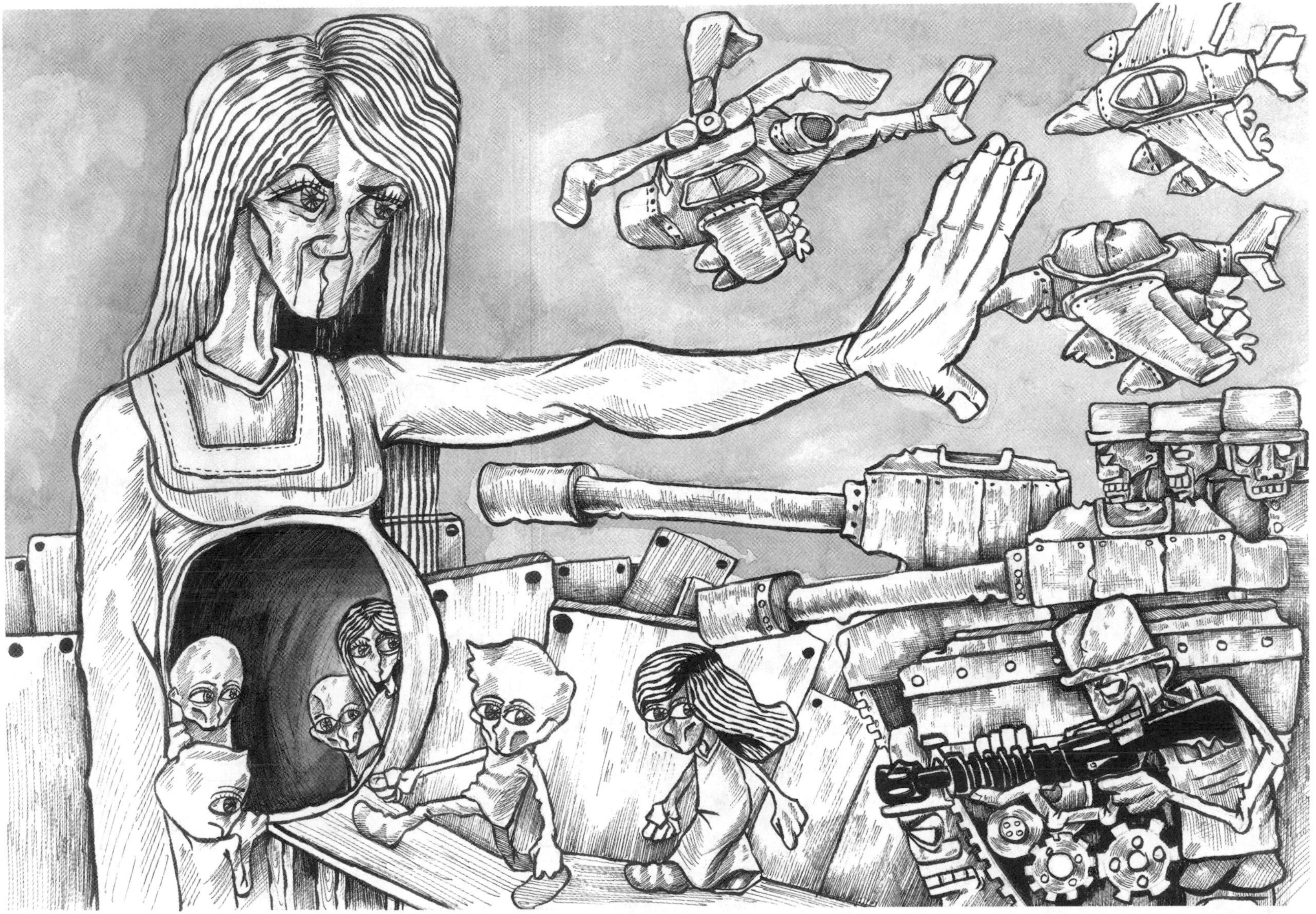

Life suspended by military occupation.

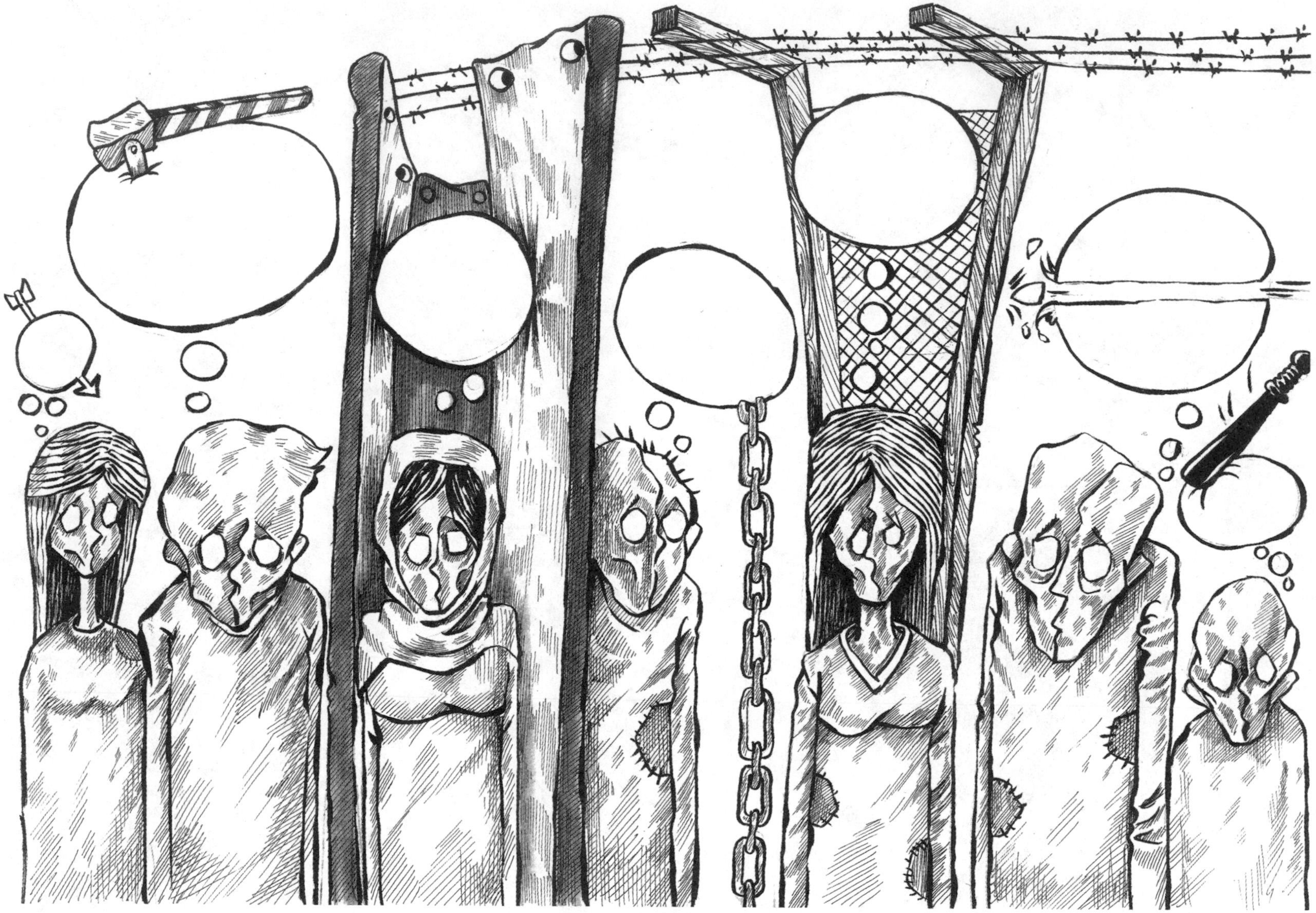

A narrative told by a scared bullet.

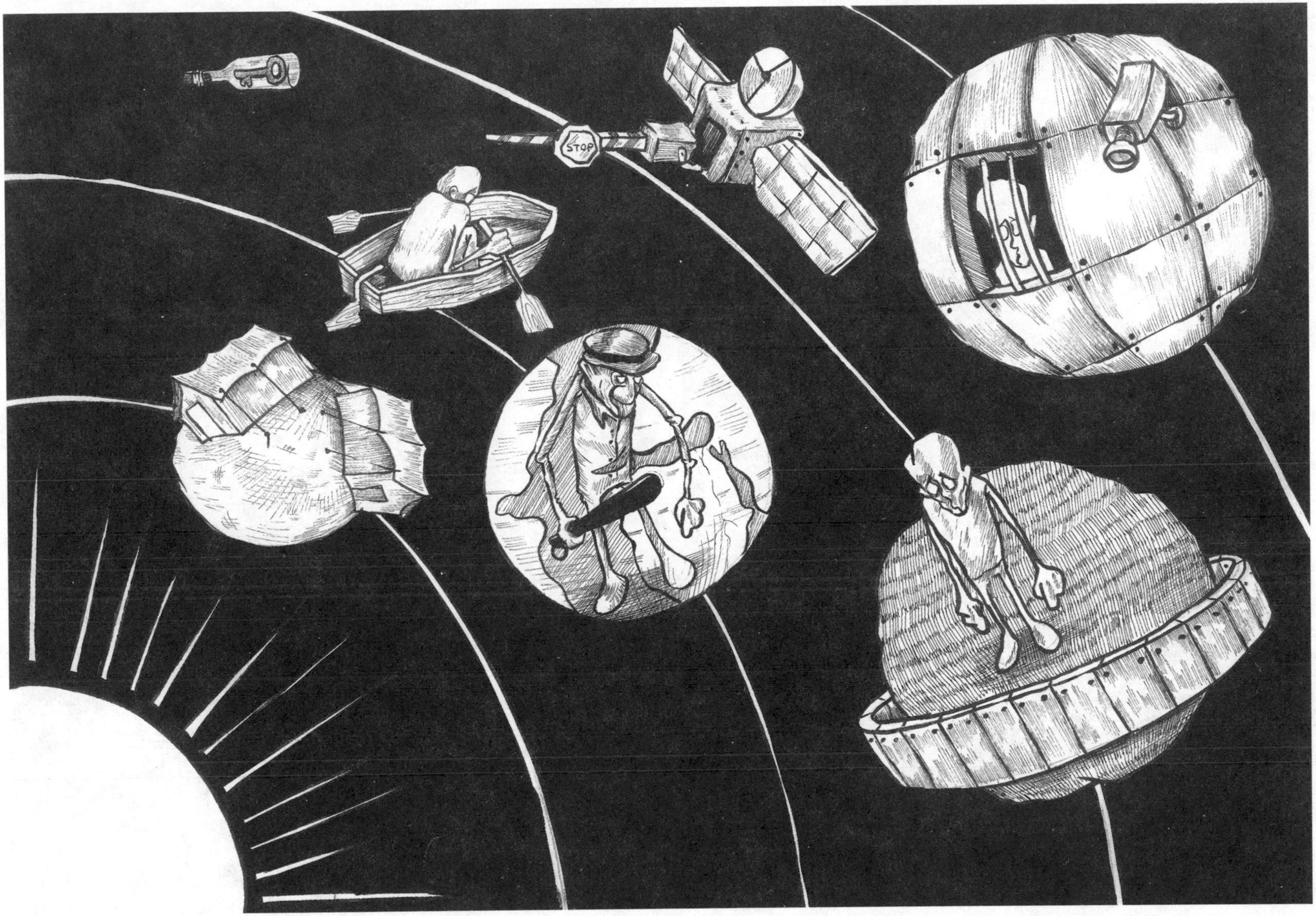
STOP

The orbits are created by a system, but our regimes control our orbits.

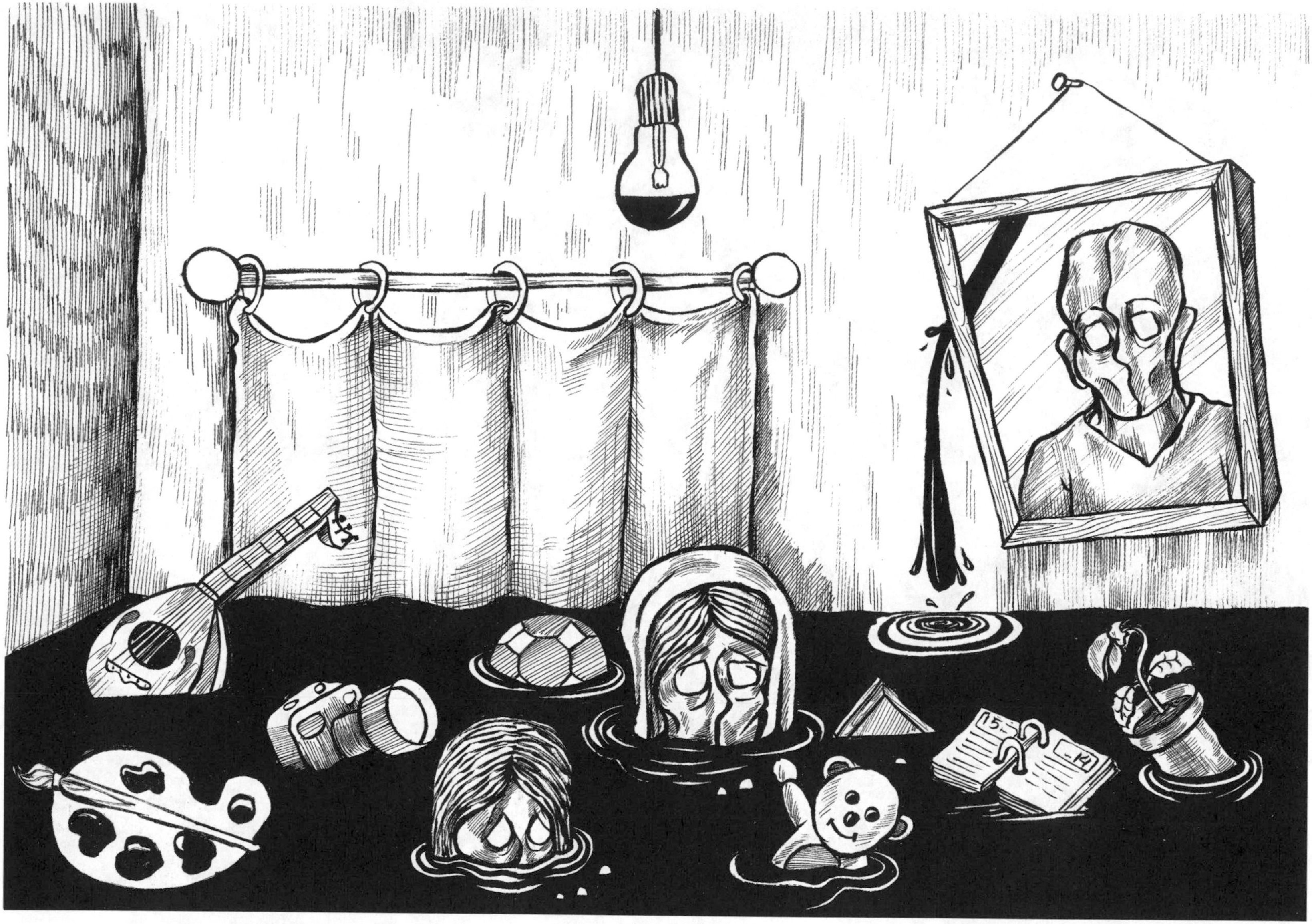

Past and present fight for the future.

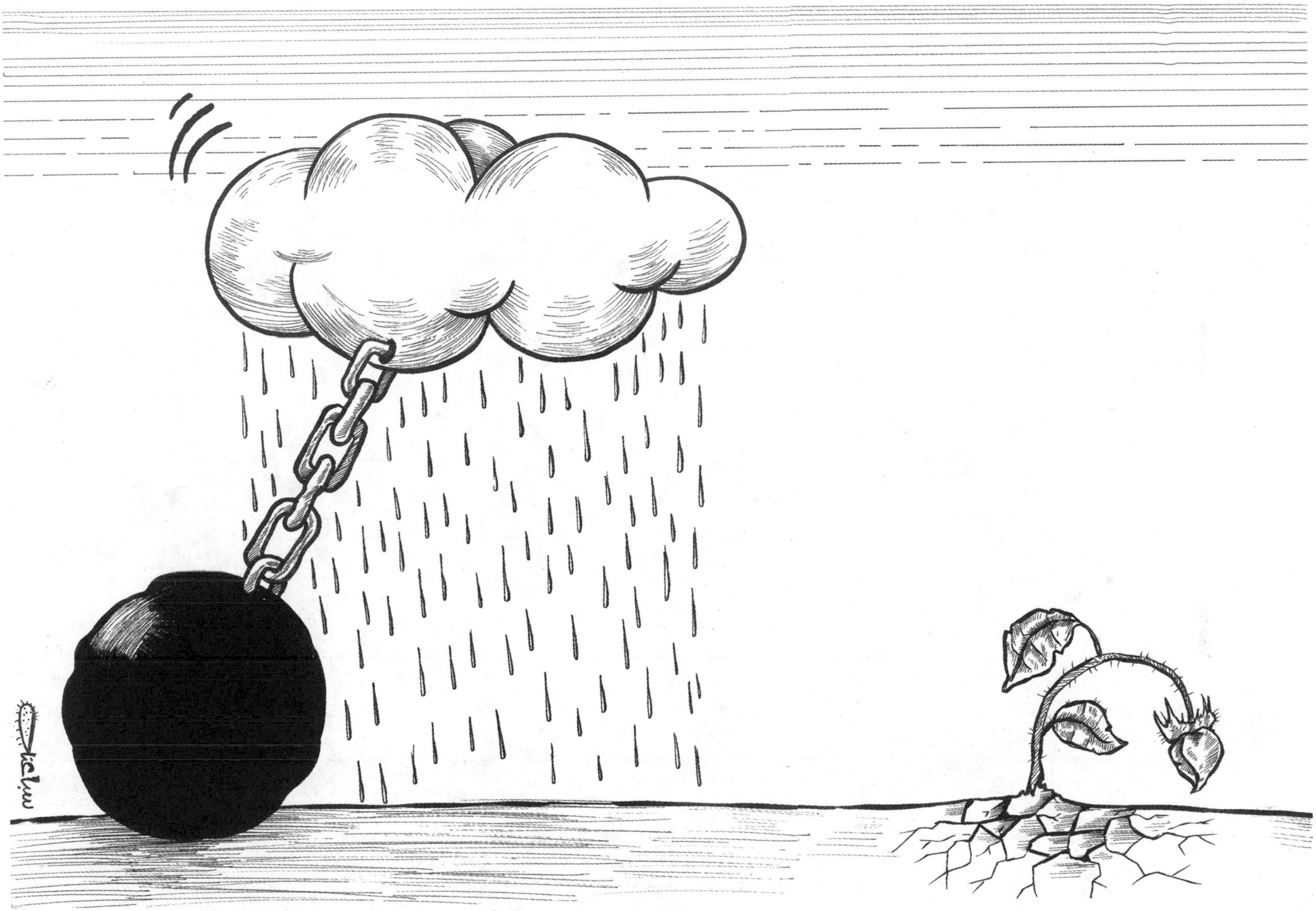

The price of controlling nature.

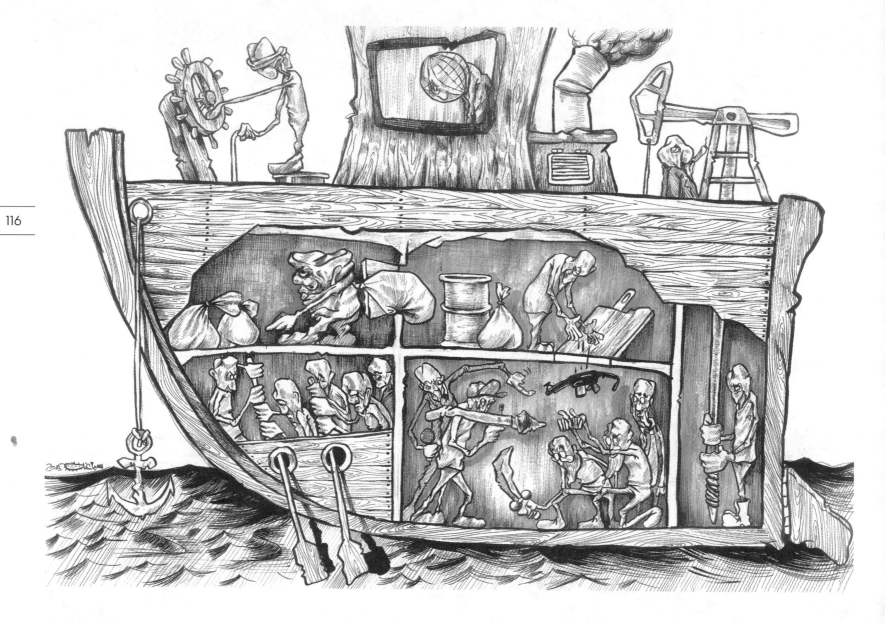

What takes place beneath the surface.

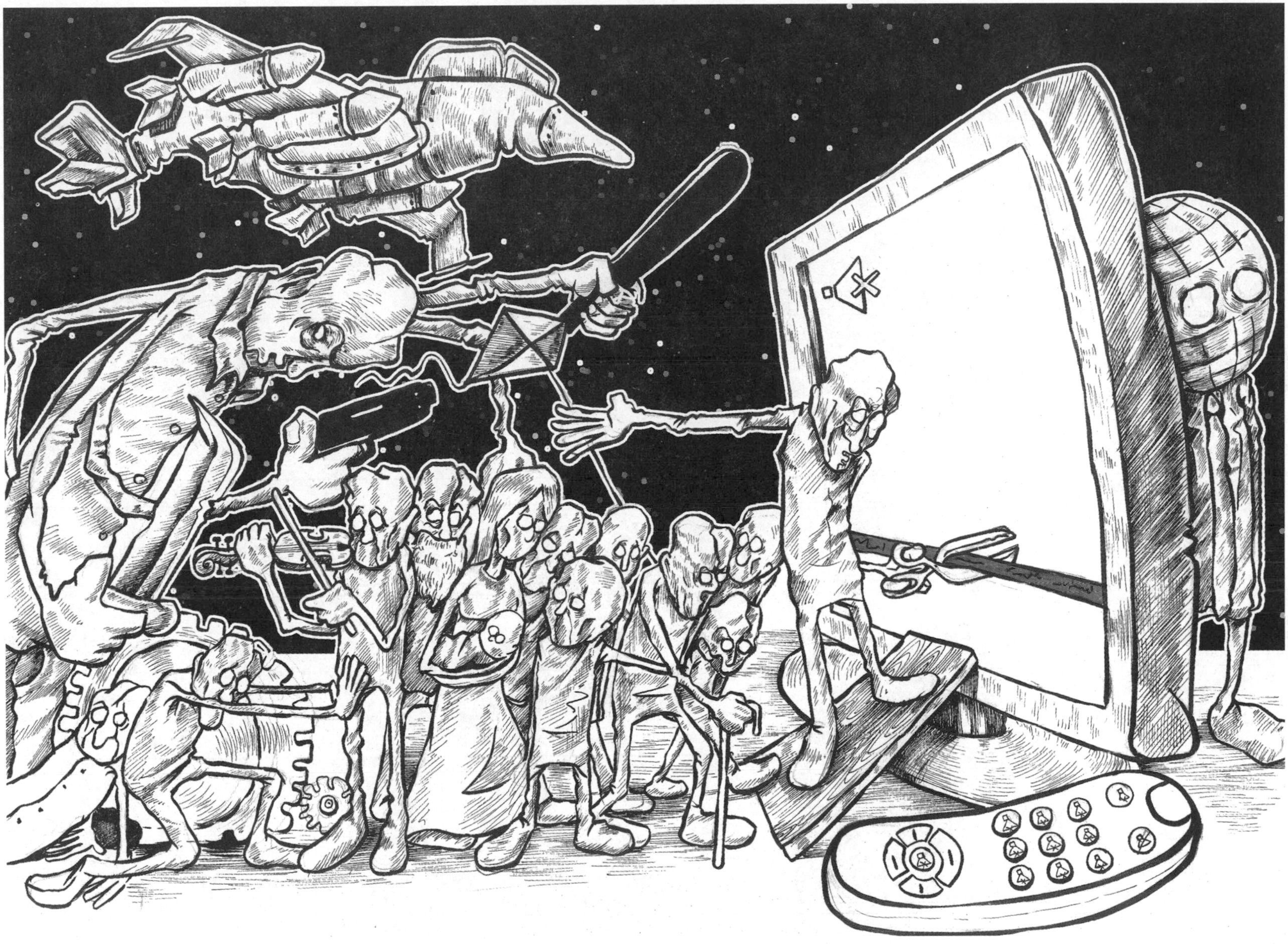

Breaking news (but keep it quiet).

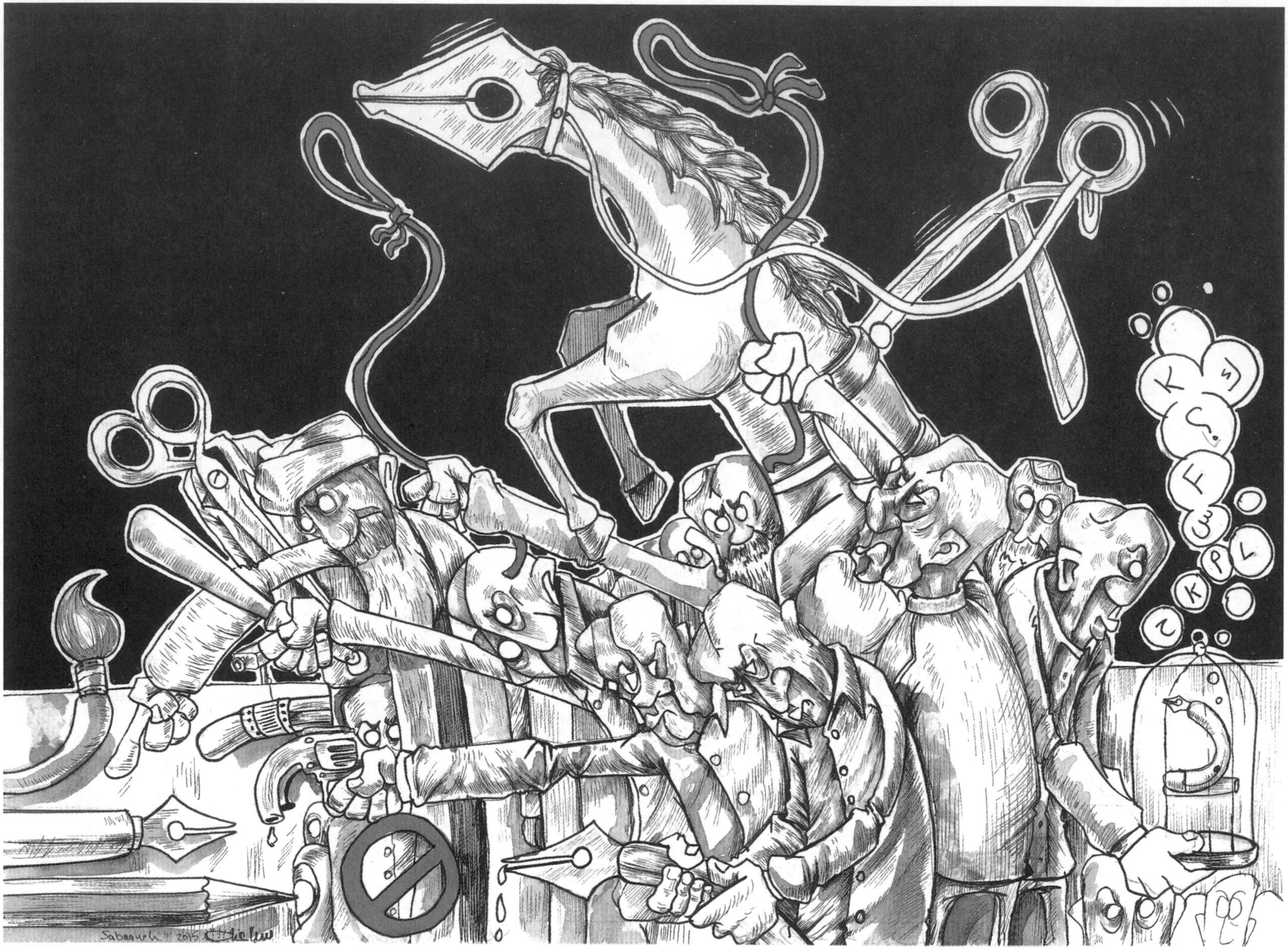

Freedom of expression as understood by religions and governments.

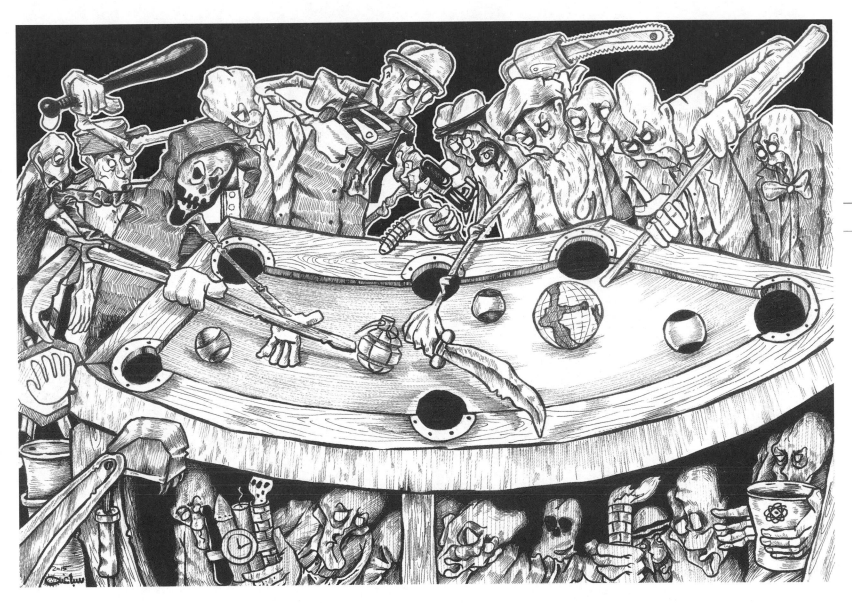

We fight for the same resources and pursue our individual interests.

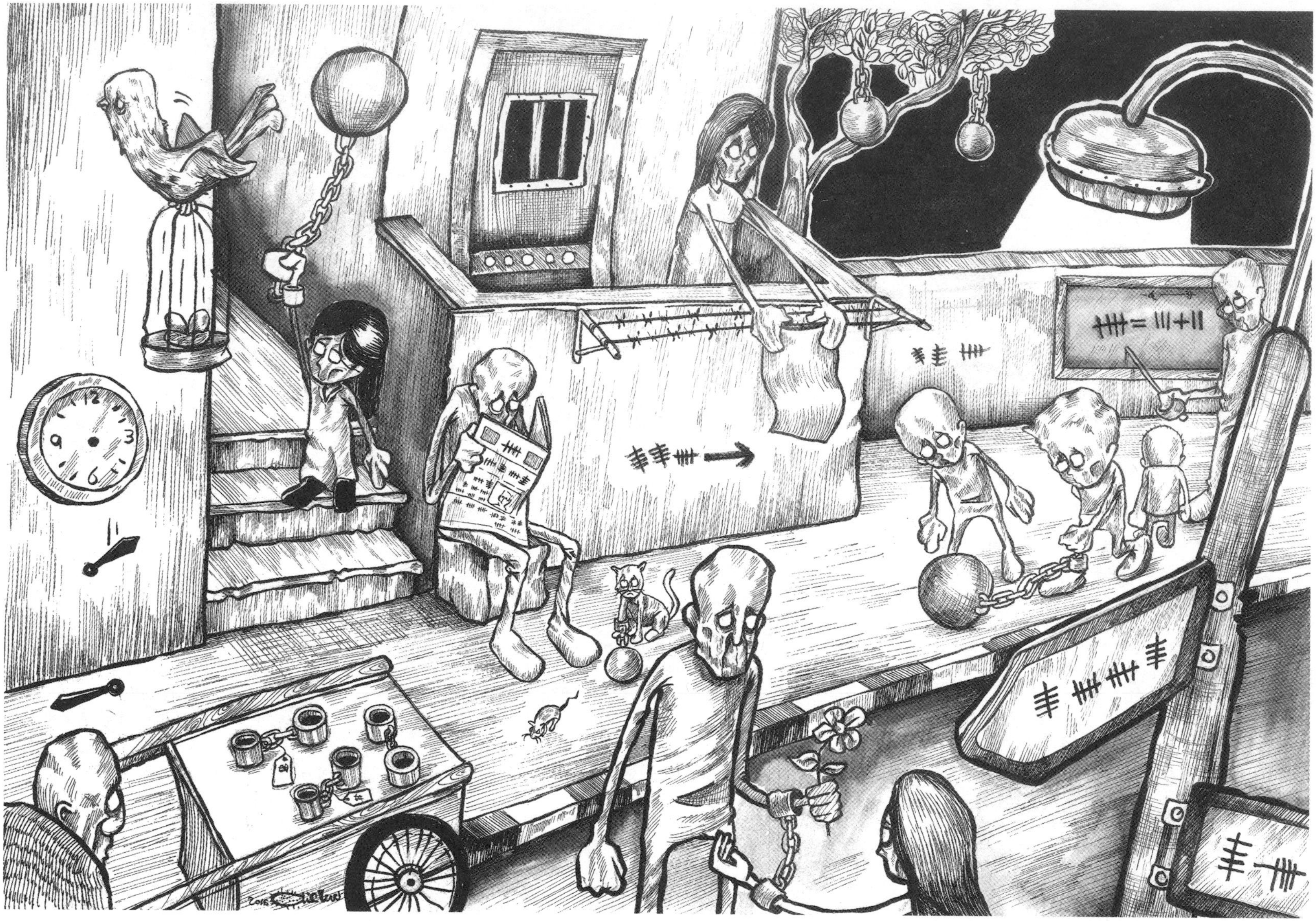

Marking time (a kind of existence).

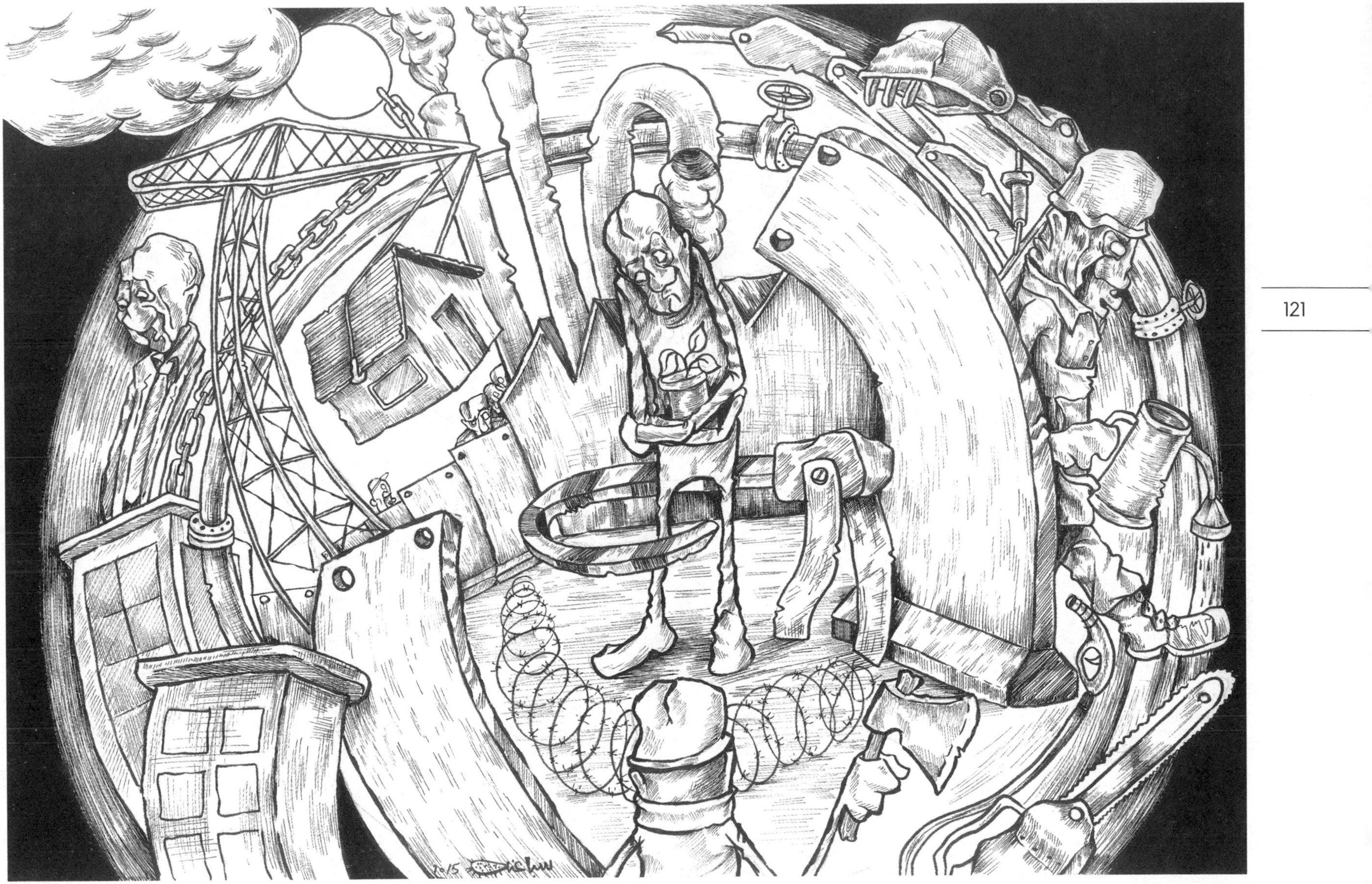

Trapped.

We sing freedom.

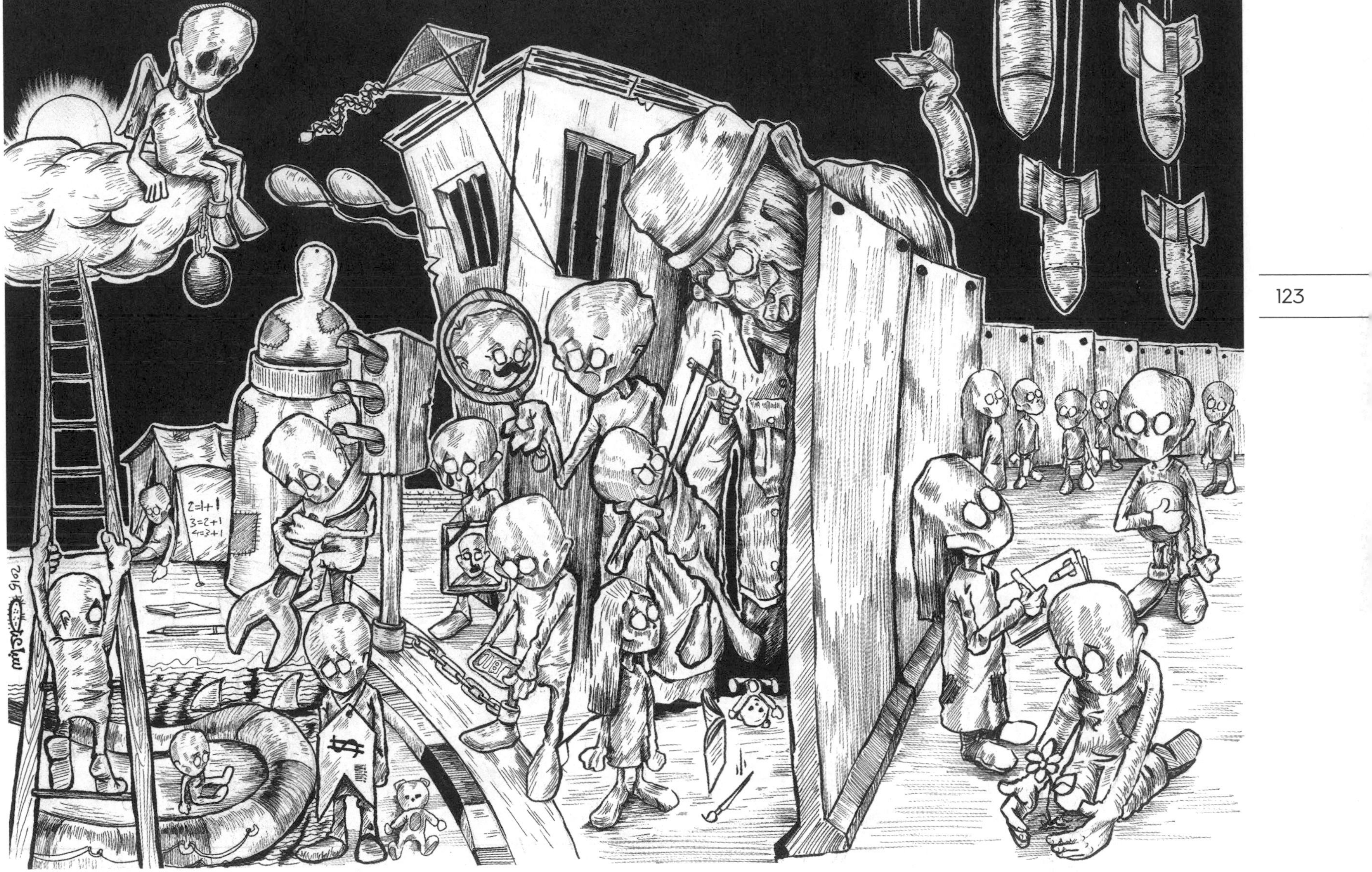
2=1+1
3=2+1
4=3+1

Each child is a potential.

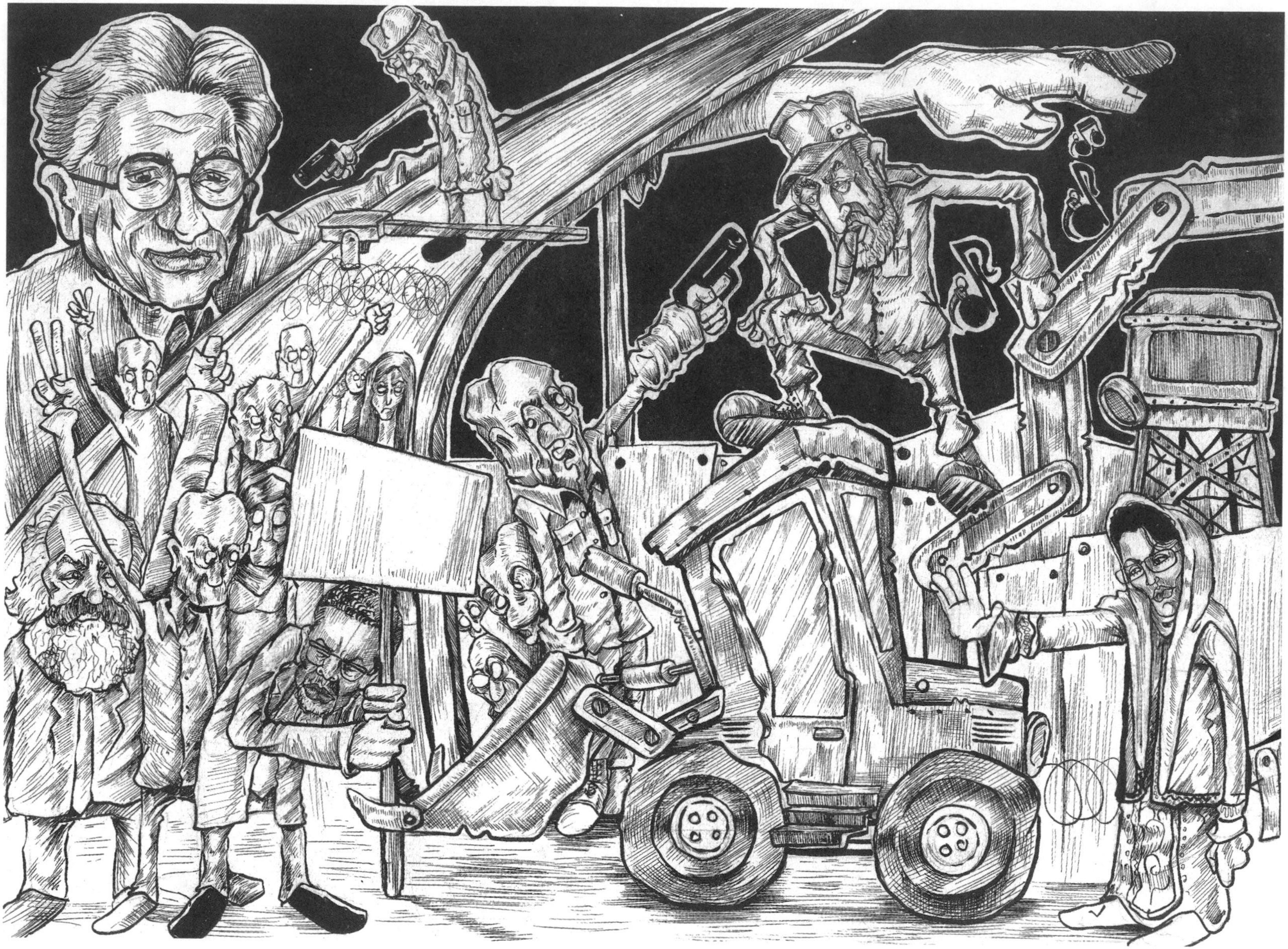

How will history judge the torment of Palestine?

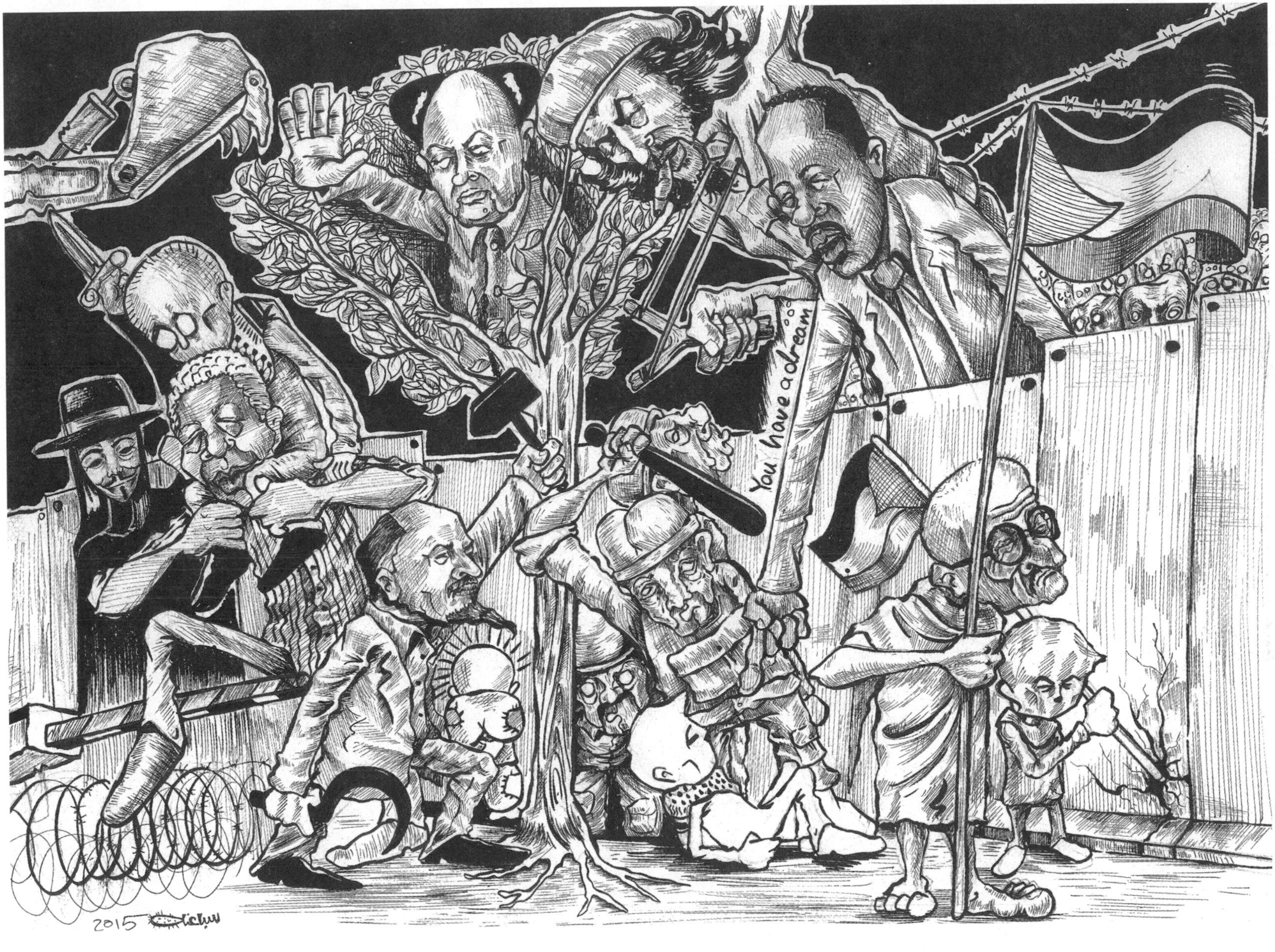
You have a dream
2015

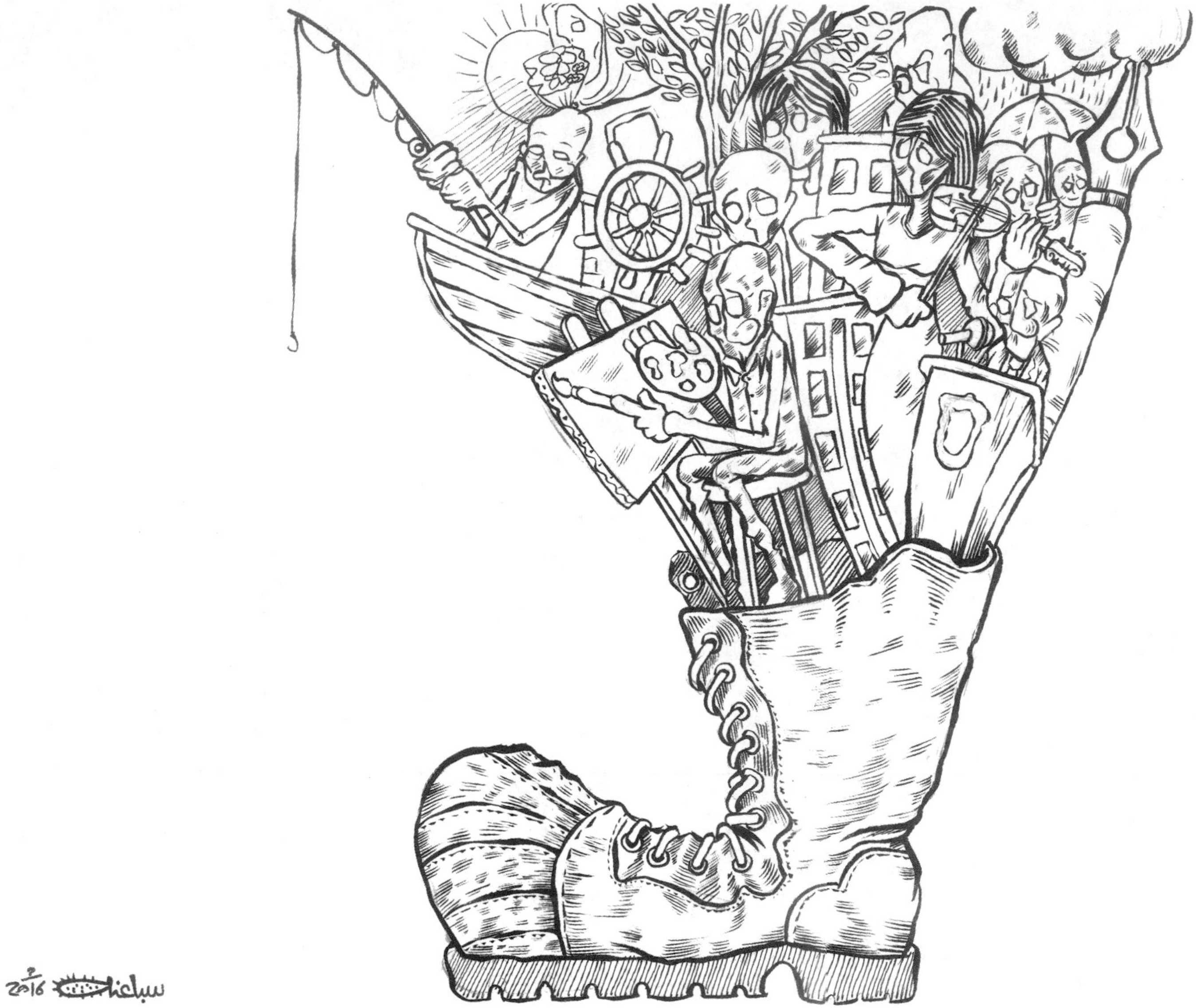

The army passed this way.

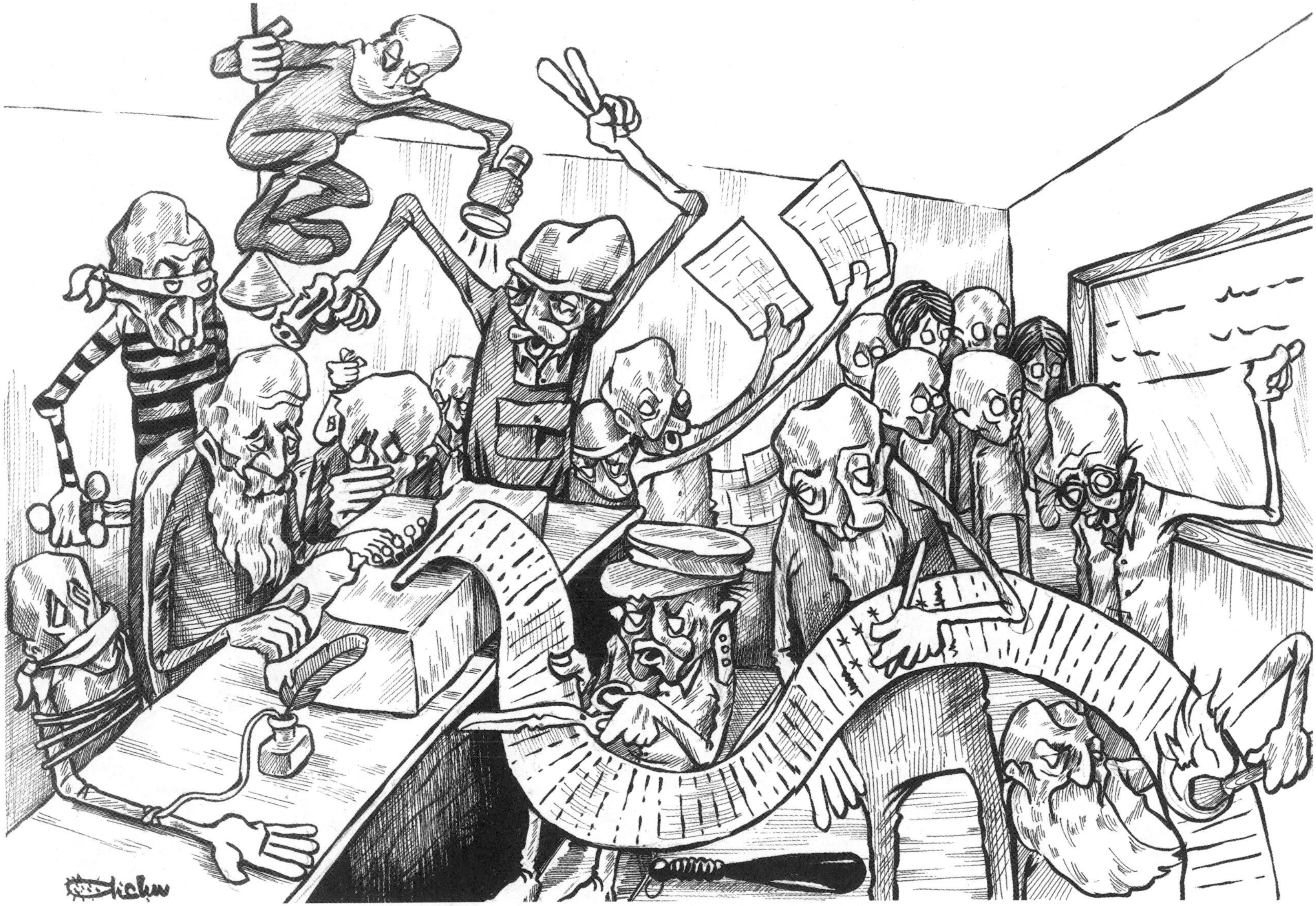

How will history be written, and by whom?

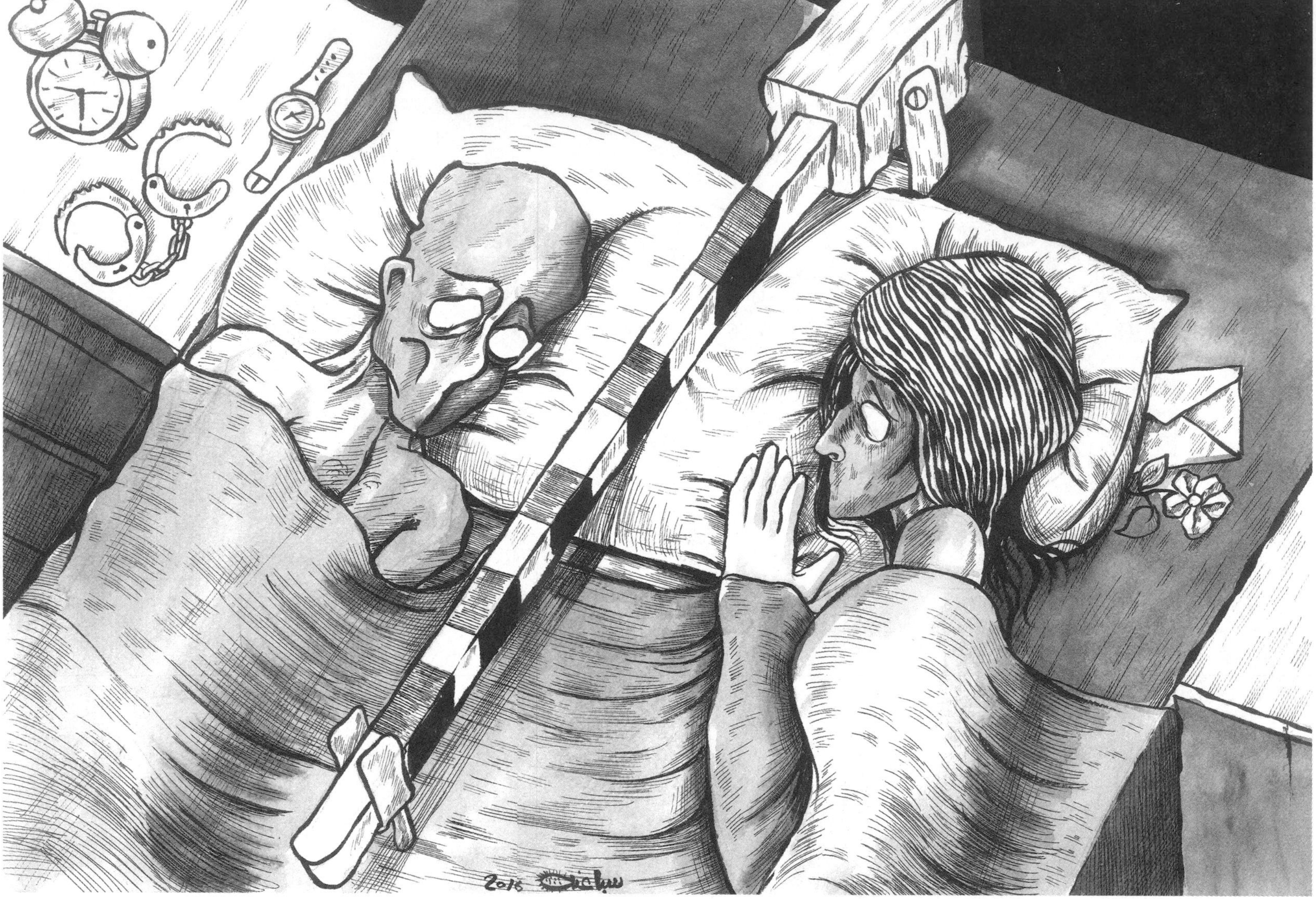

Someday we'll meet.

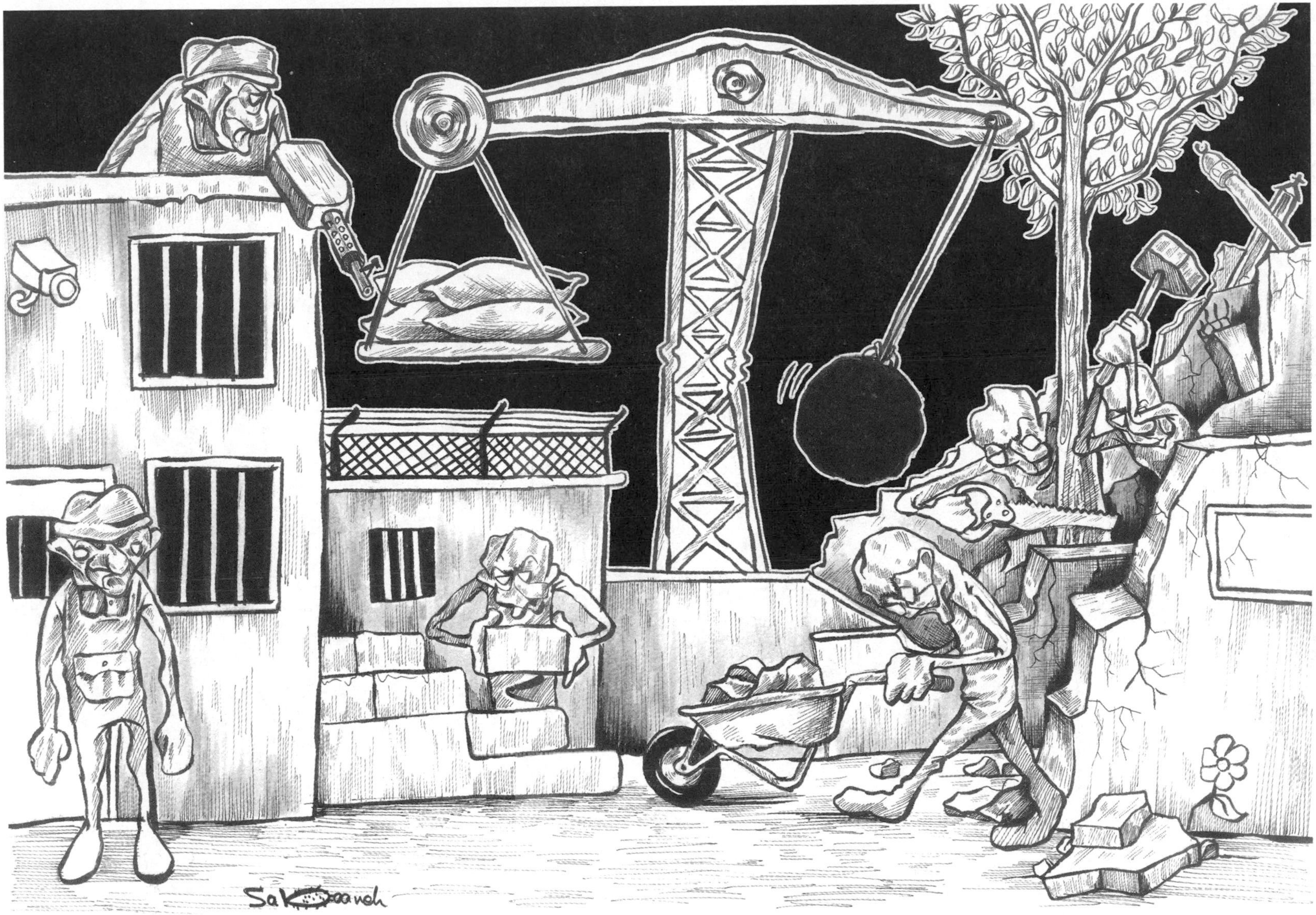
SaKhnanah

Warm homes make cold prisons.

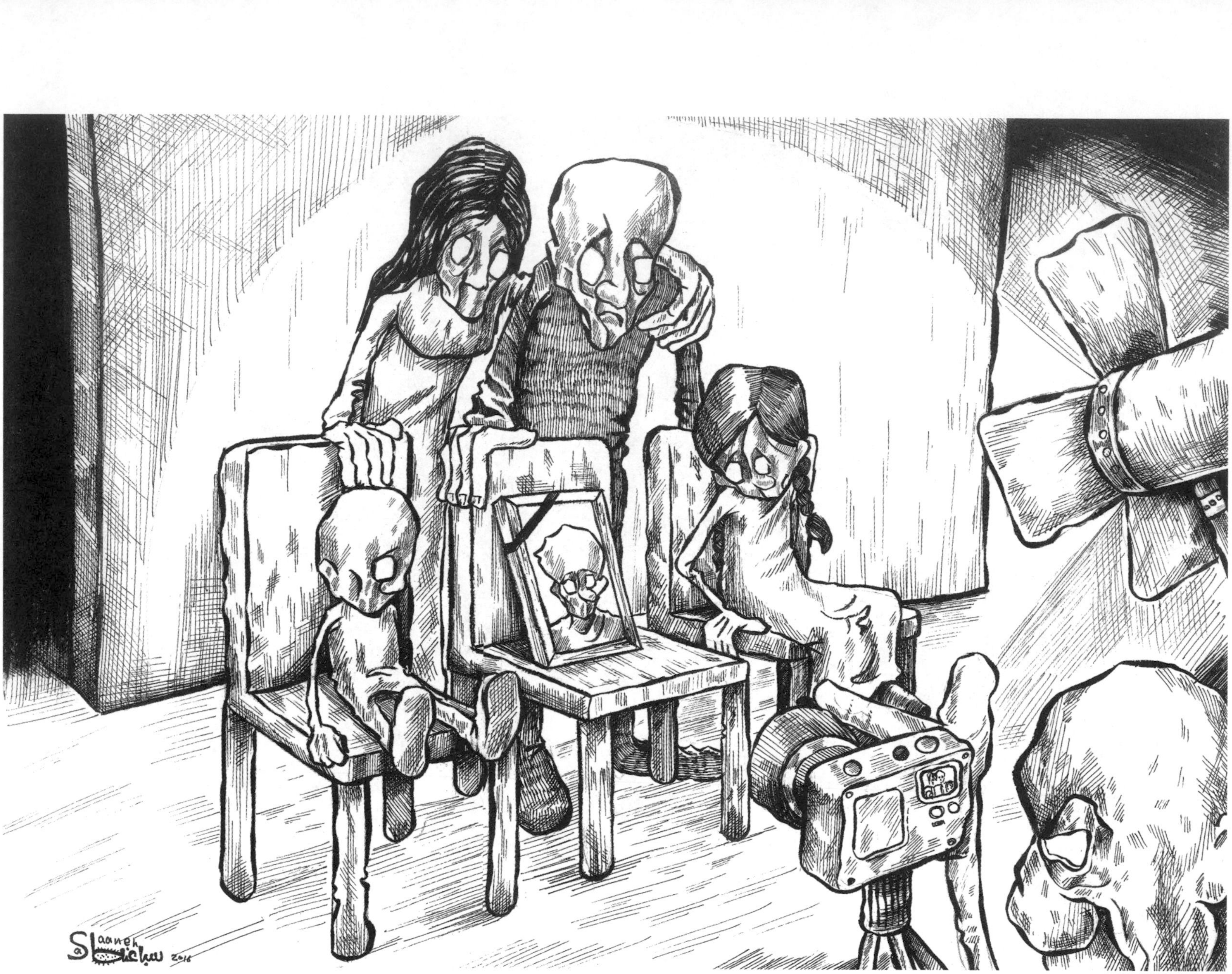

A family photo.

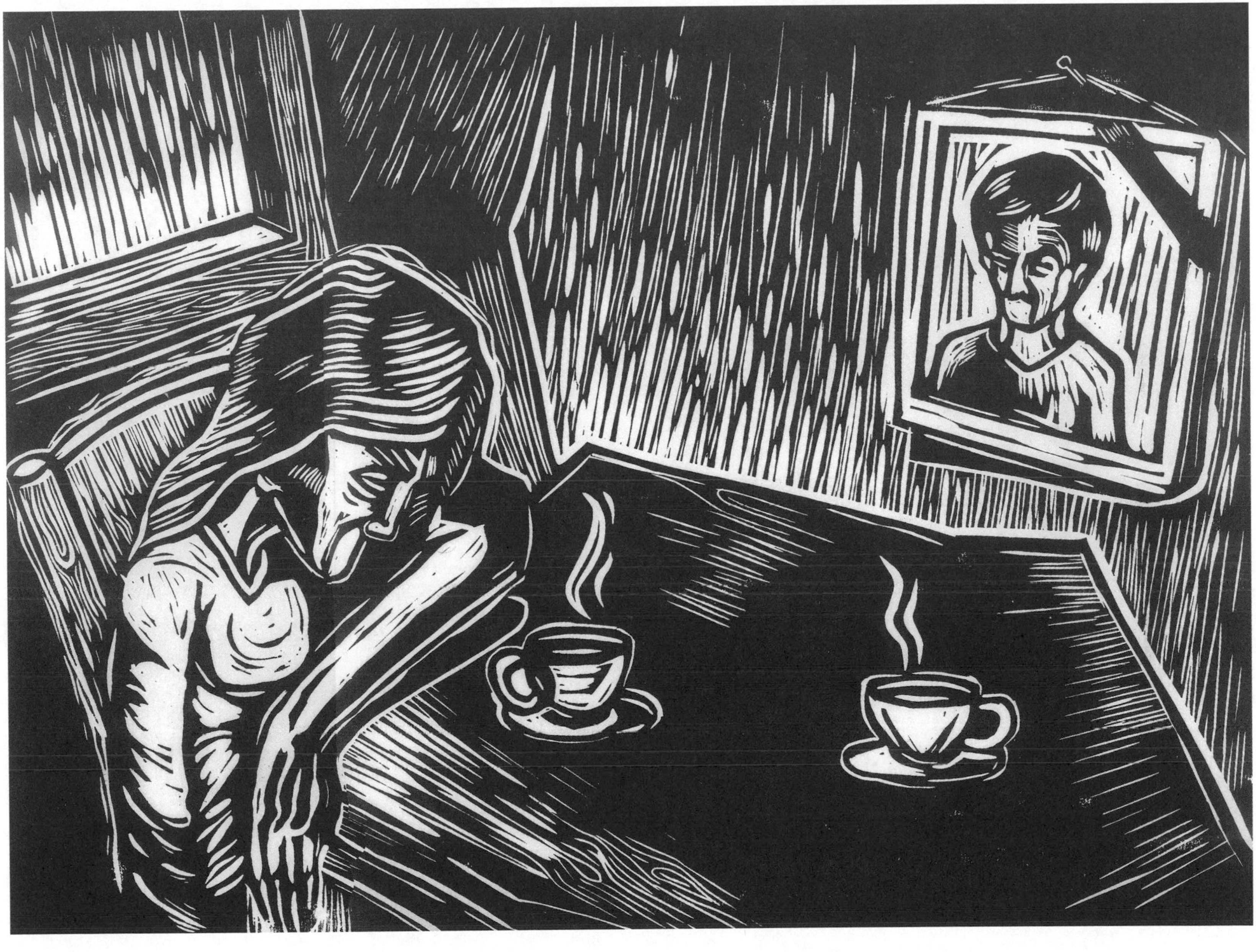

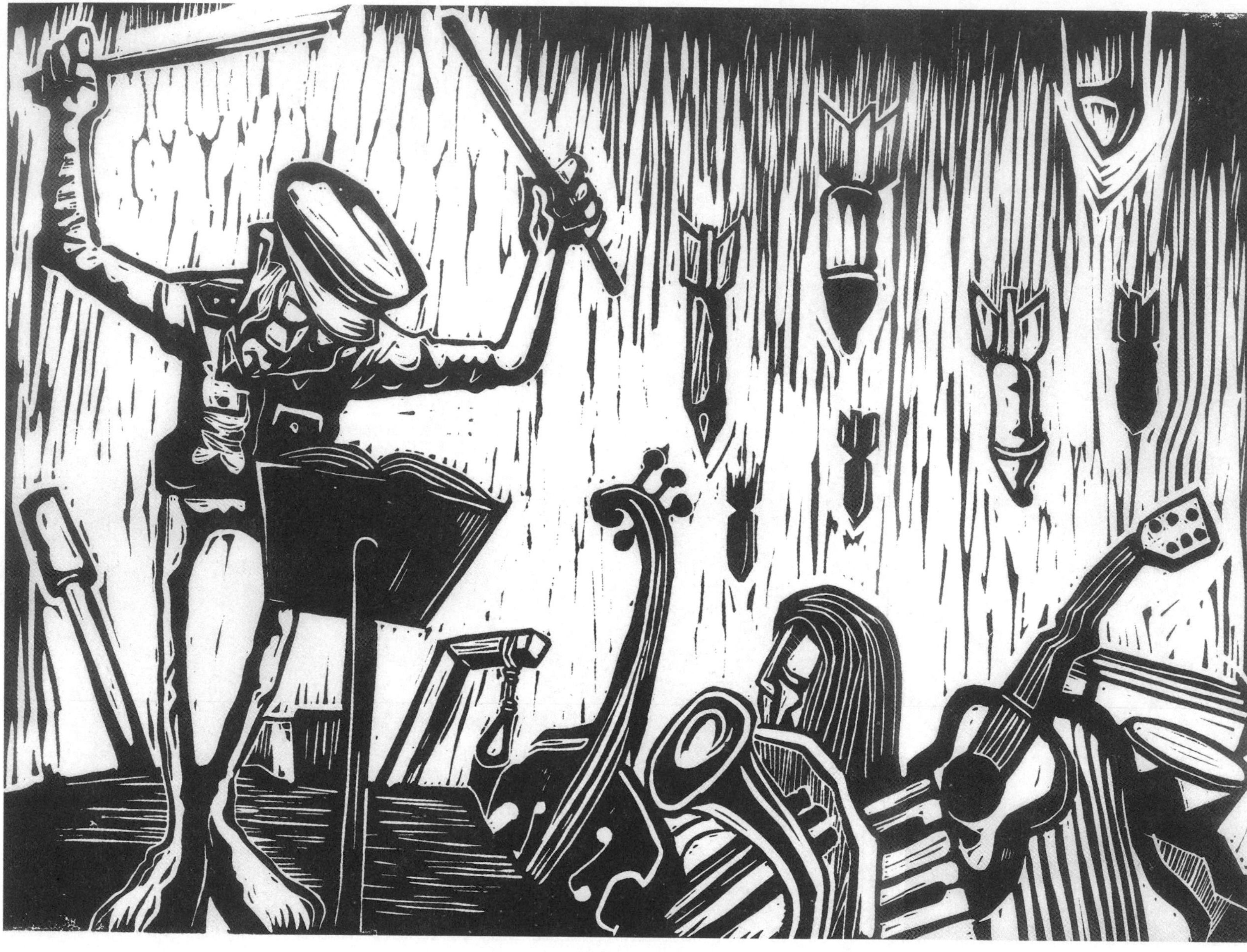

The dictator's melody.

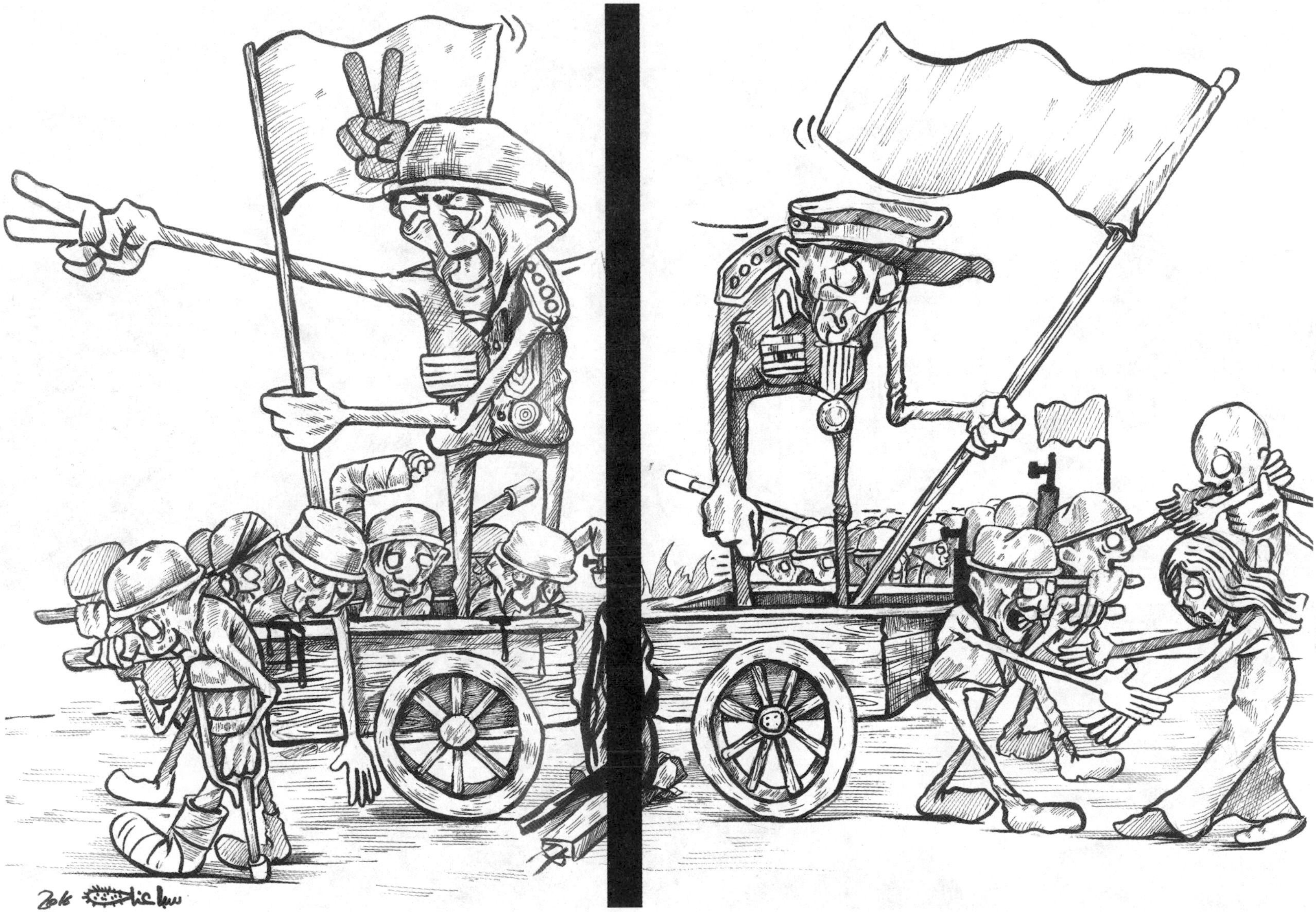

What does victory mean to a family that lost a soldier in their battles?

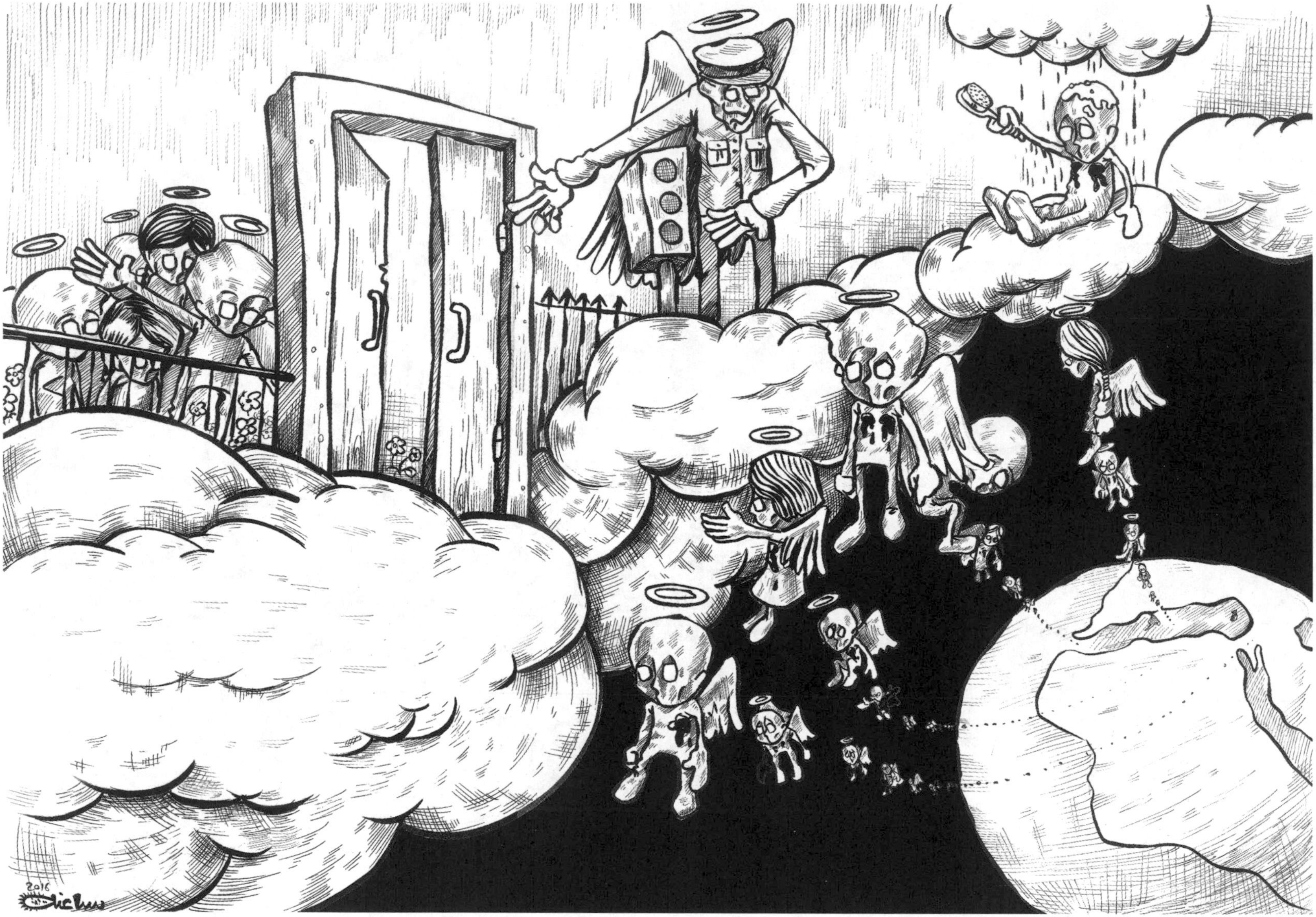

Child overcrowding.

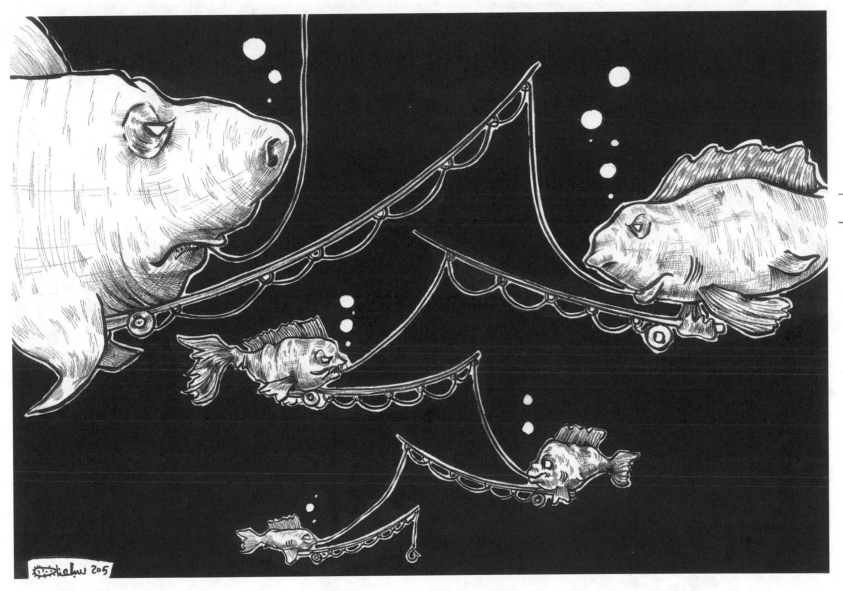

How the world works.

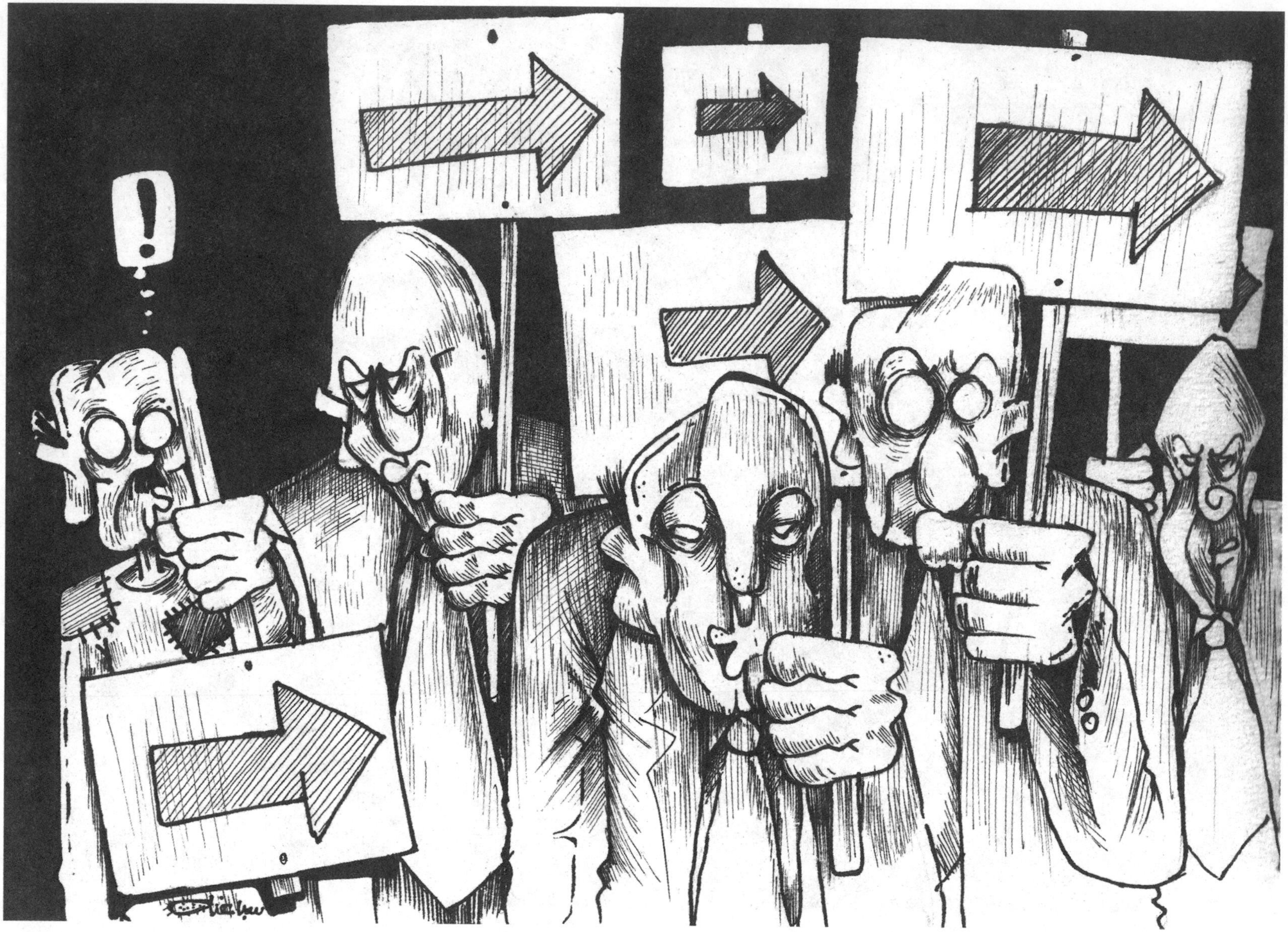
!

Swimming with the current.

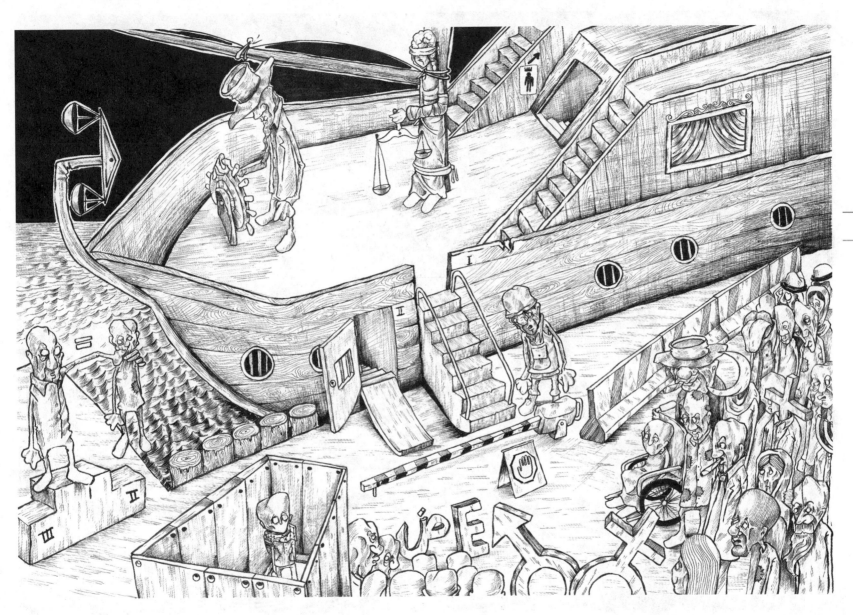

Who makes it into the boat?

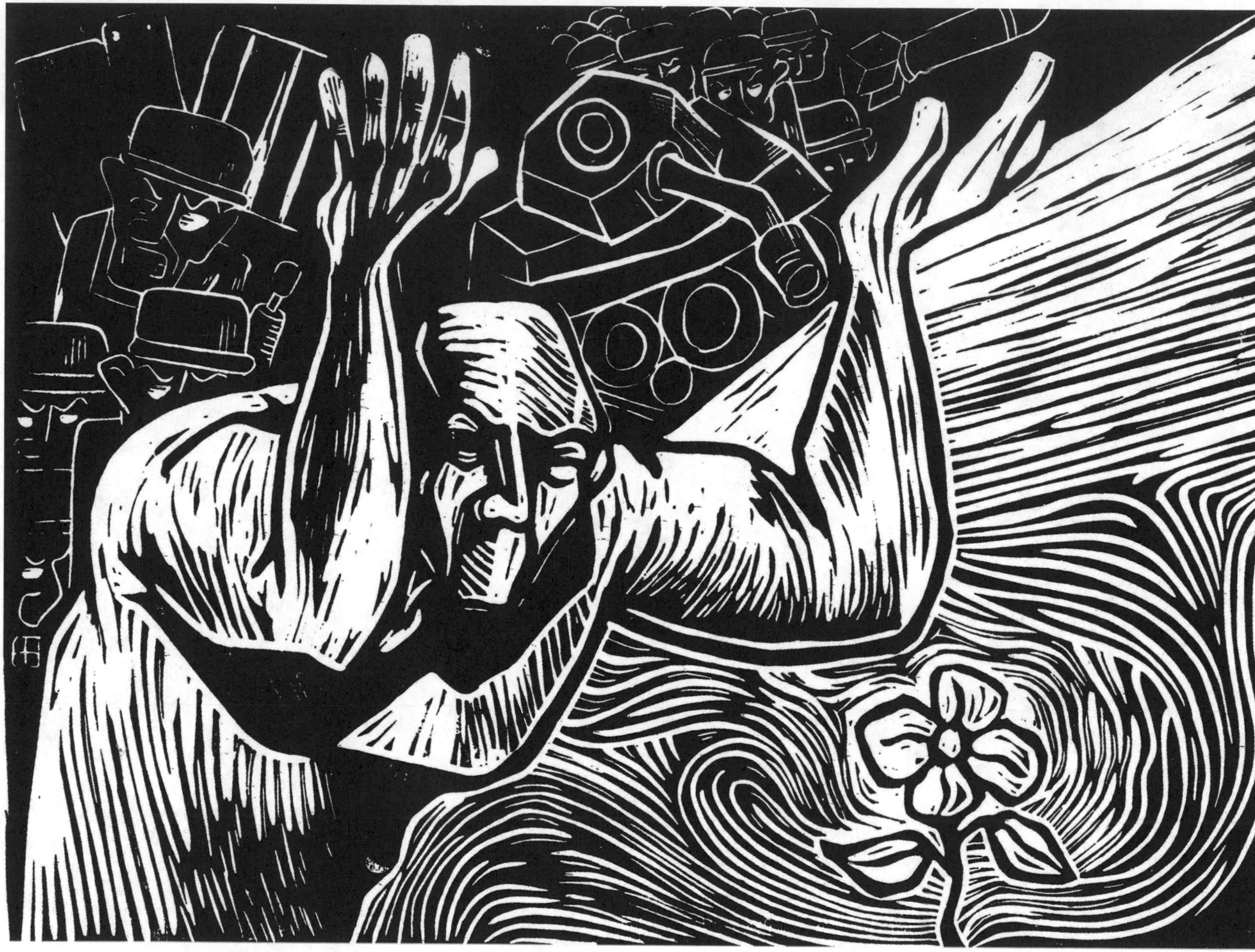

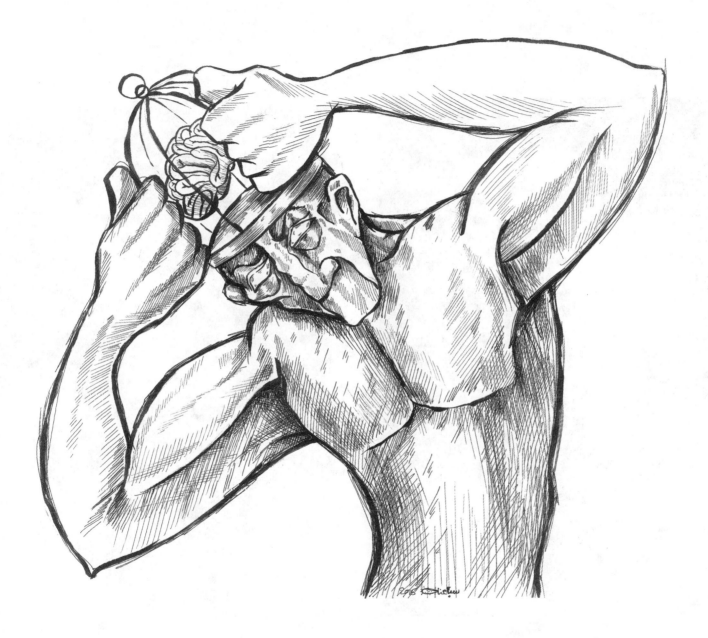

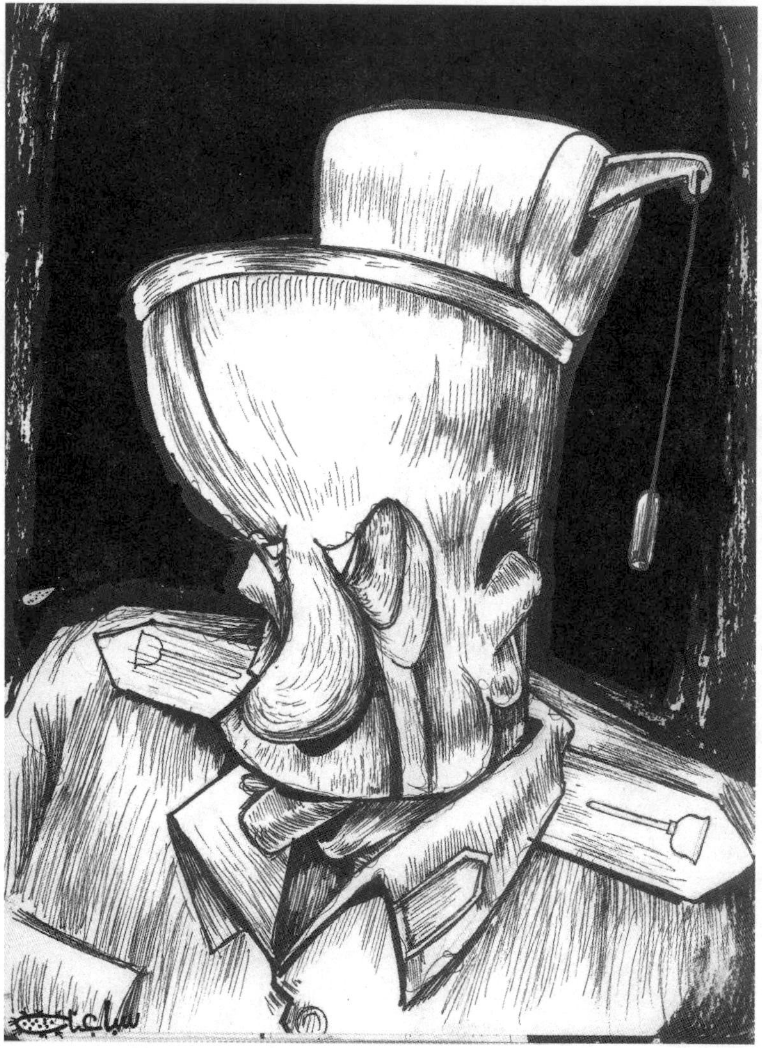

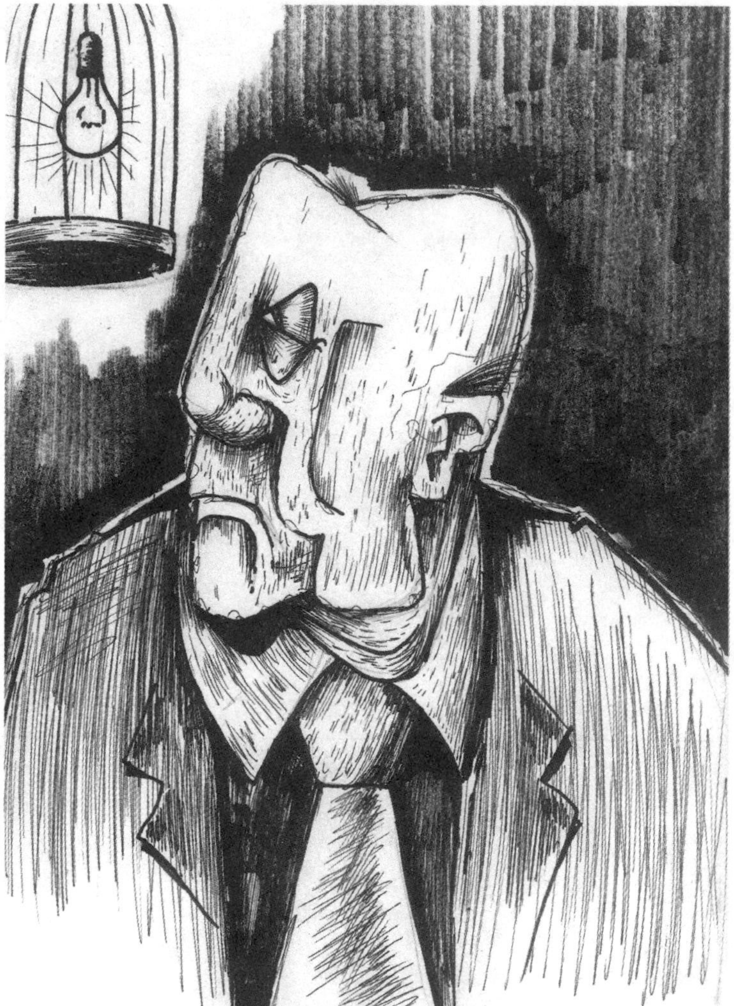

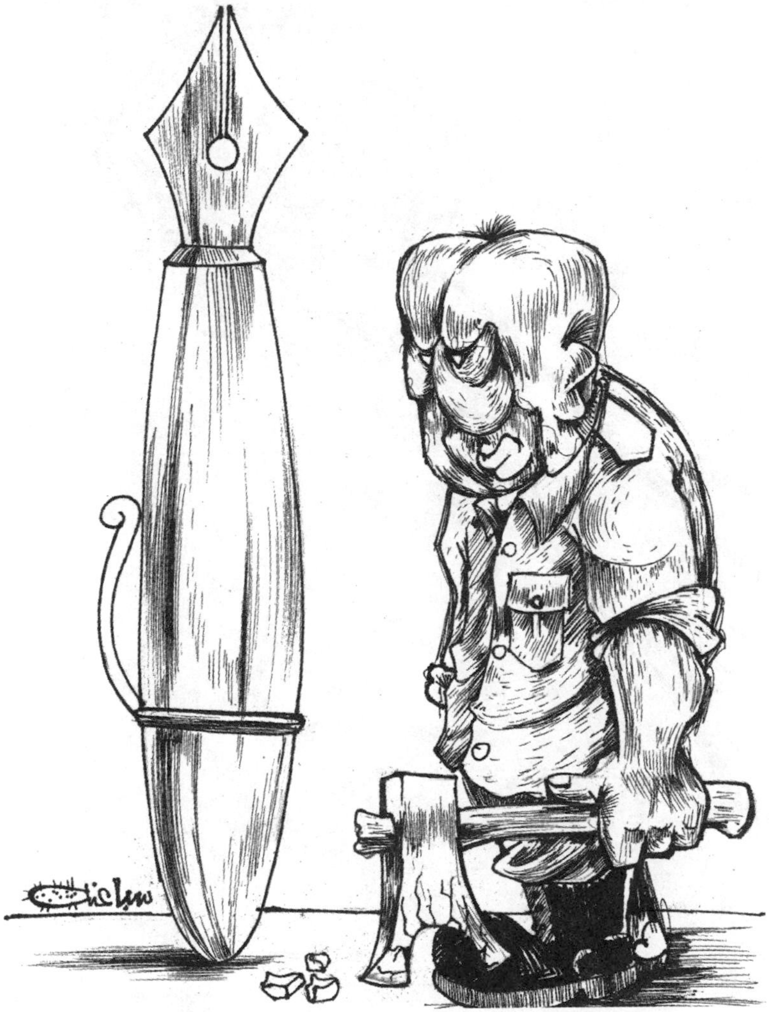

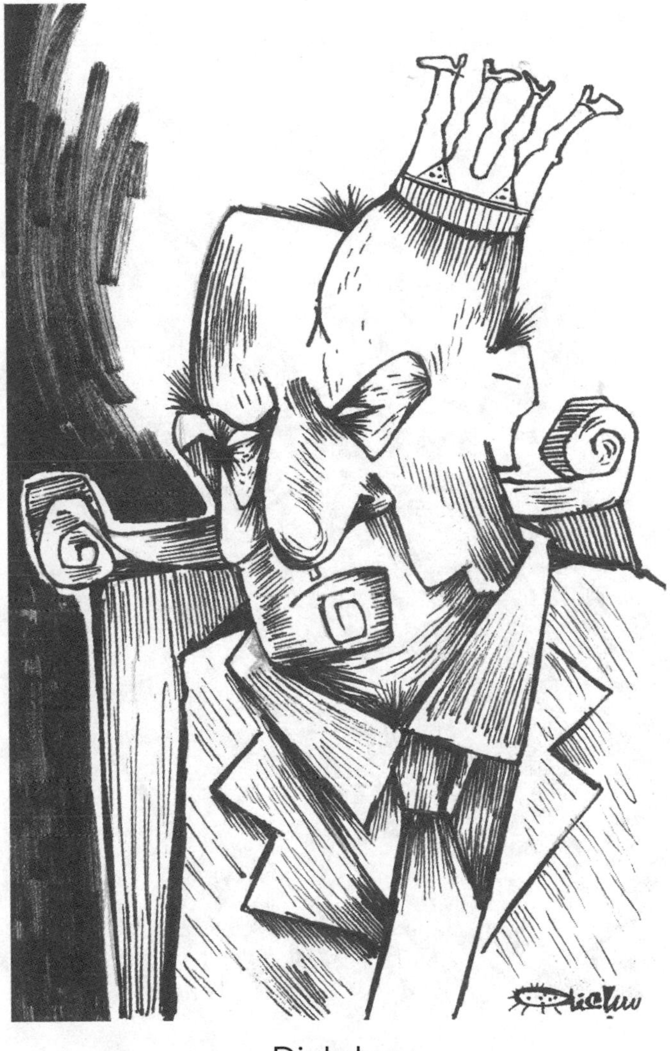

Dictator.

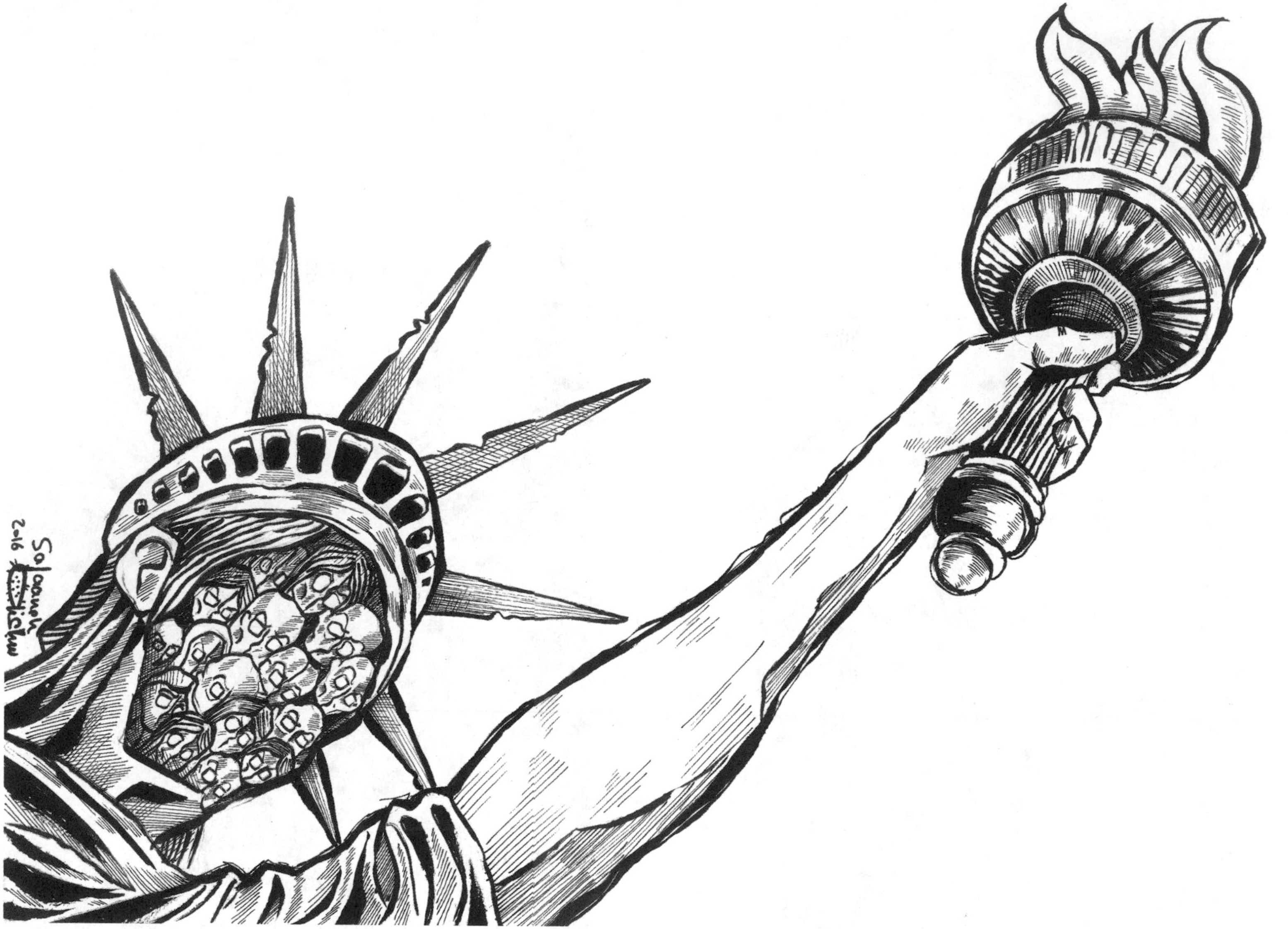

Nations are the symbols of freedom.

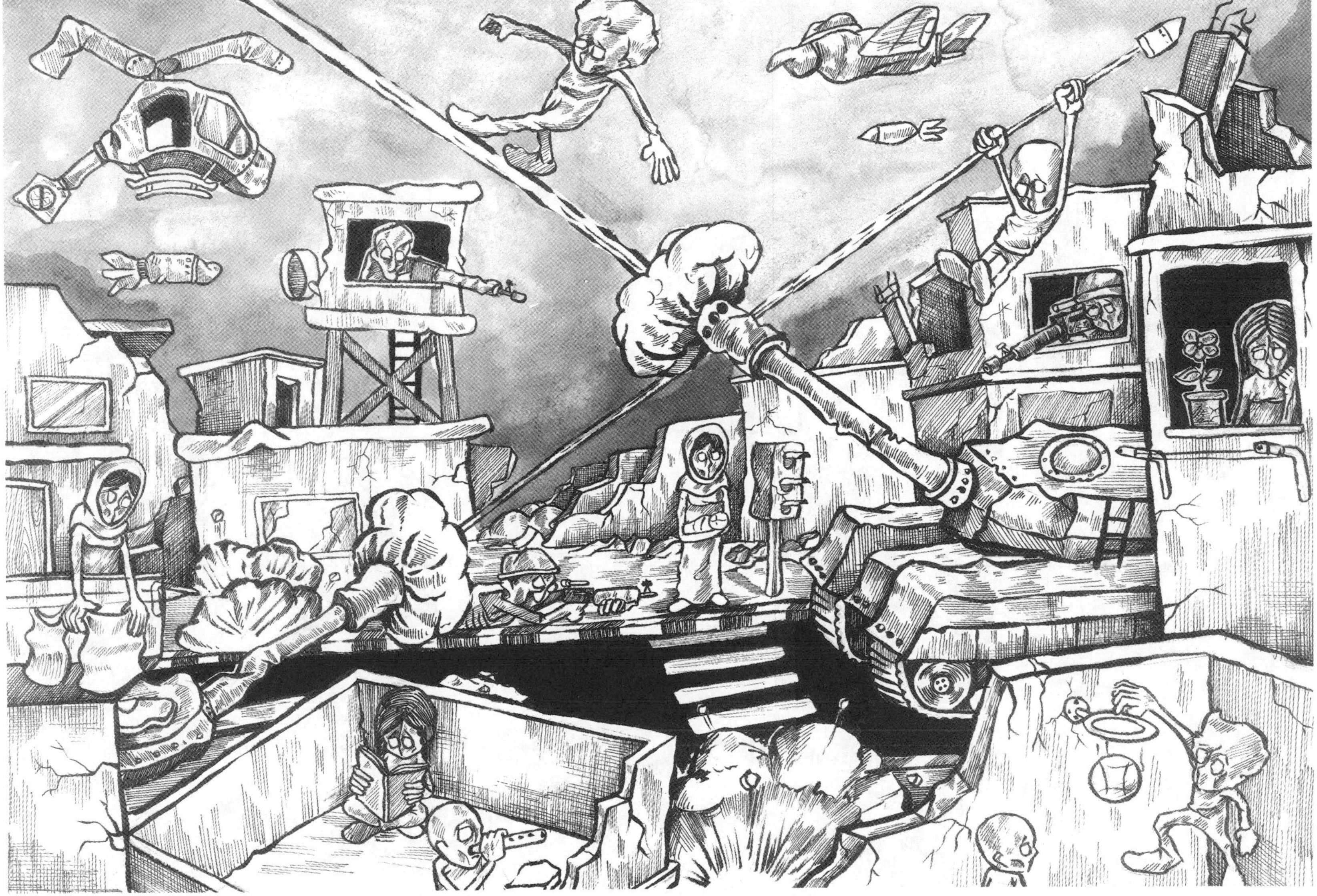

We need space to live amid the crush of death.

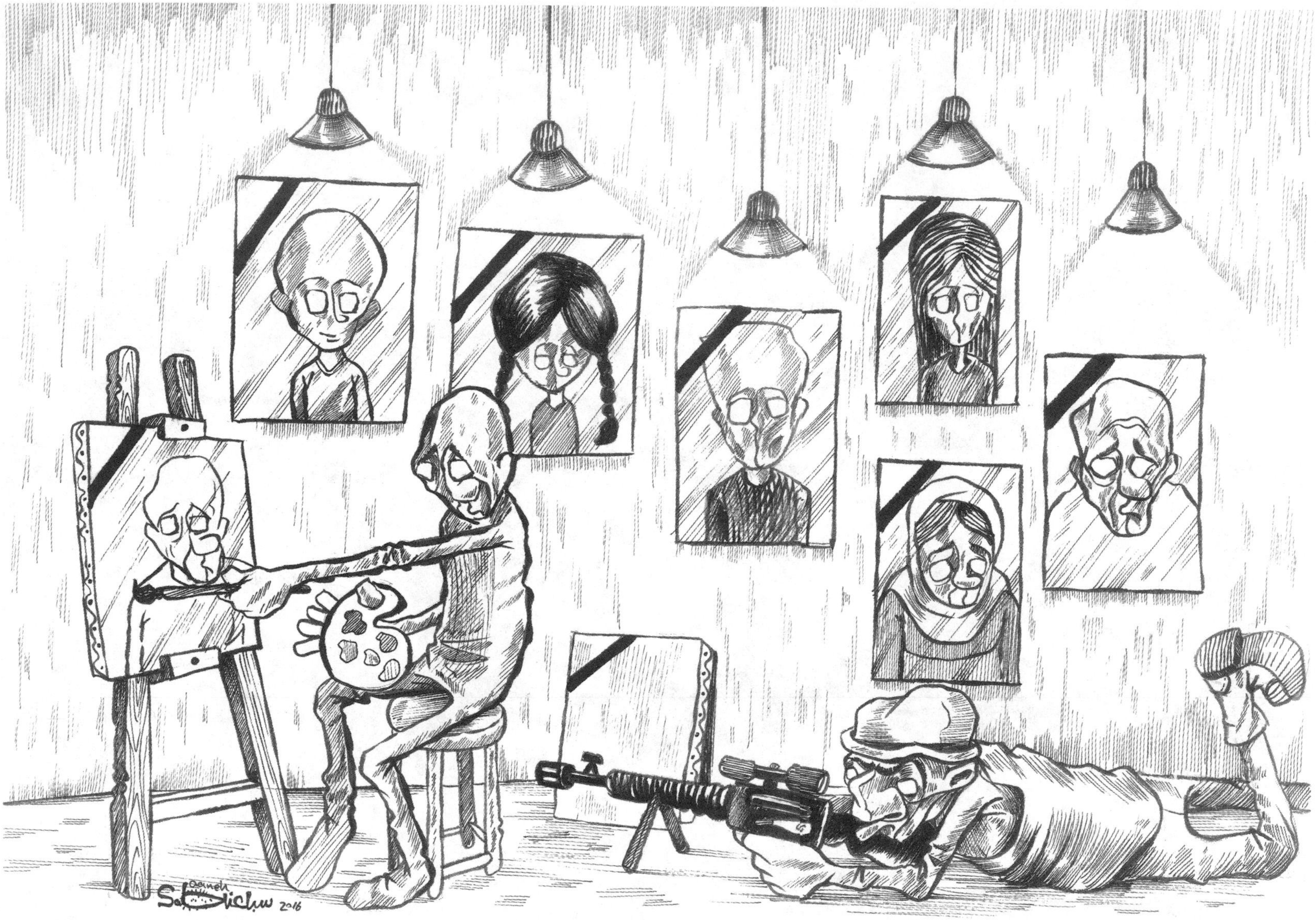

And I am a victim.

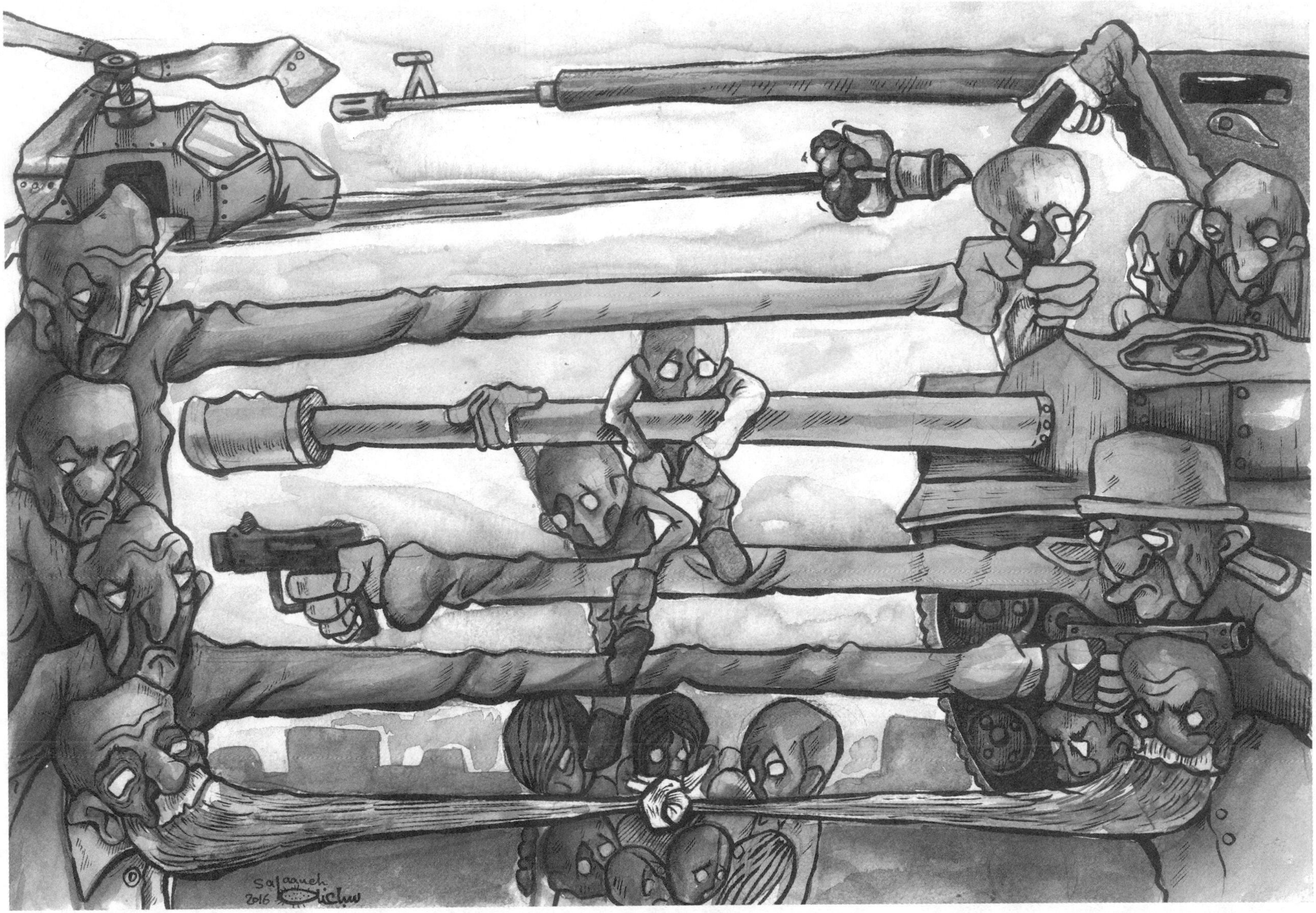
Safaaneh
2016

War is never-ending.

CHAPTER 4

SHORT STORIES

Palestinians have not always managed to convey our stories in a way that elicited understanding or empathy. The cartoons in this chapter present Palestinians who are like everyone else that you and I are likely to meet—people with stories worth telling.

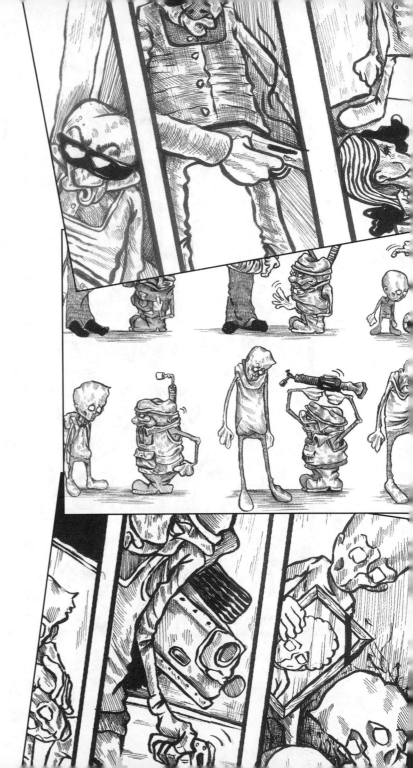

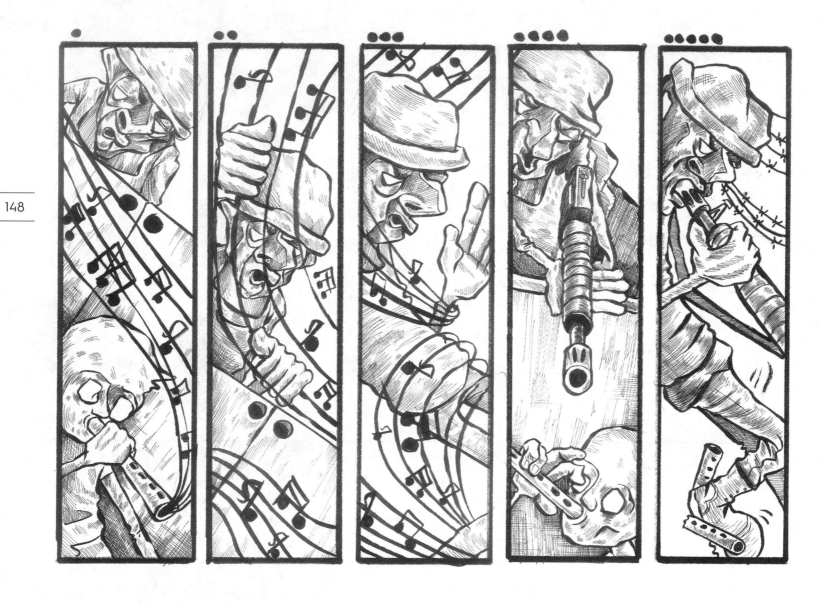

Each of us has a song.

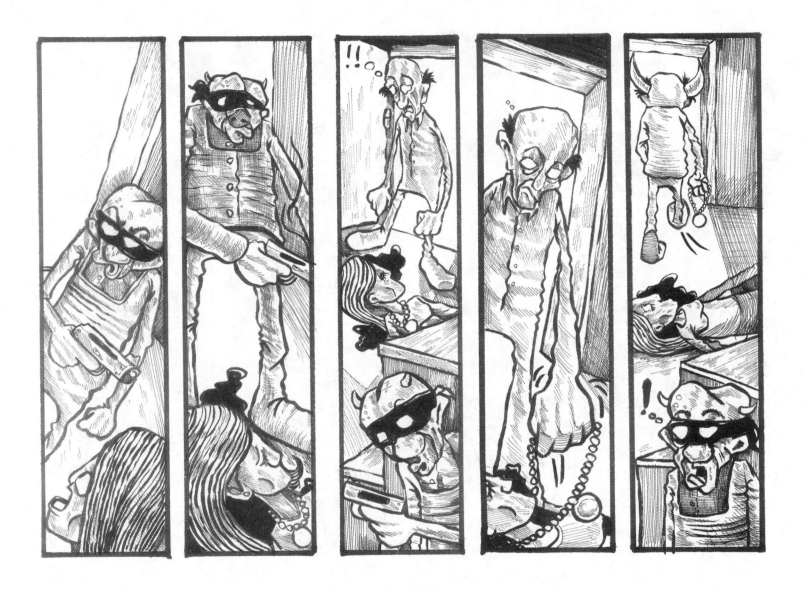

Compounding the crime.

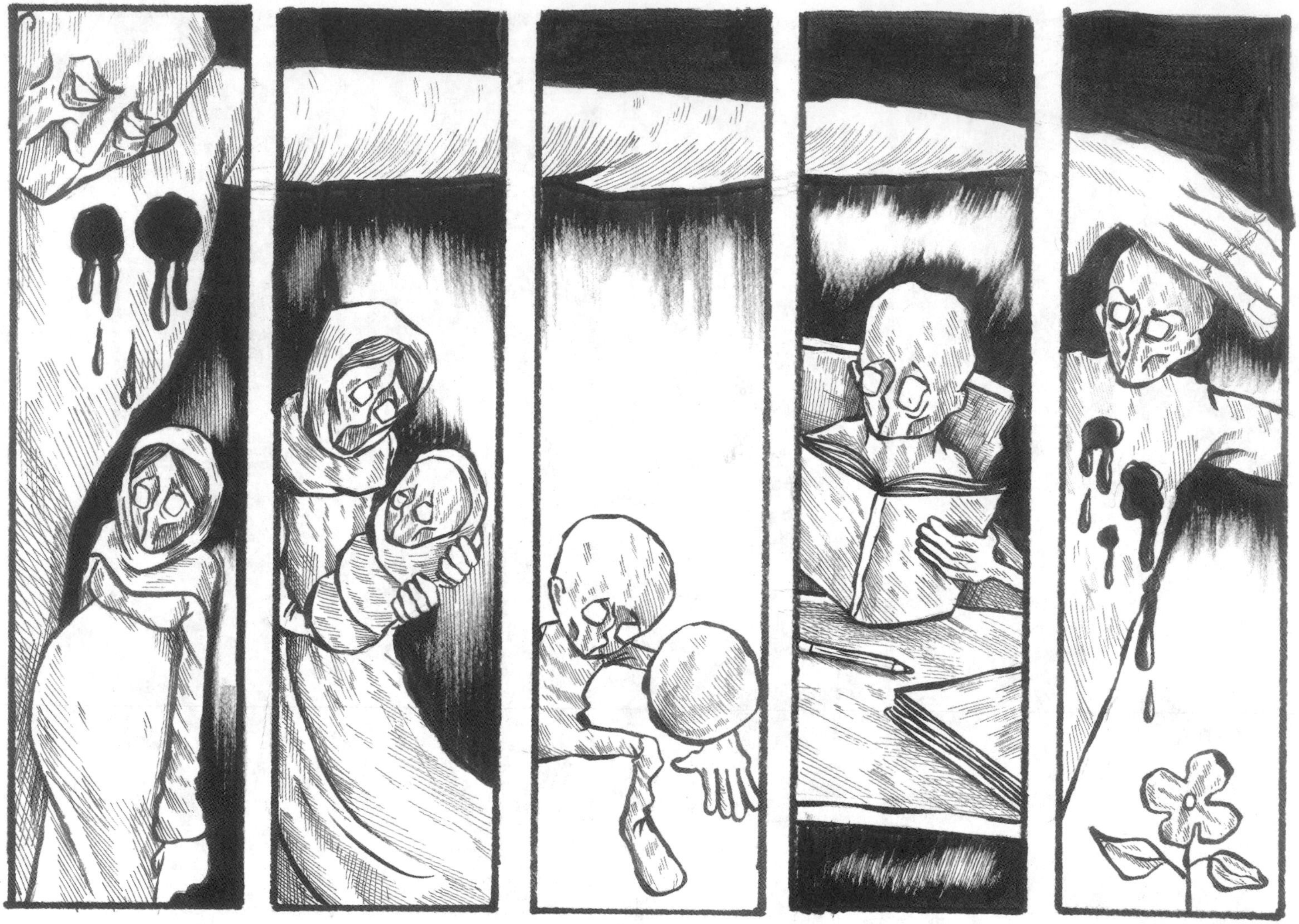

Let the tale continue.

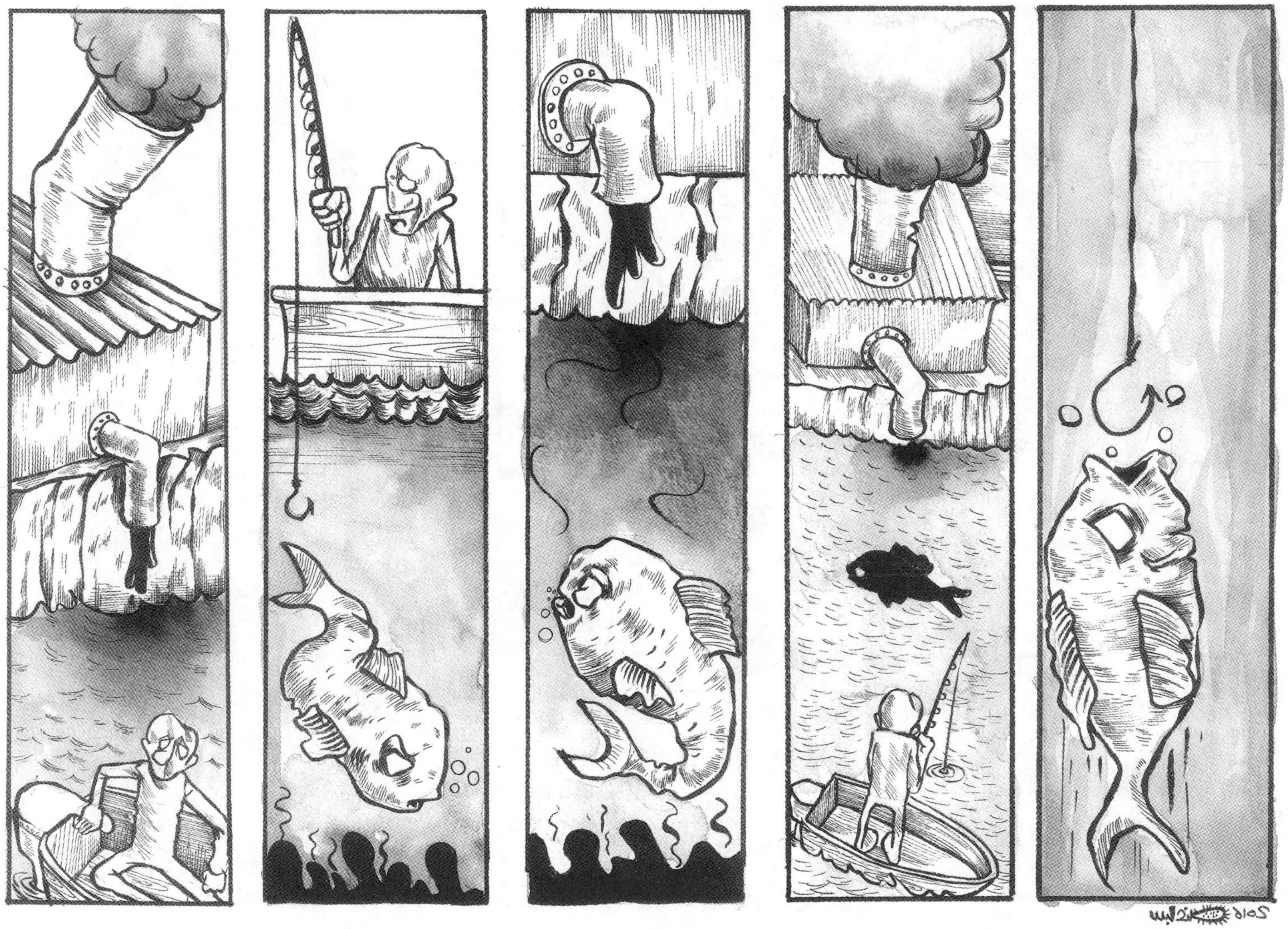

Pollution.

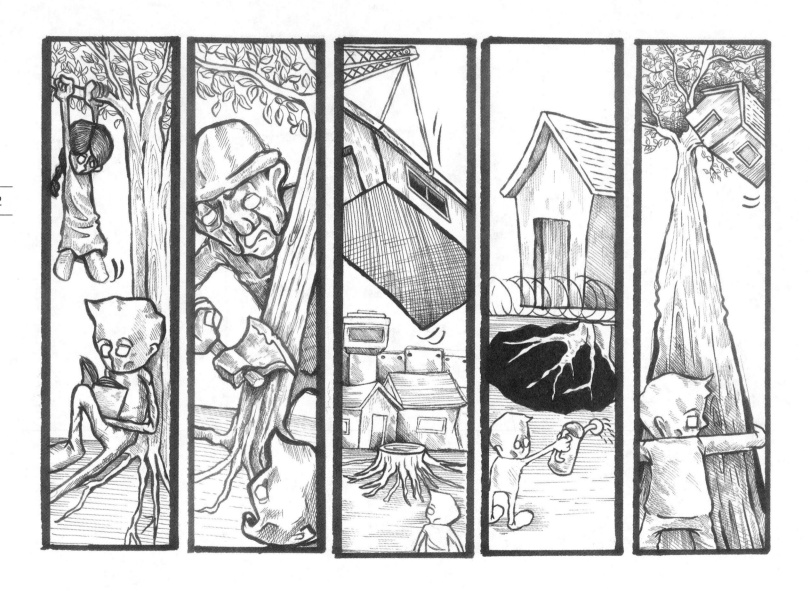

We have roots.

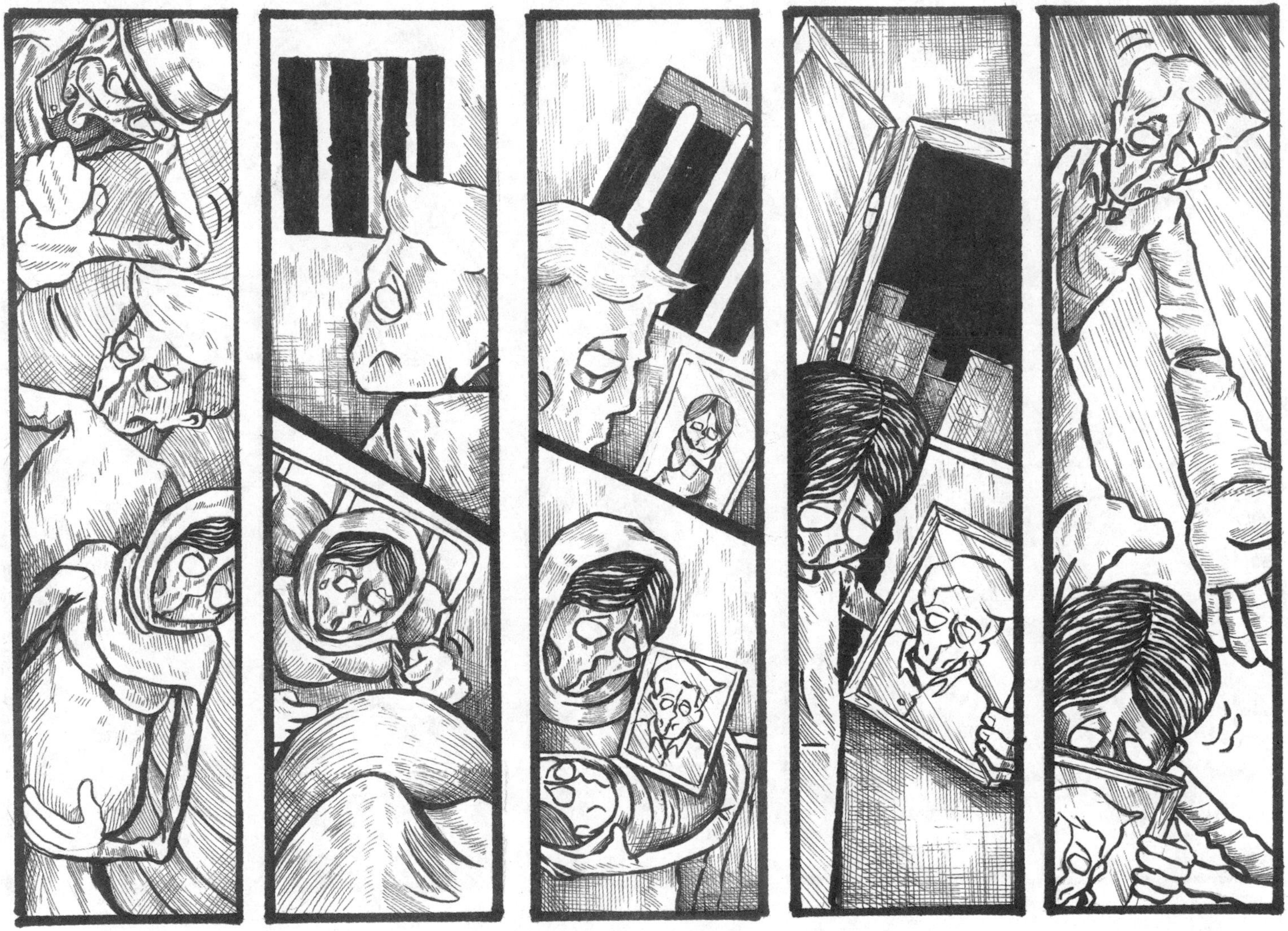

Tales of prisoners I: Some children know their fathers only through photographs.

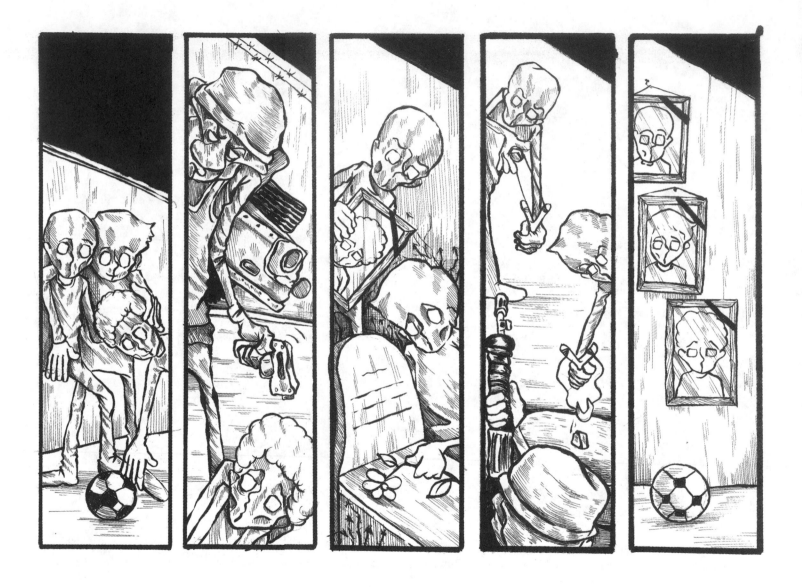

Together in life and death.

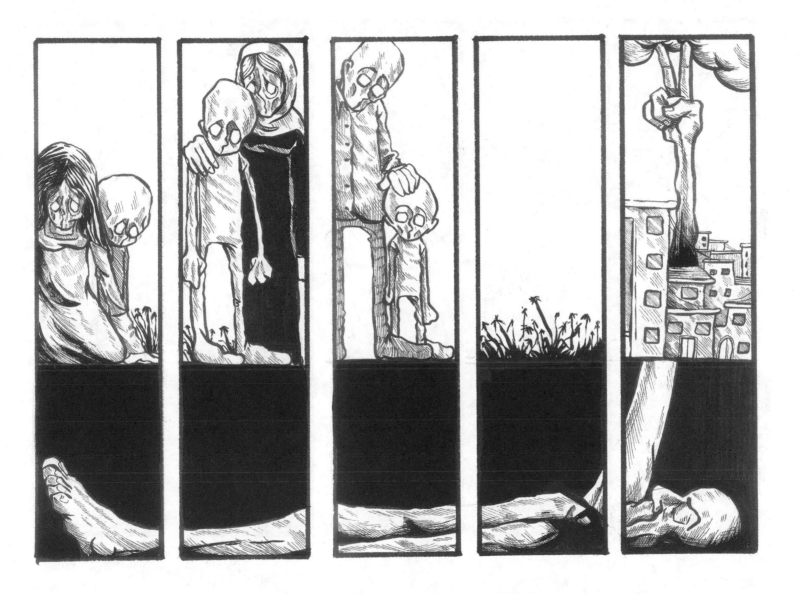

Buried but not gone.

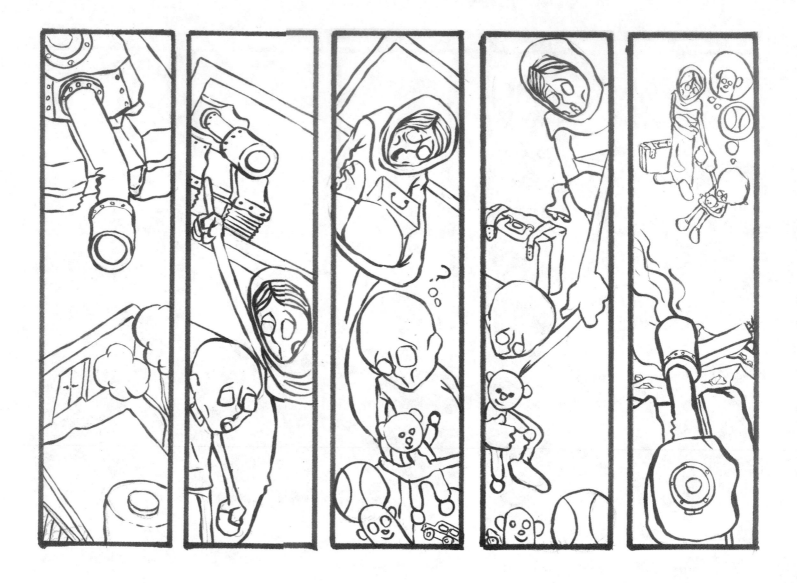

What shall I take with me? What gets left behind?

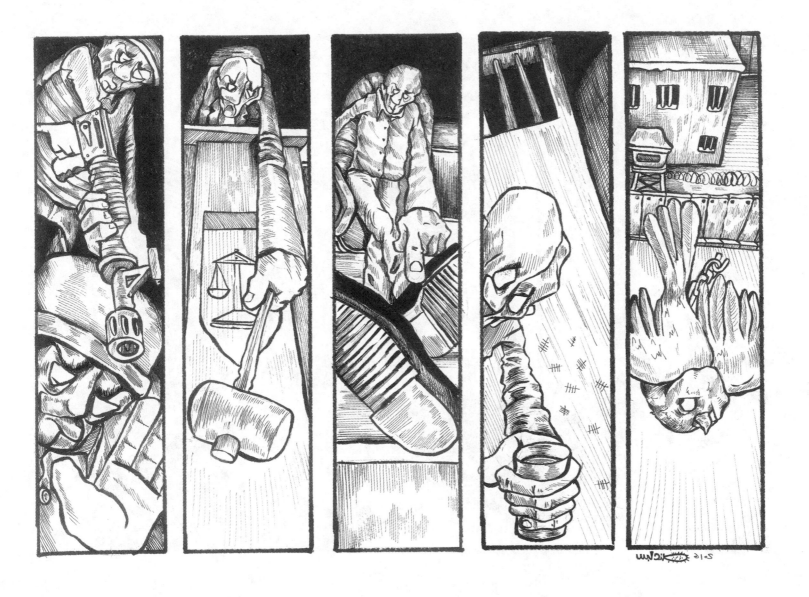

Tales of prisoners II: Some prisoners care for birds in their cells.

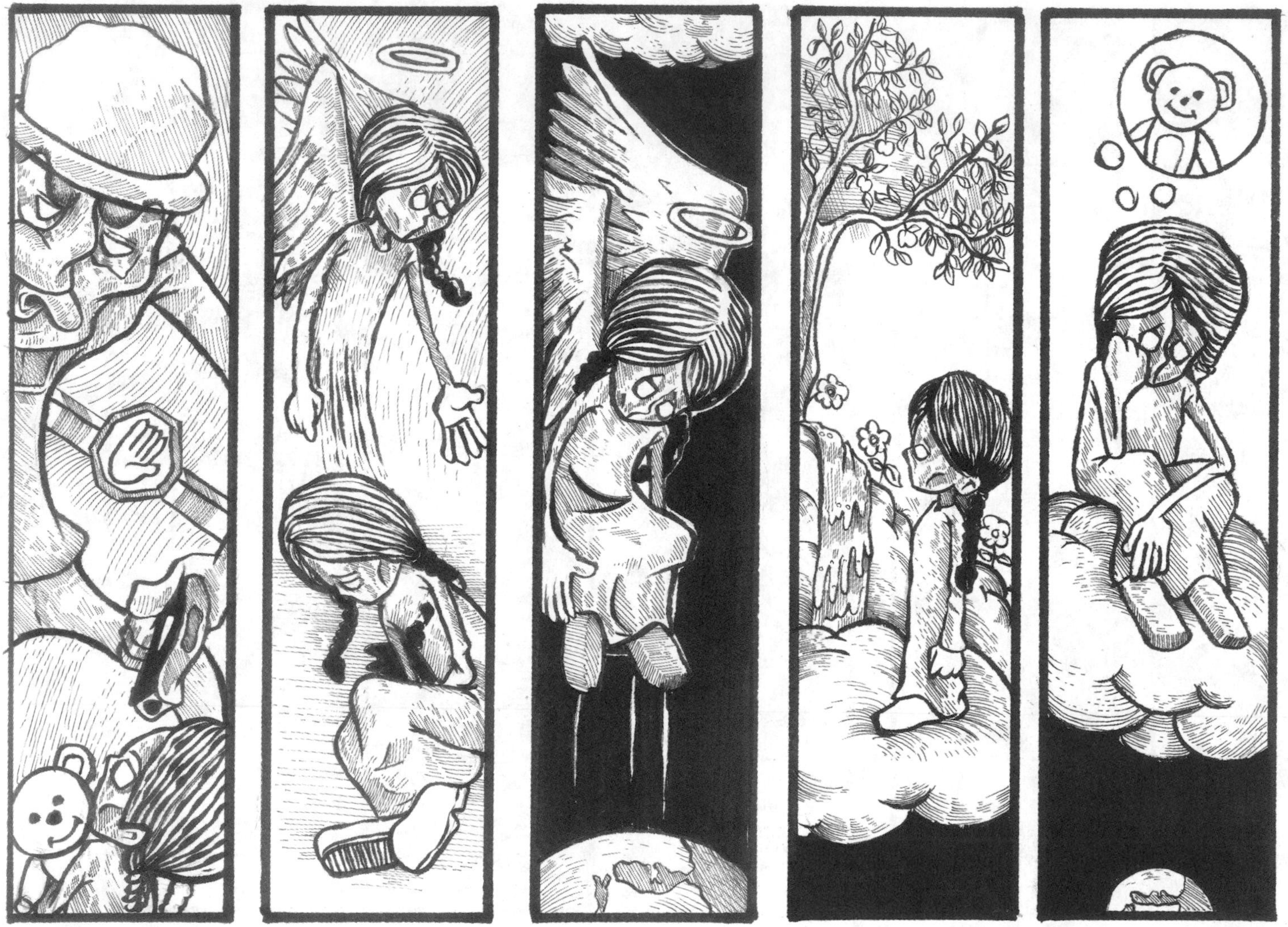

There are some things heaven can't provide.

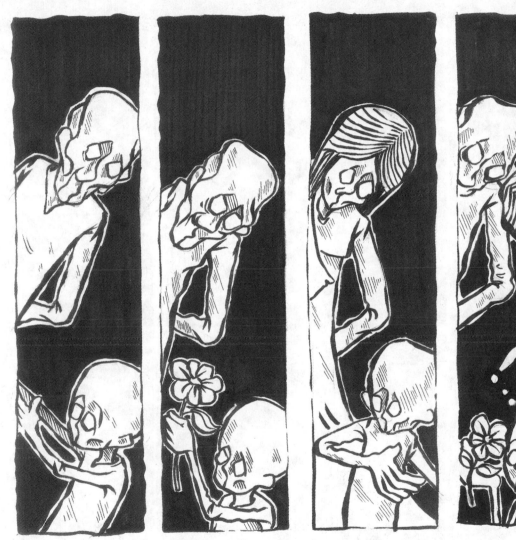

Prophets.

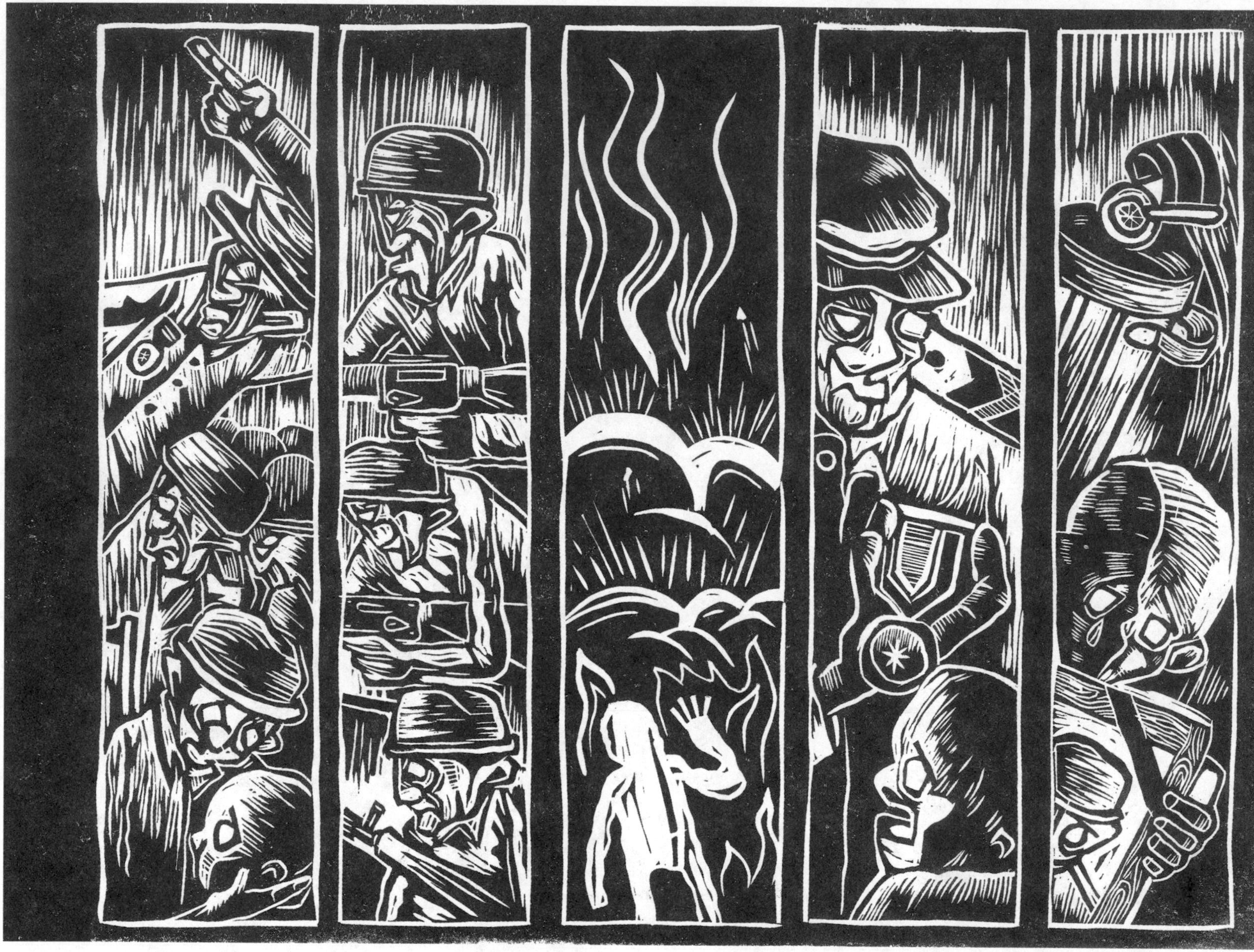

You have your victory, and I have my sorrow.

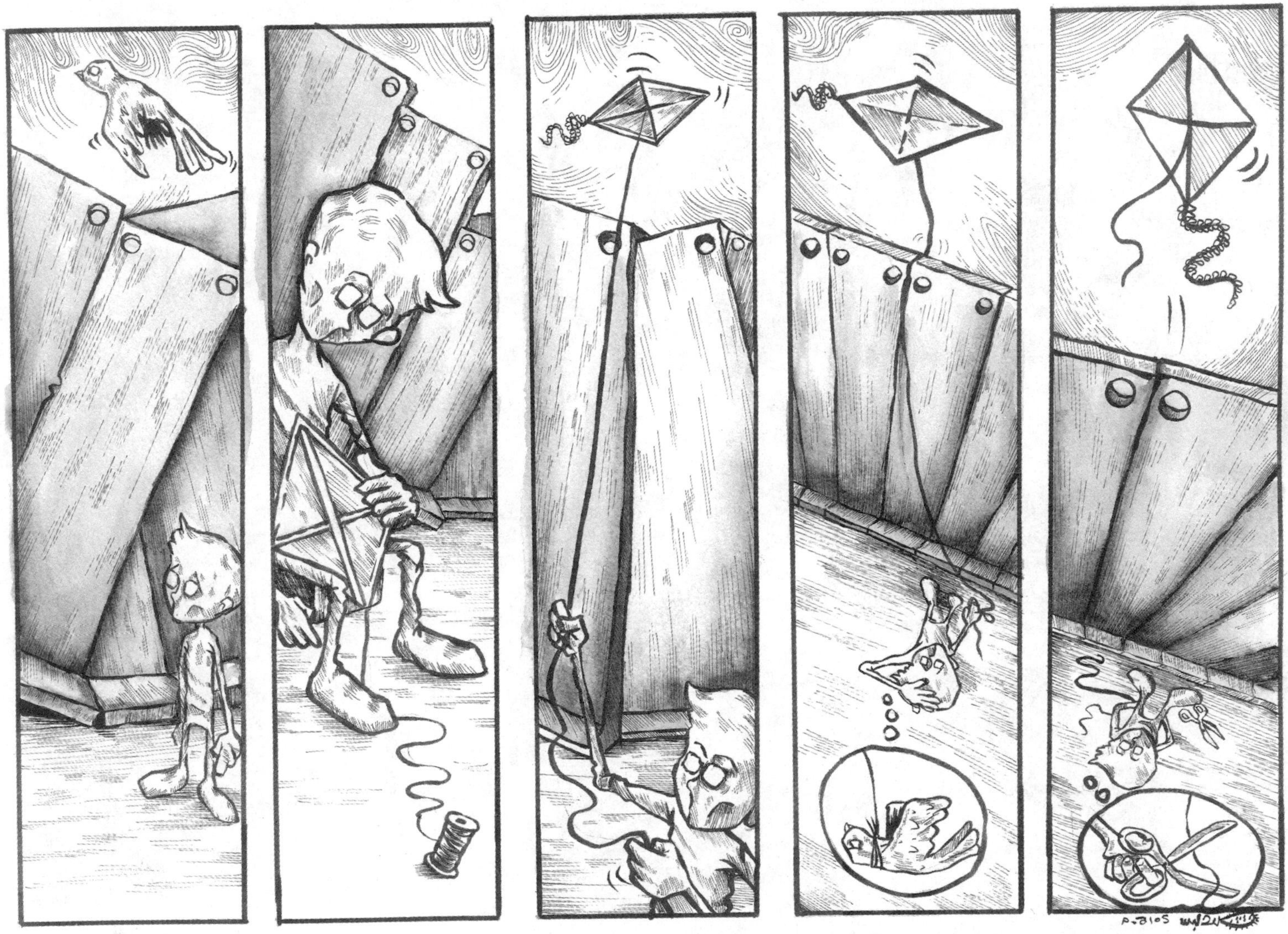

A choice.

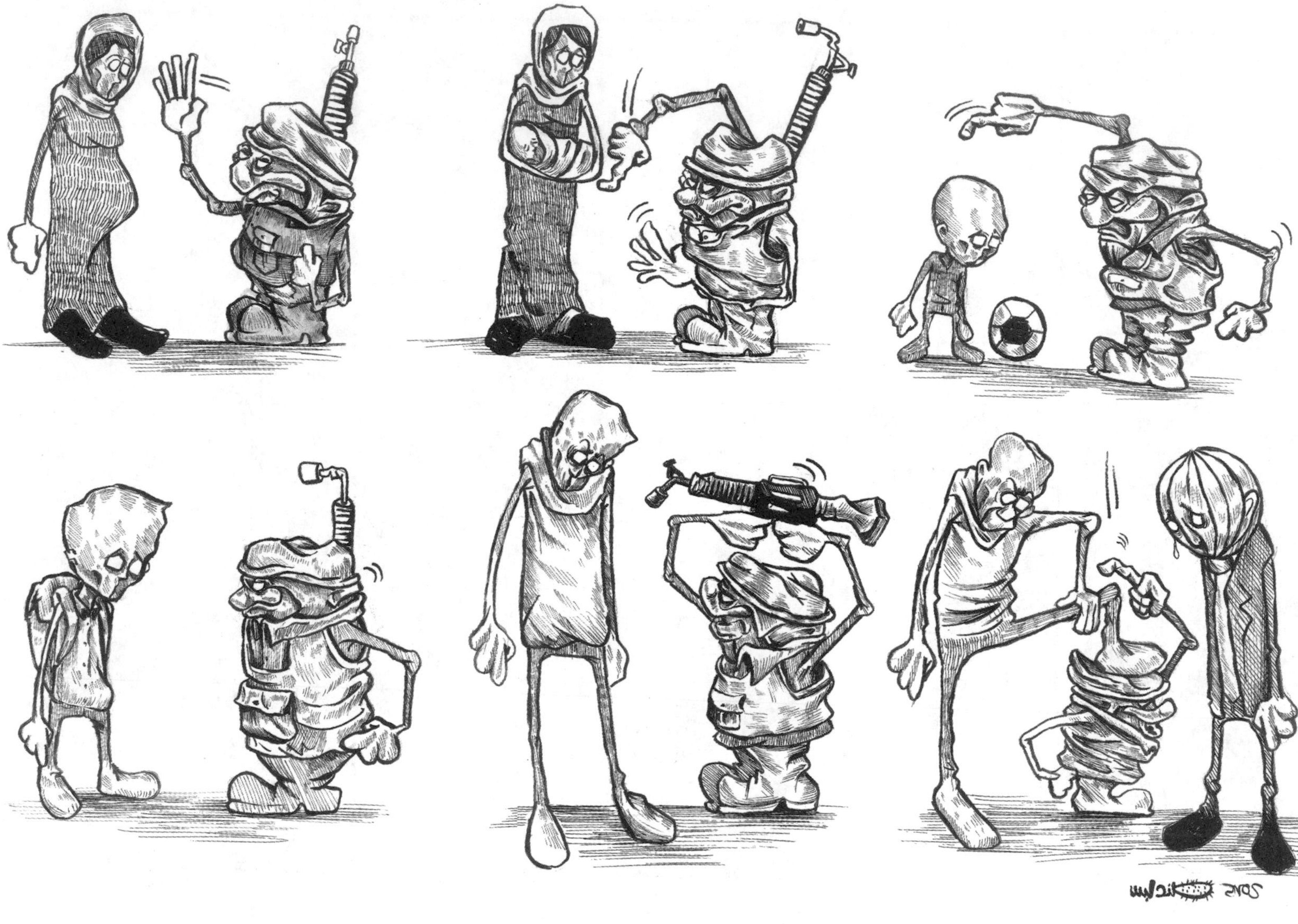

You remain a victim.

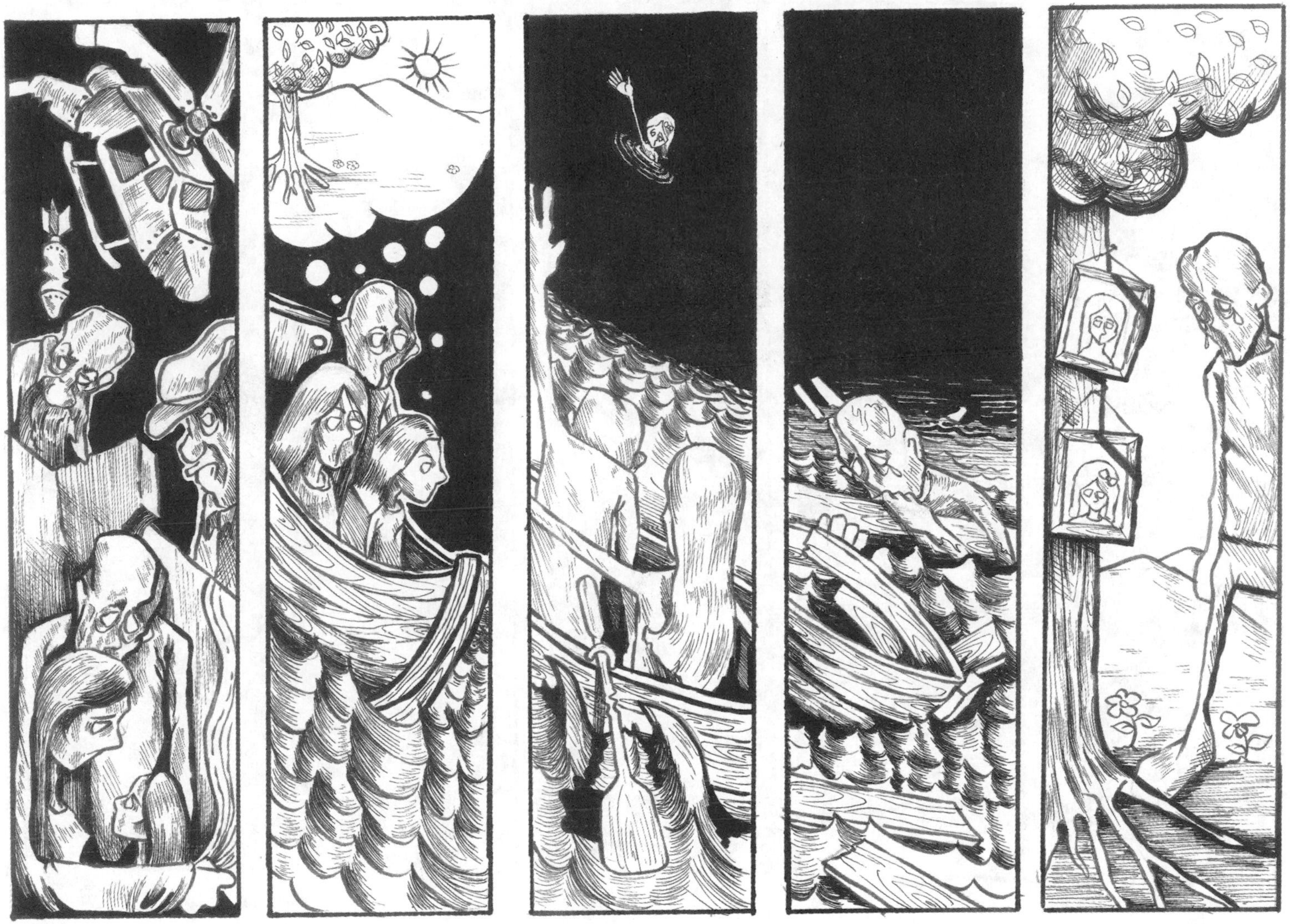

Fleeing death and finding another death.

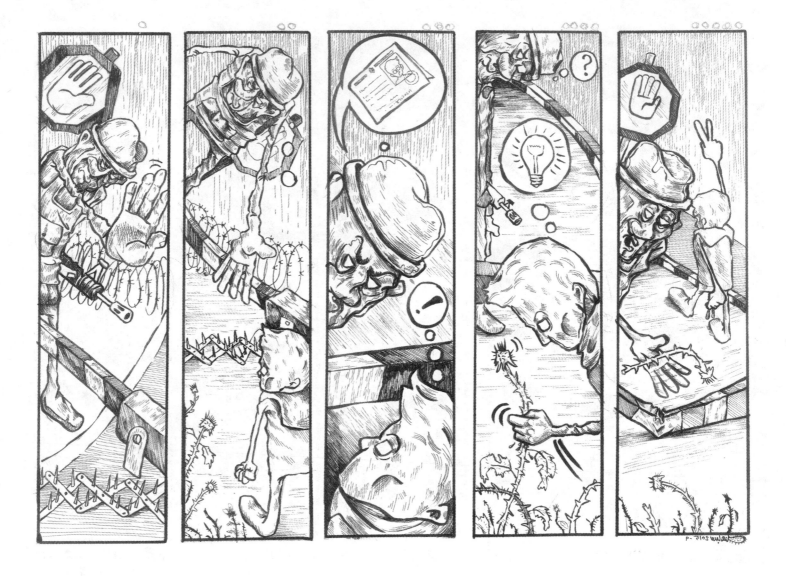

Identity card.

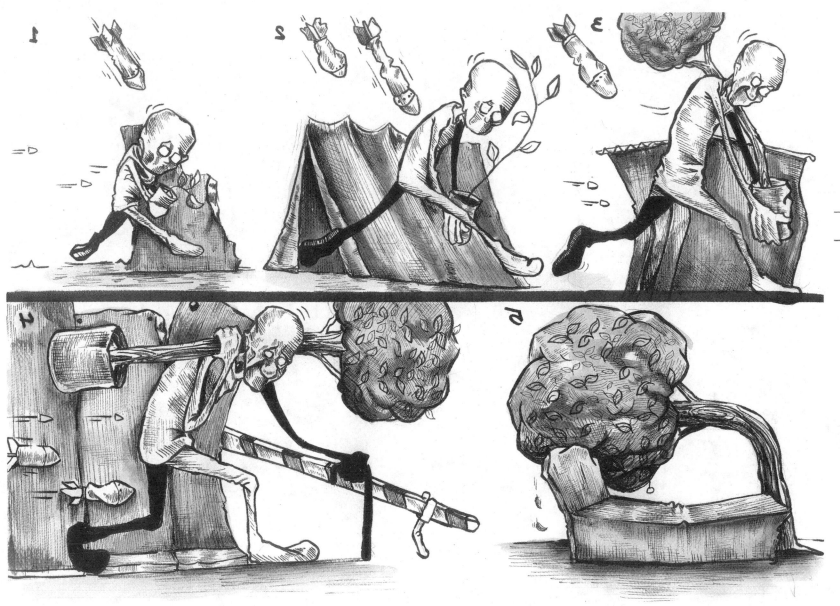

Diaspora.

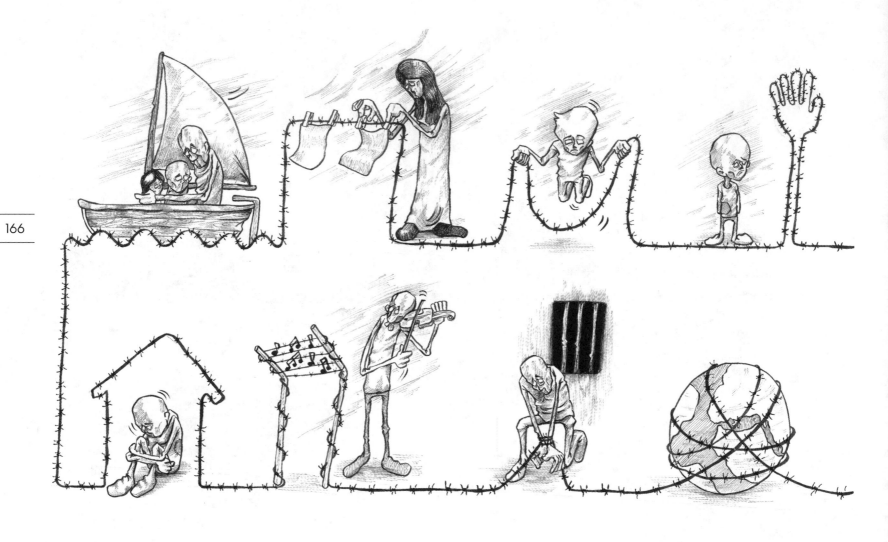

Chains.

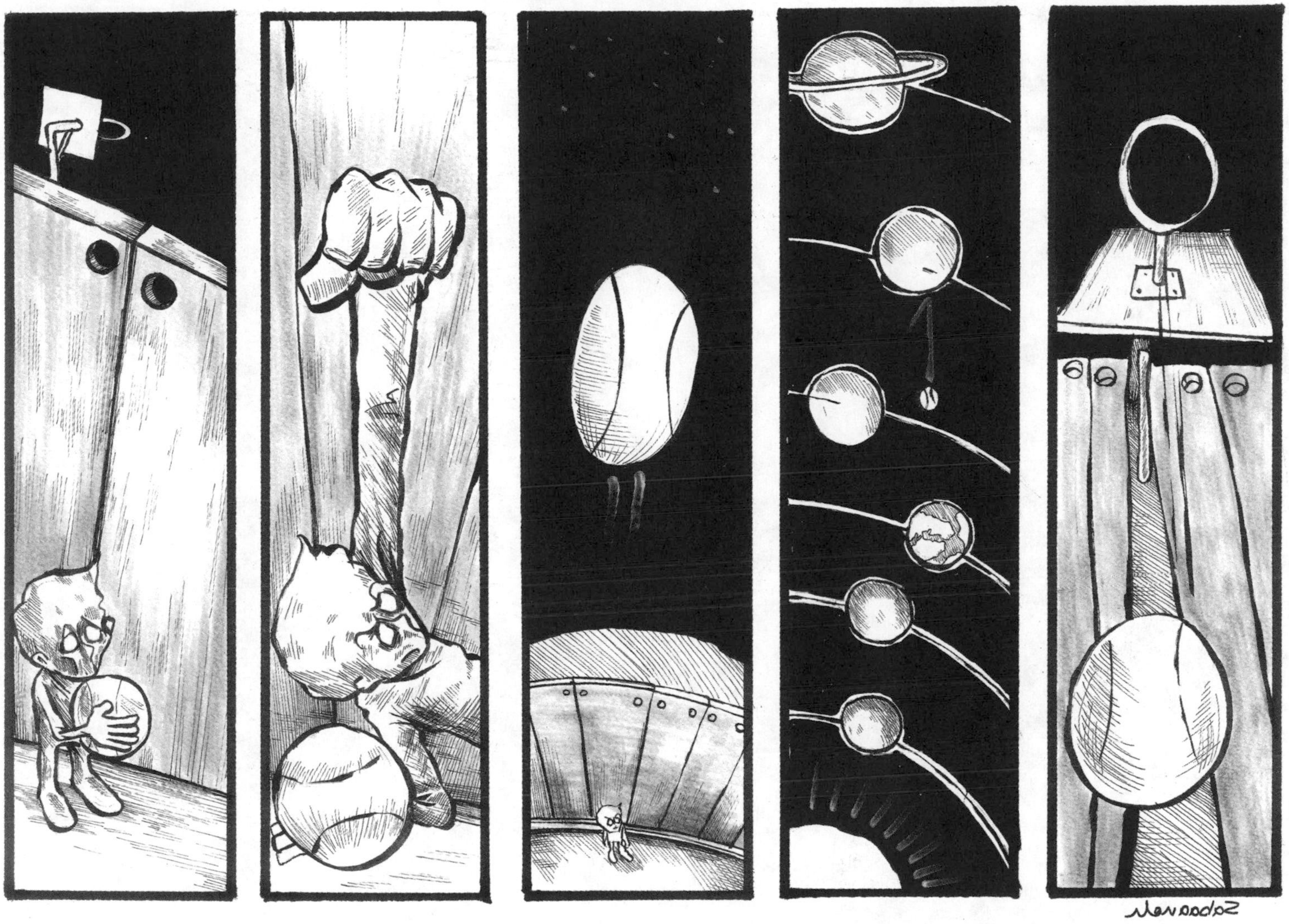

There are no shortcuts.

CHAPTER 5

POLITICAL PRISONERS

The cartoons in this chapter, whose outlines were sketched while I was in prison, dispense with the idea of the prisoner as a legendary figure and present subjects of greater immediacy, such as his sharp longing for family and his occasional fear, illness, and hunger. Even much-anticipated family visits are difficult occasions because prisoners are separated from their loved ones, and on the infrequent visits when they are allowed to be in the same room with family members, their young children often do not recognize them and so are reluctant to be held by someone they regard as a stranger. The images I drew conveyed the stiffness and sometimes the ugliness of the occupation and the oppressor. I could not find beauty anywhere in my surroundings—not in my jailer and not even in his victims.

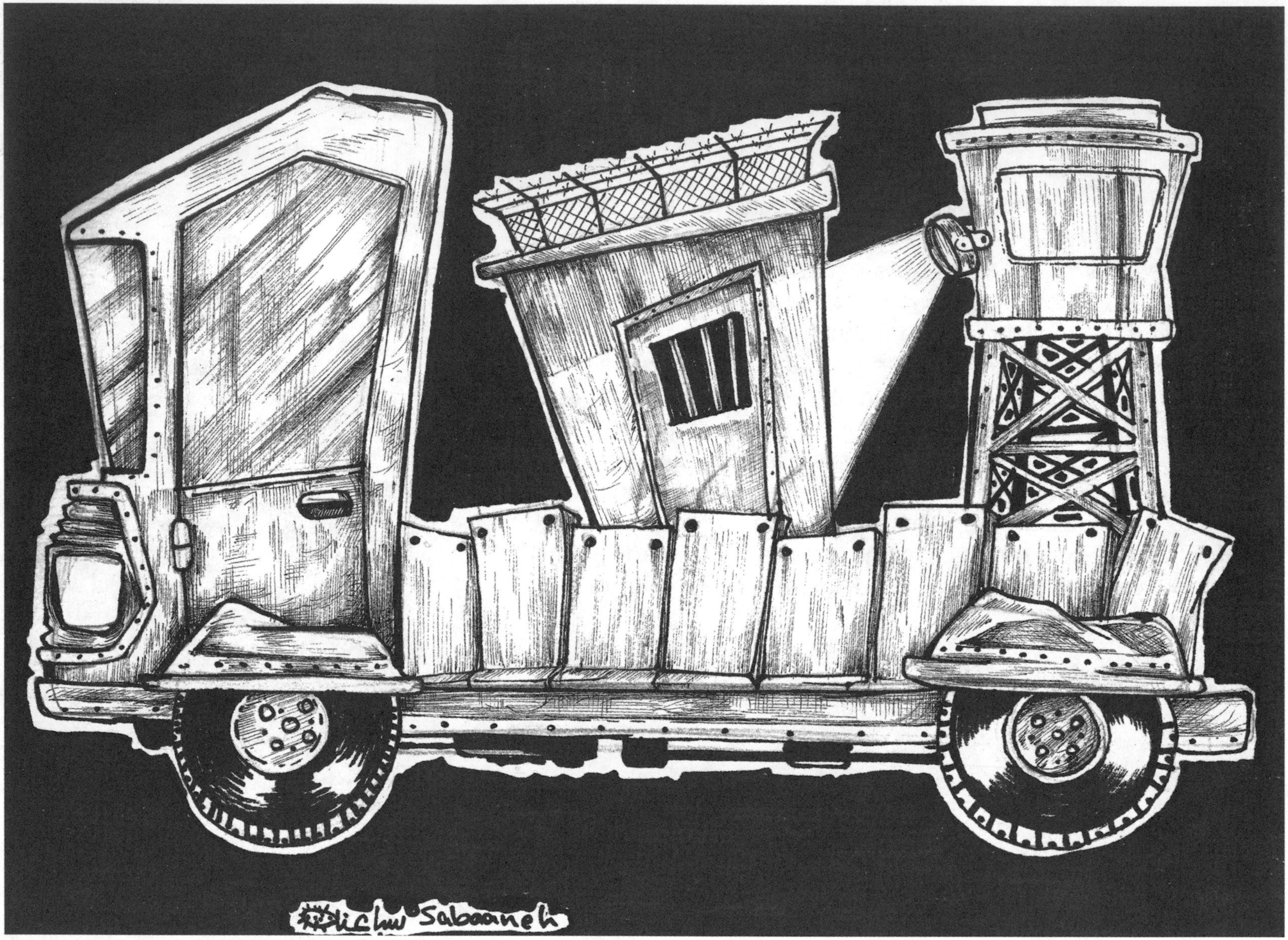

Prisoner express.

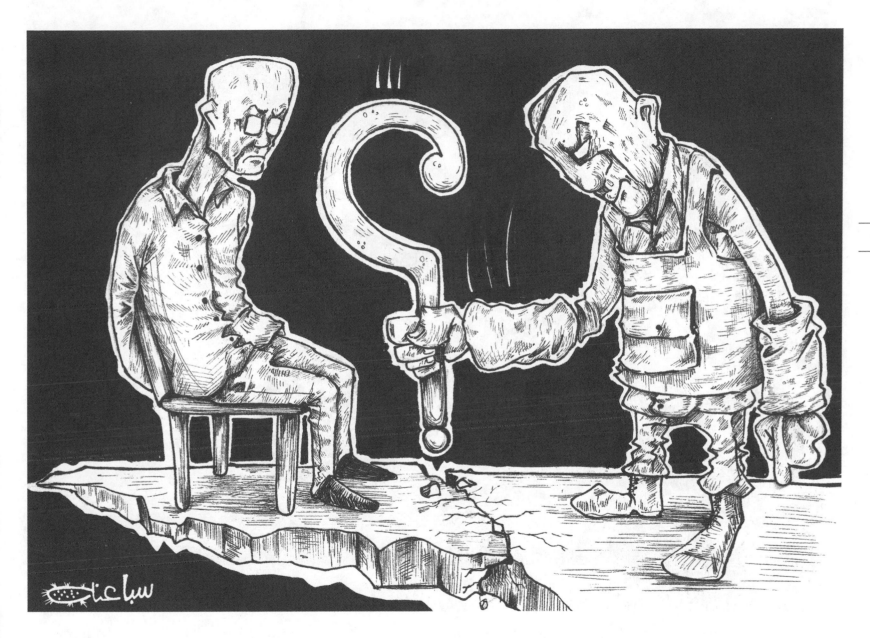

The prisoner's only weapon during interrogation is patience.

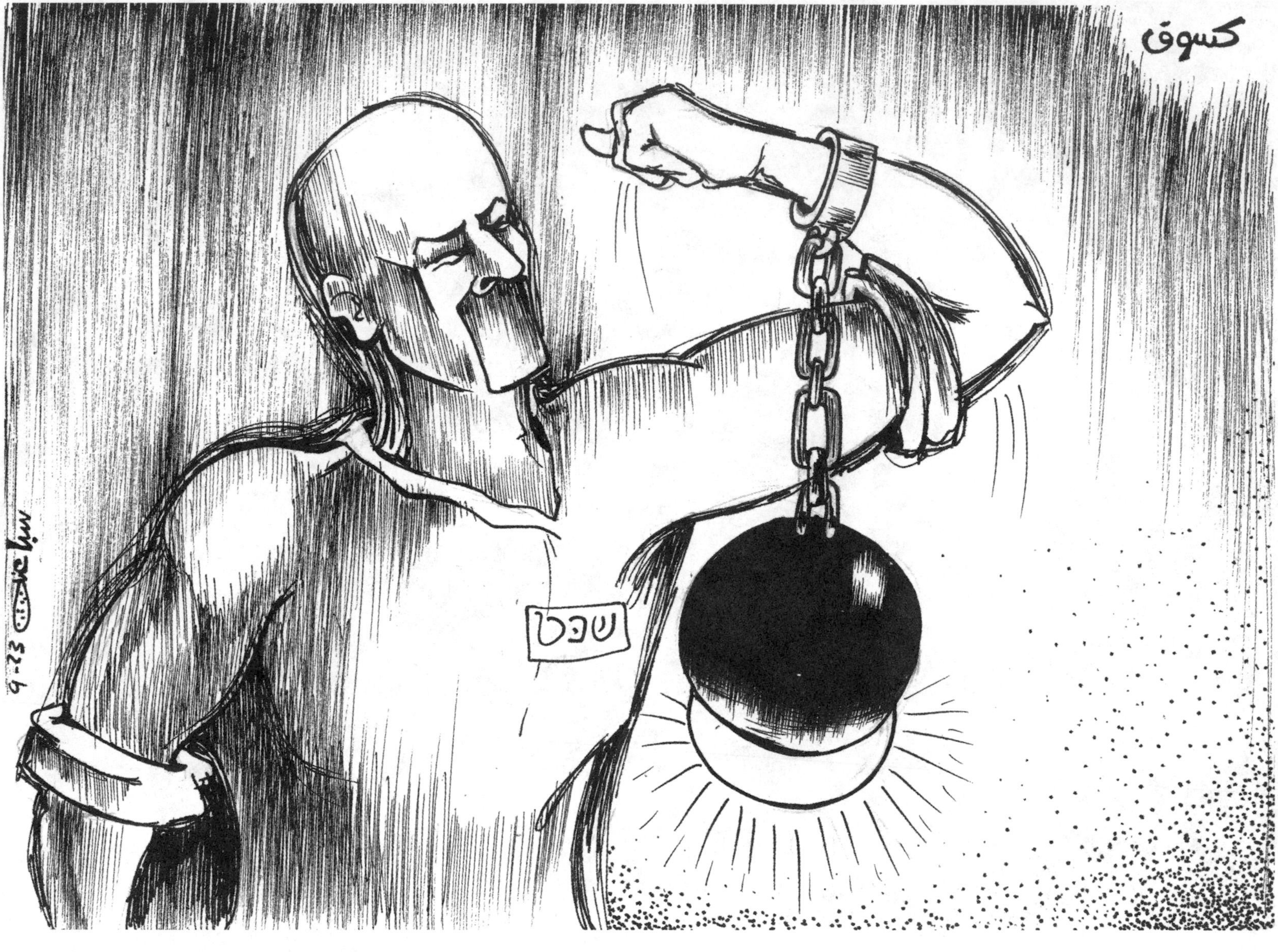
كسوف
שפט

Our sun never sets.

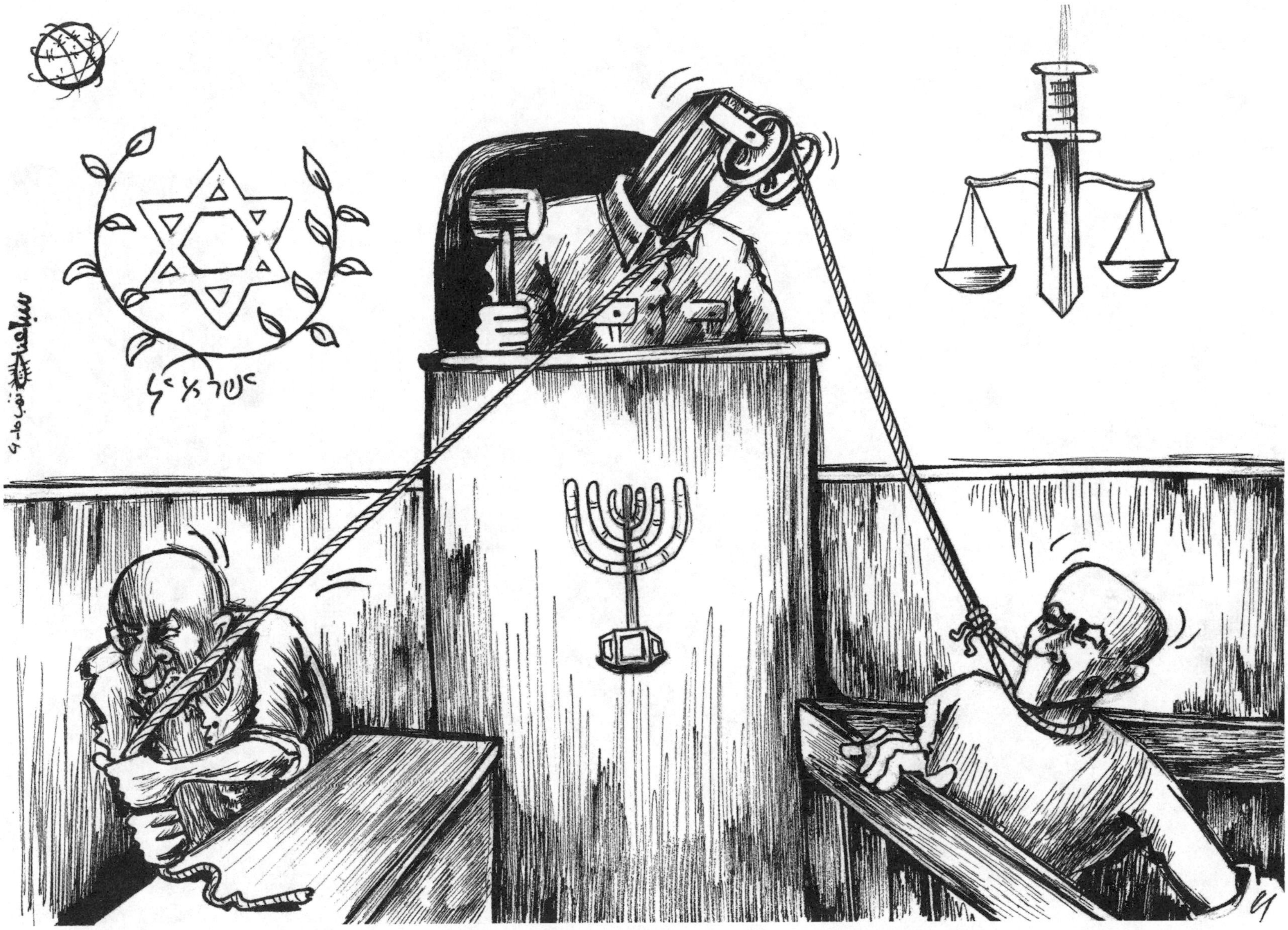

The judiciary is just another tool in the hands of the jailer.

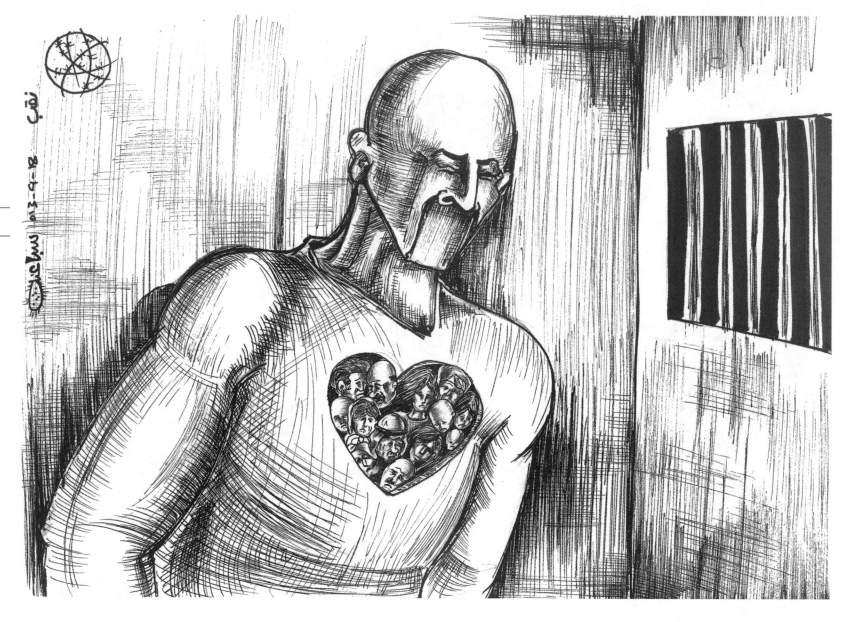

My homeland lives in my heart.

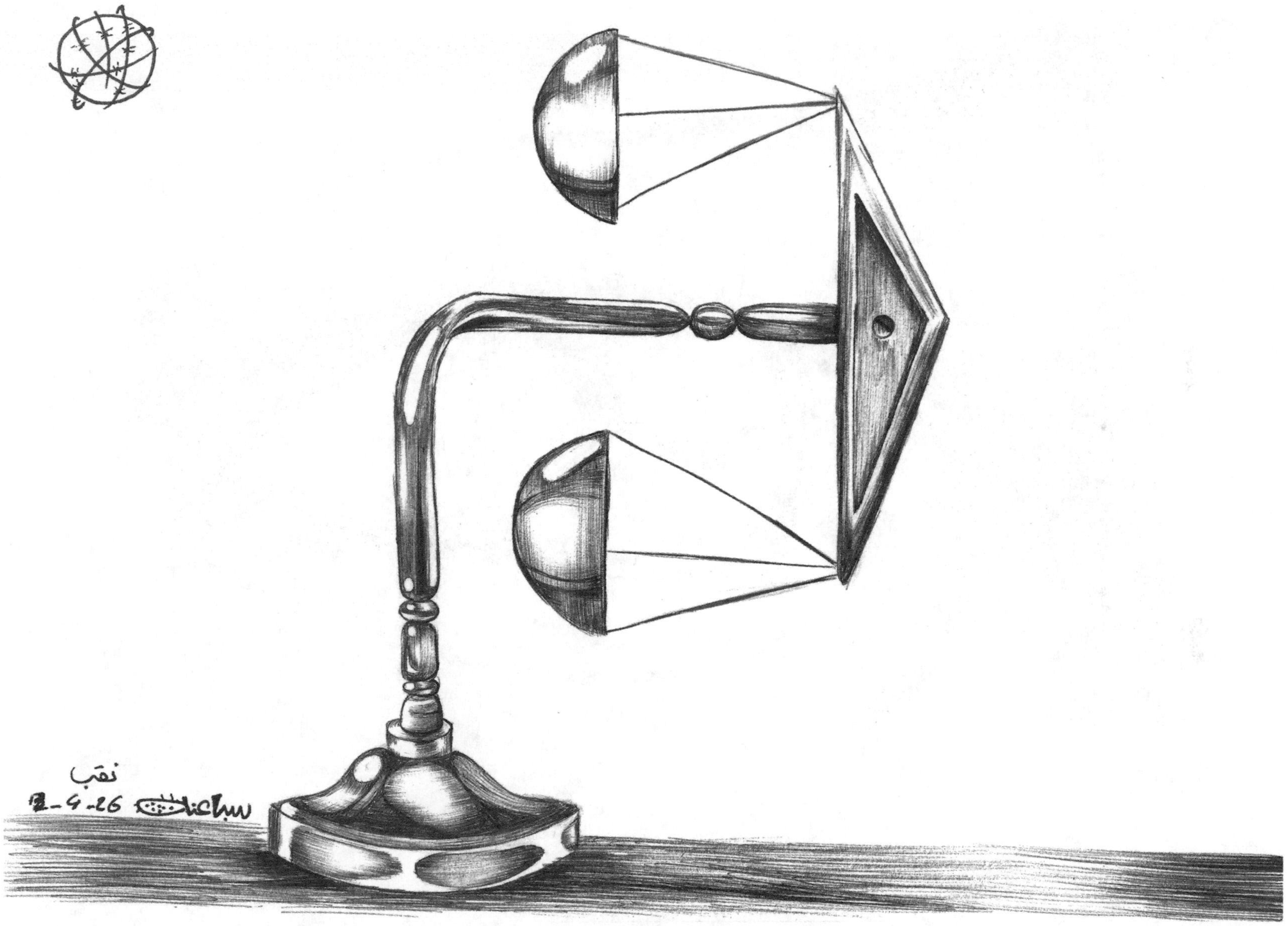
نقب

Scales of “justice.”

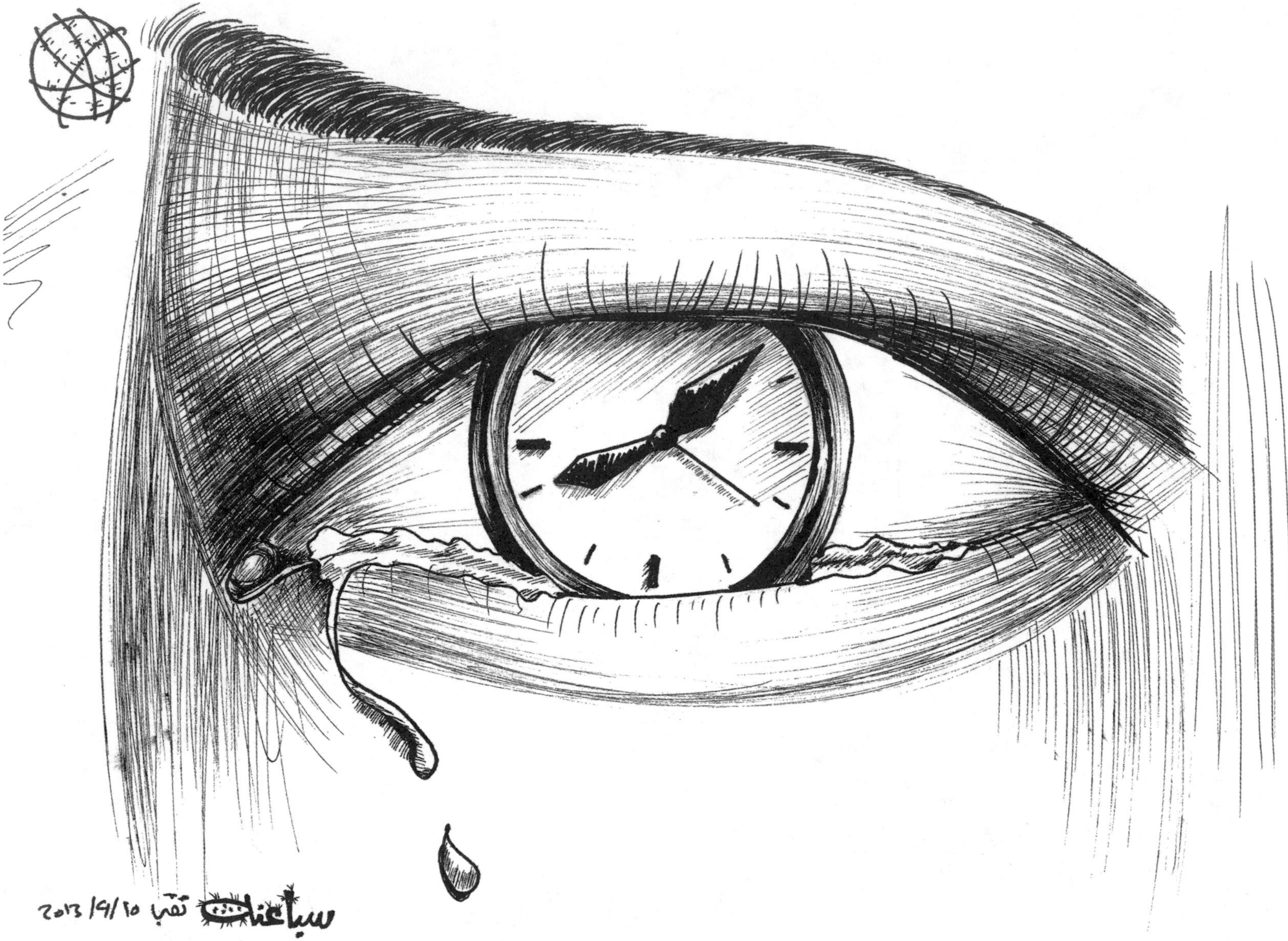

For prisoners, time = tears + blood.

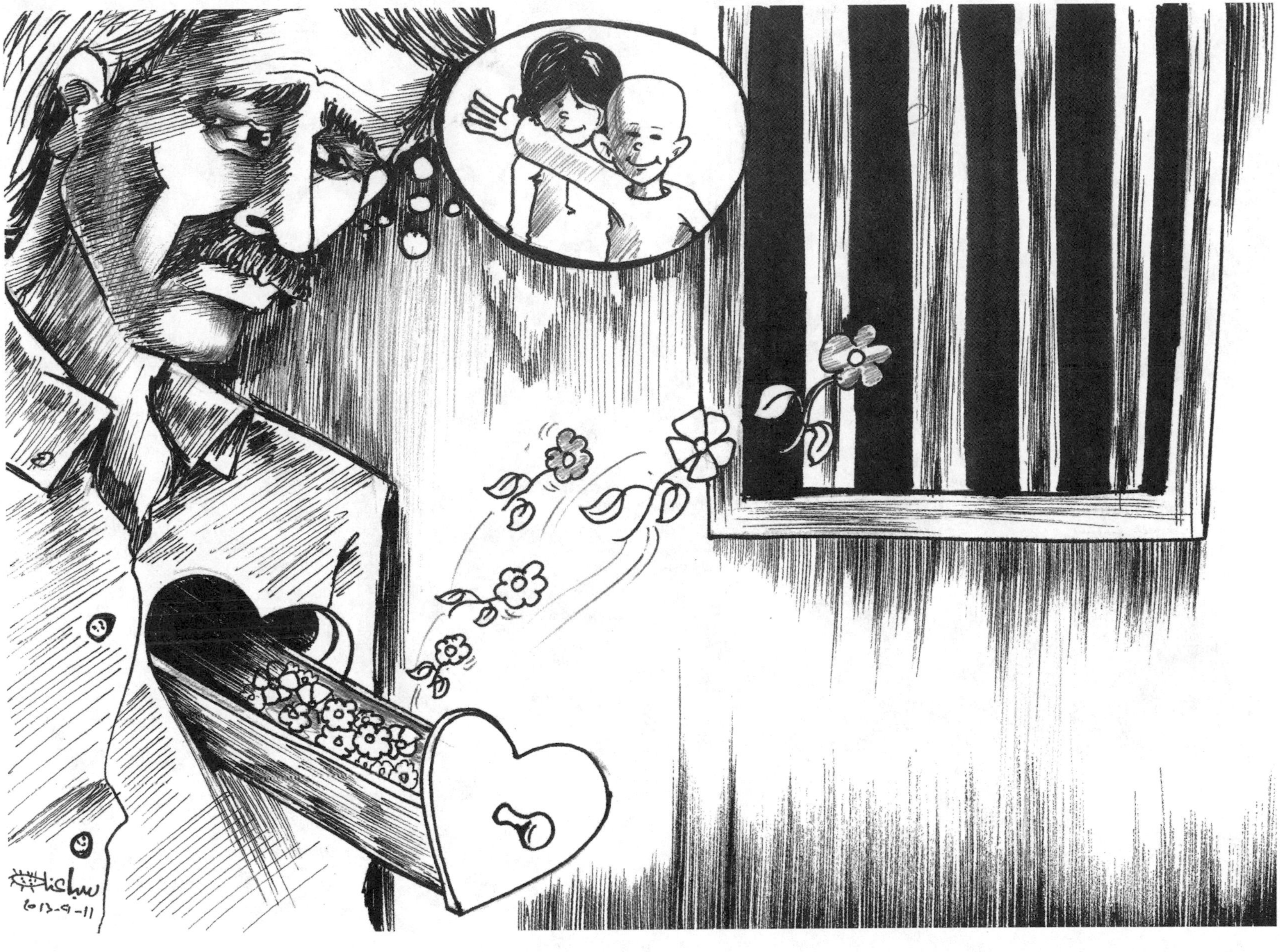
2013-9-11

Walls can't keep out heartache and longing.

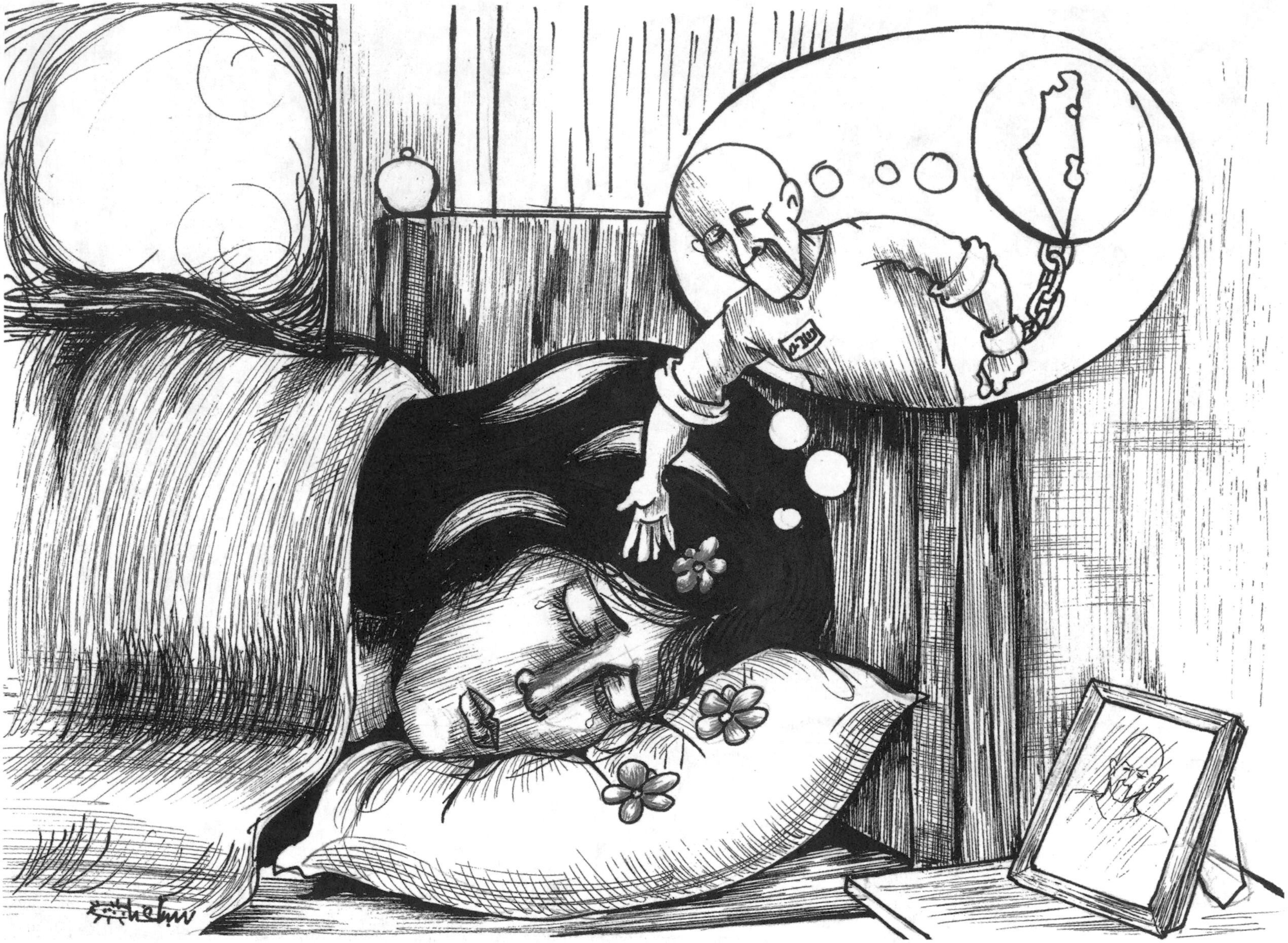

Memories.

The judiciary is not authorized to reach a verdict.

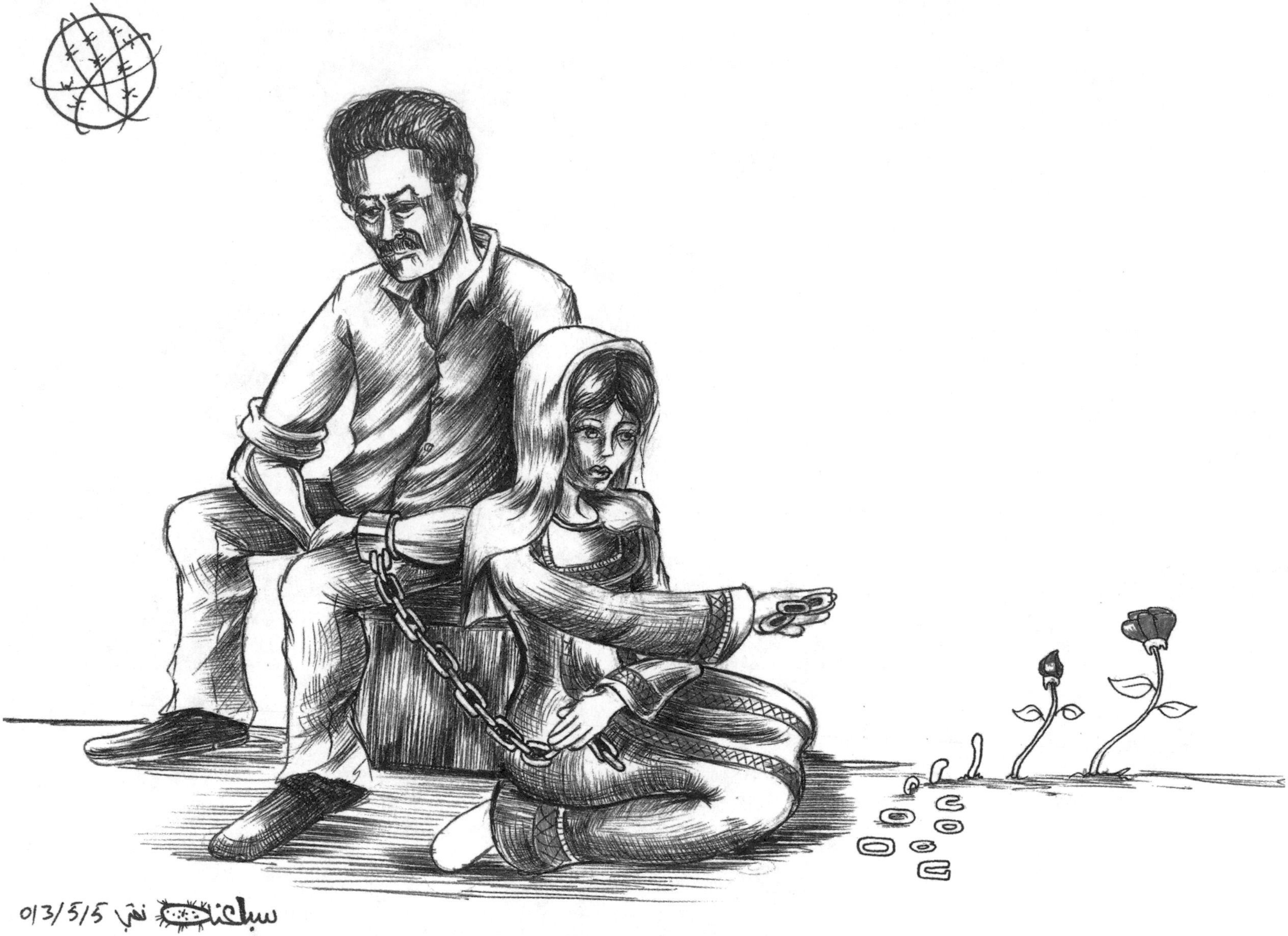

Prisoners and their wives—two sides of the same coin.

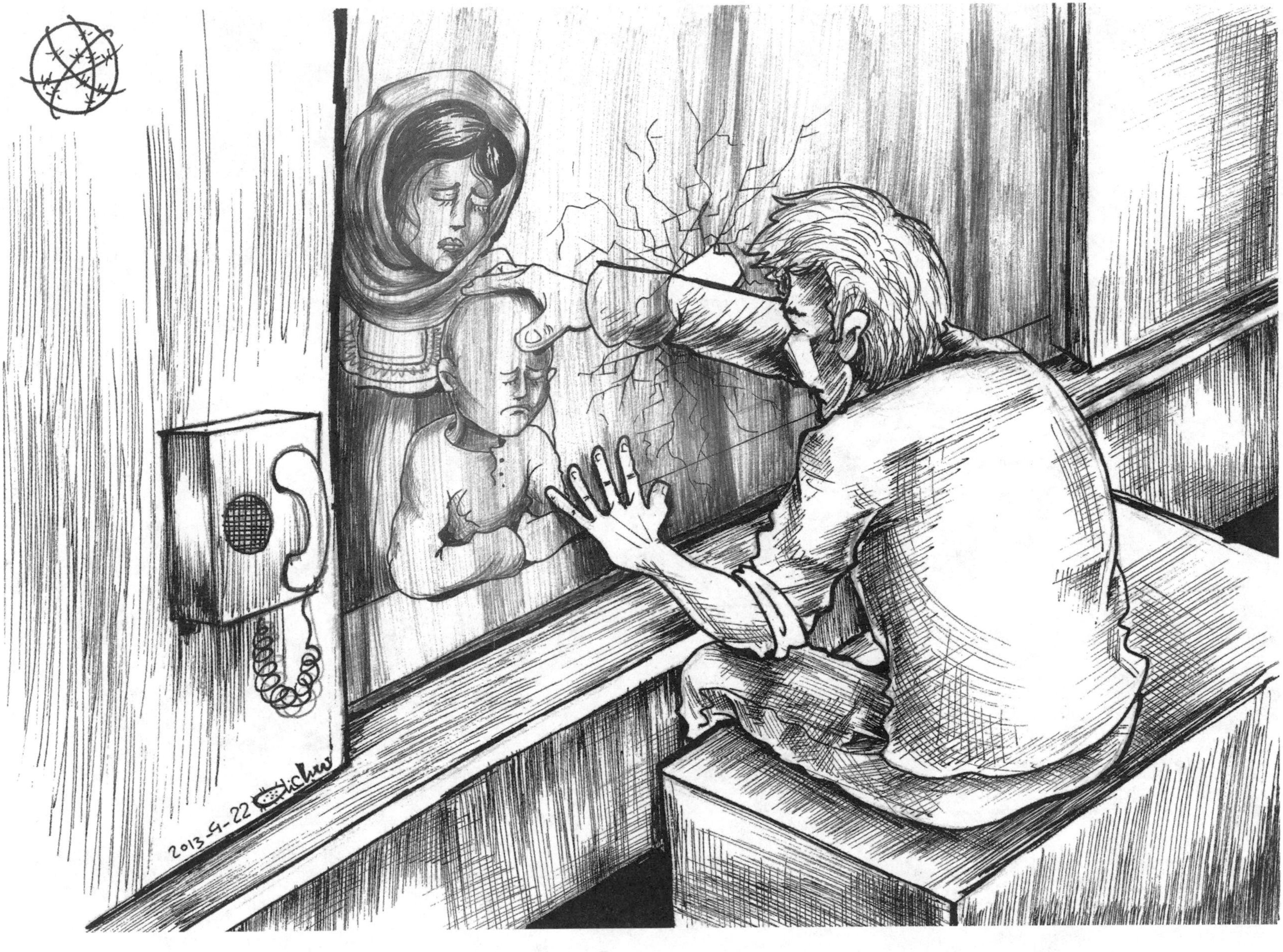
2013-4-22

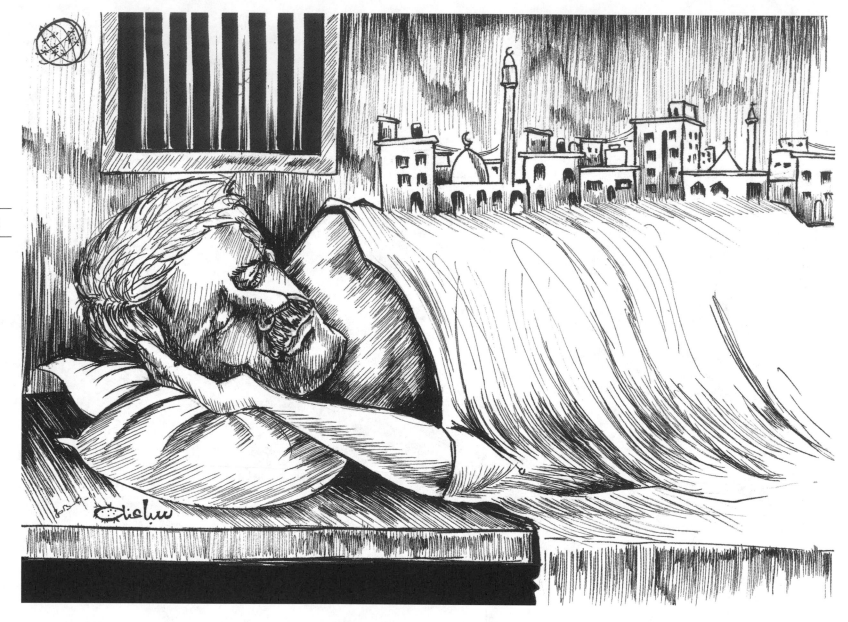

Dreaming of the homeland.

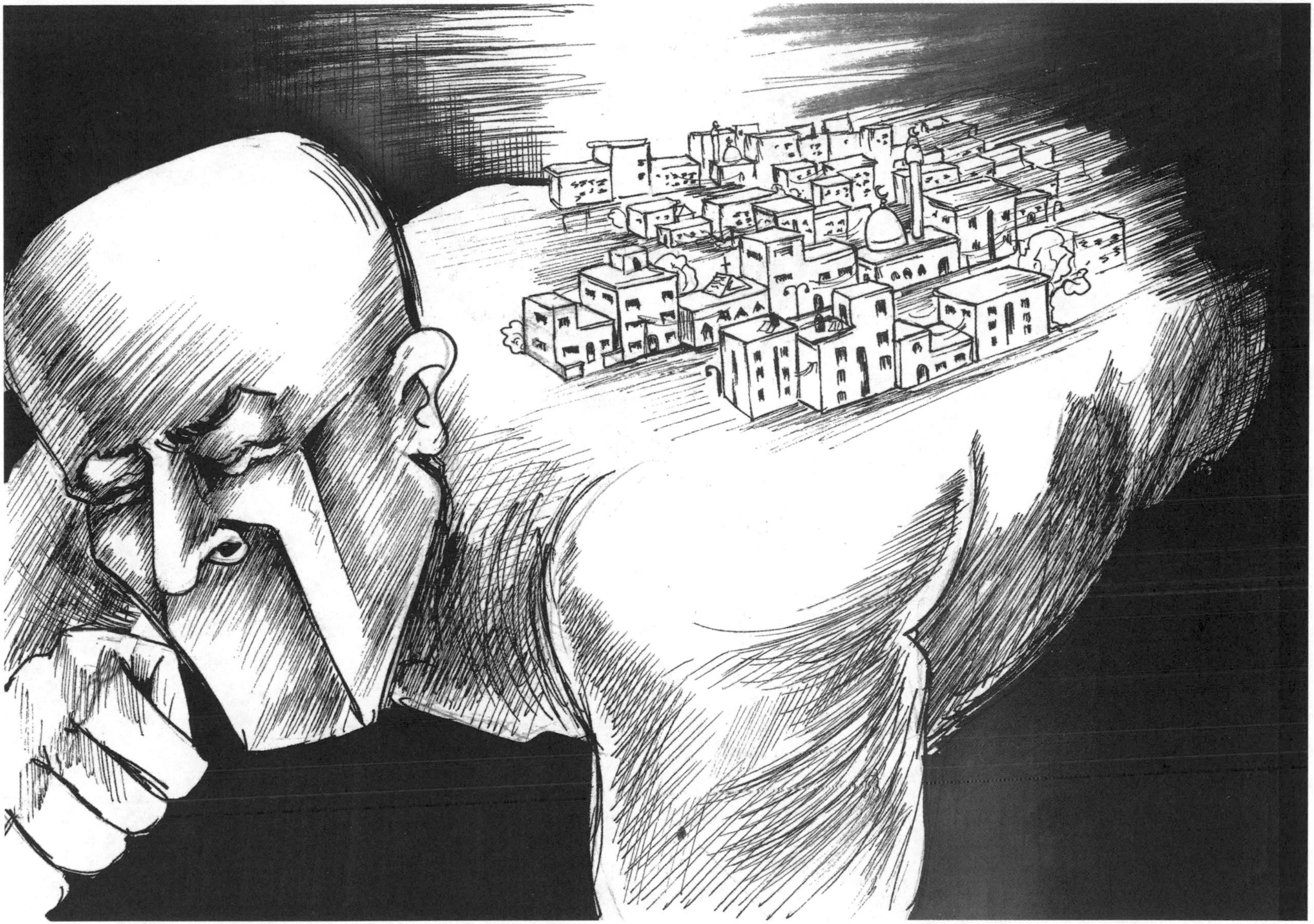

Prisoners carry the weight of their homeland.

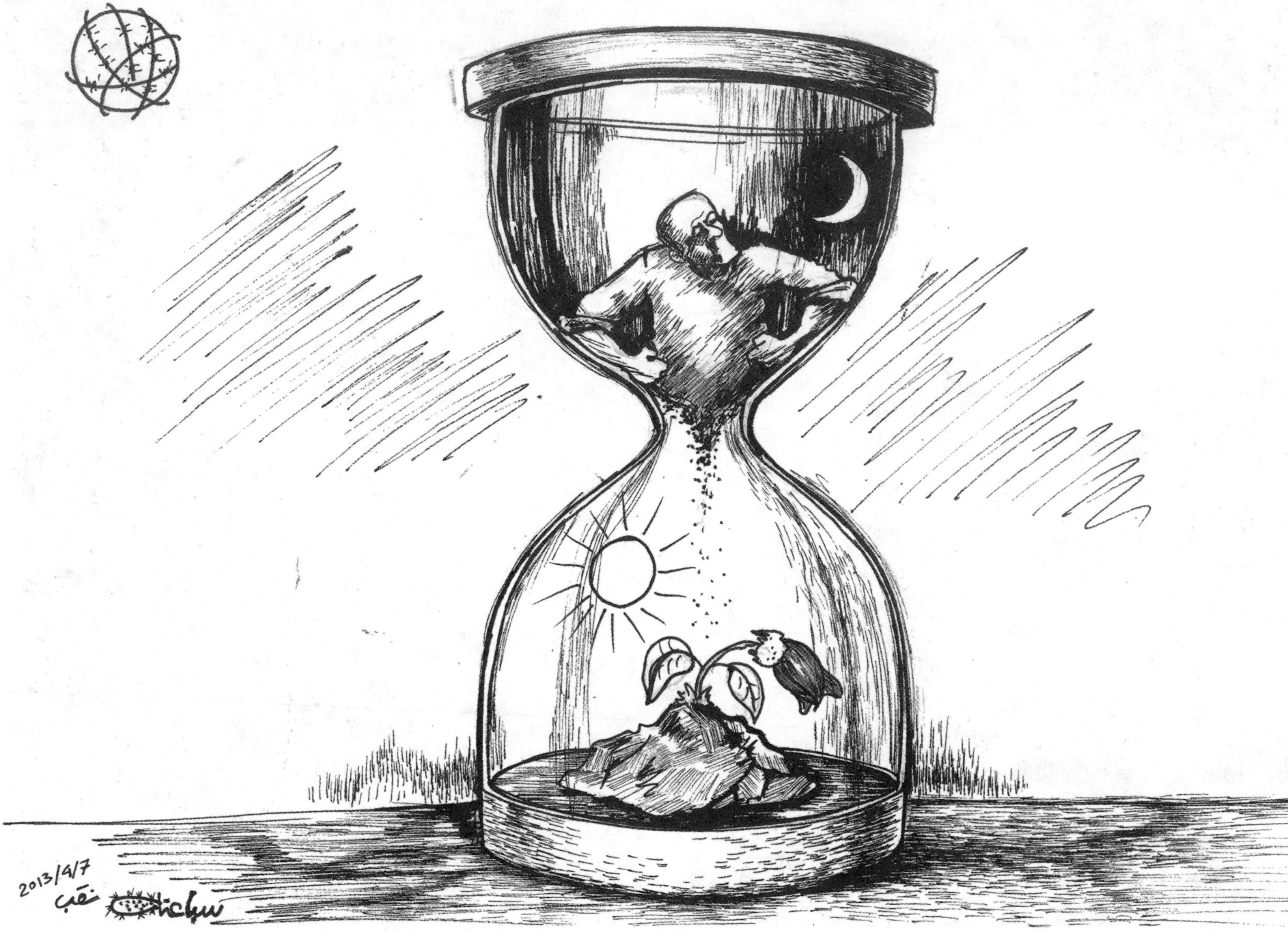
2013/4/7

They pay with the best years of their lives.

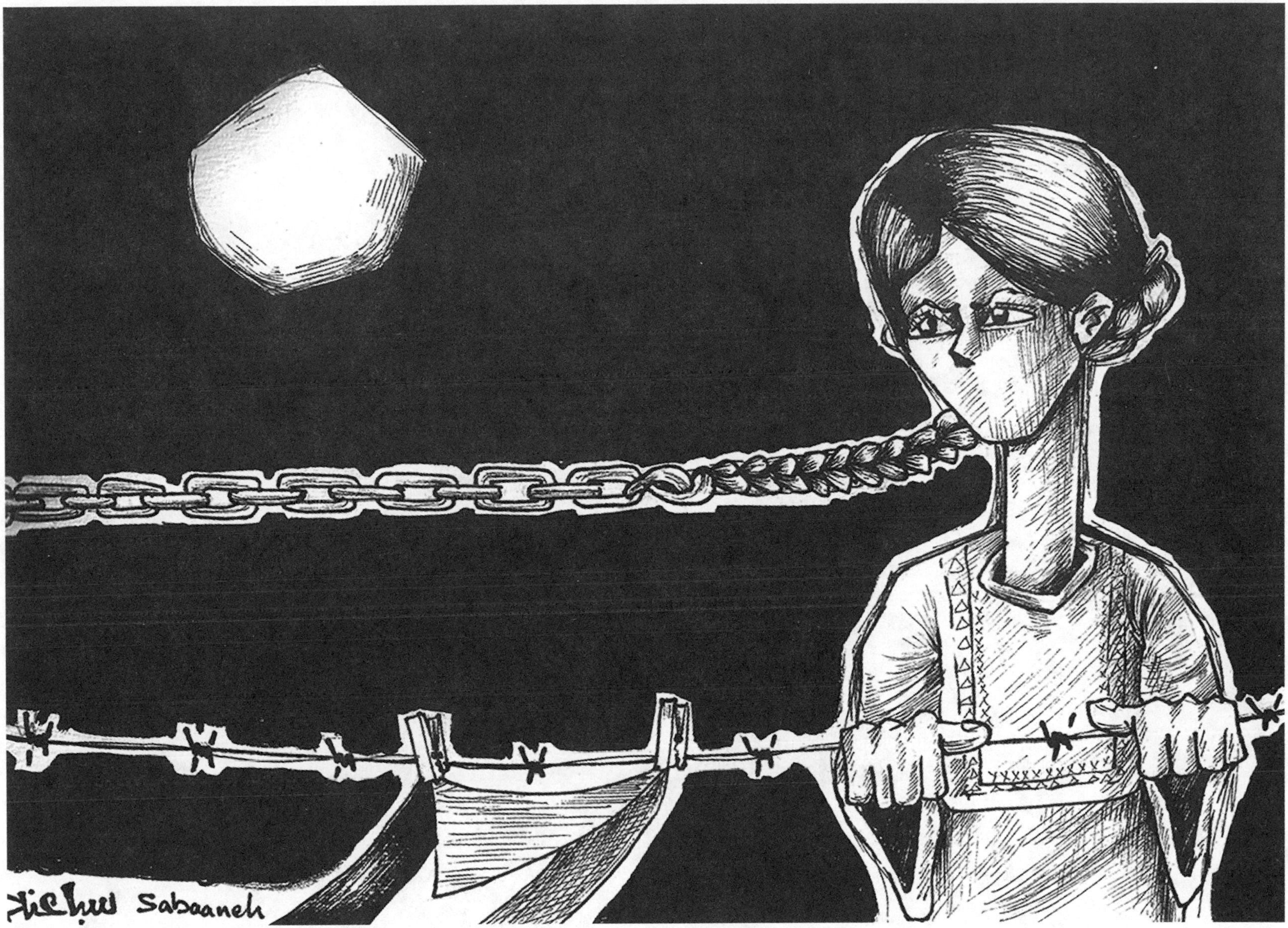
Sabaaneh

Women prisoners.

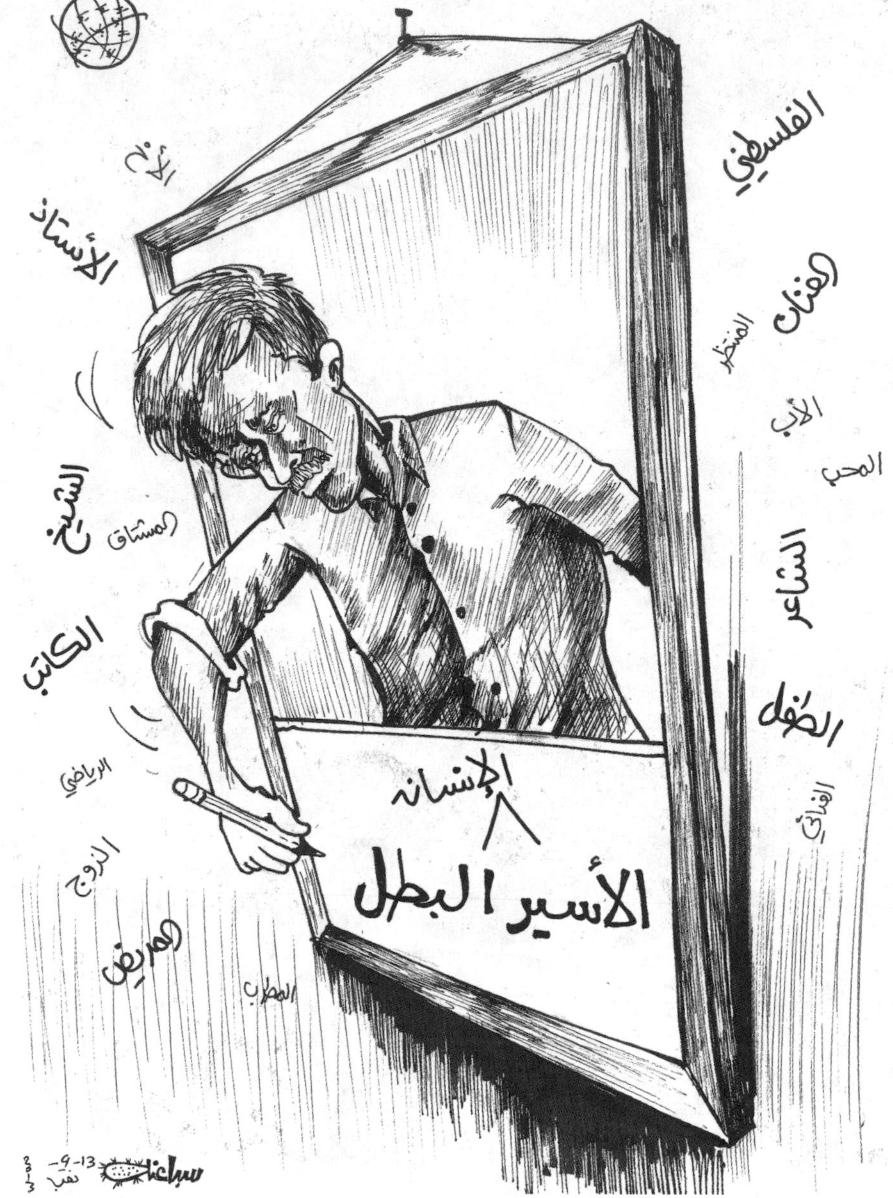
الأسير البطل
الإنسان
الفلسطيني
الفنان
المنتظر
الأب
المحب
الشاعر
الطفل
الفدائي
الأخ
الأستاذ
الشيخ
المشتاق
الكاتب
الرياضي
الزوج
المريض
الطالب

The "hero-prisoner" is a father, brother, poet, teacher—and a human being.

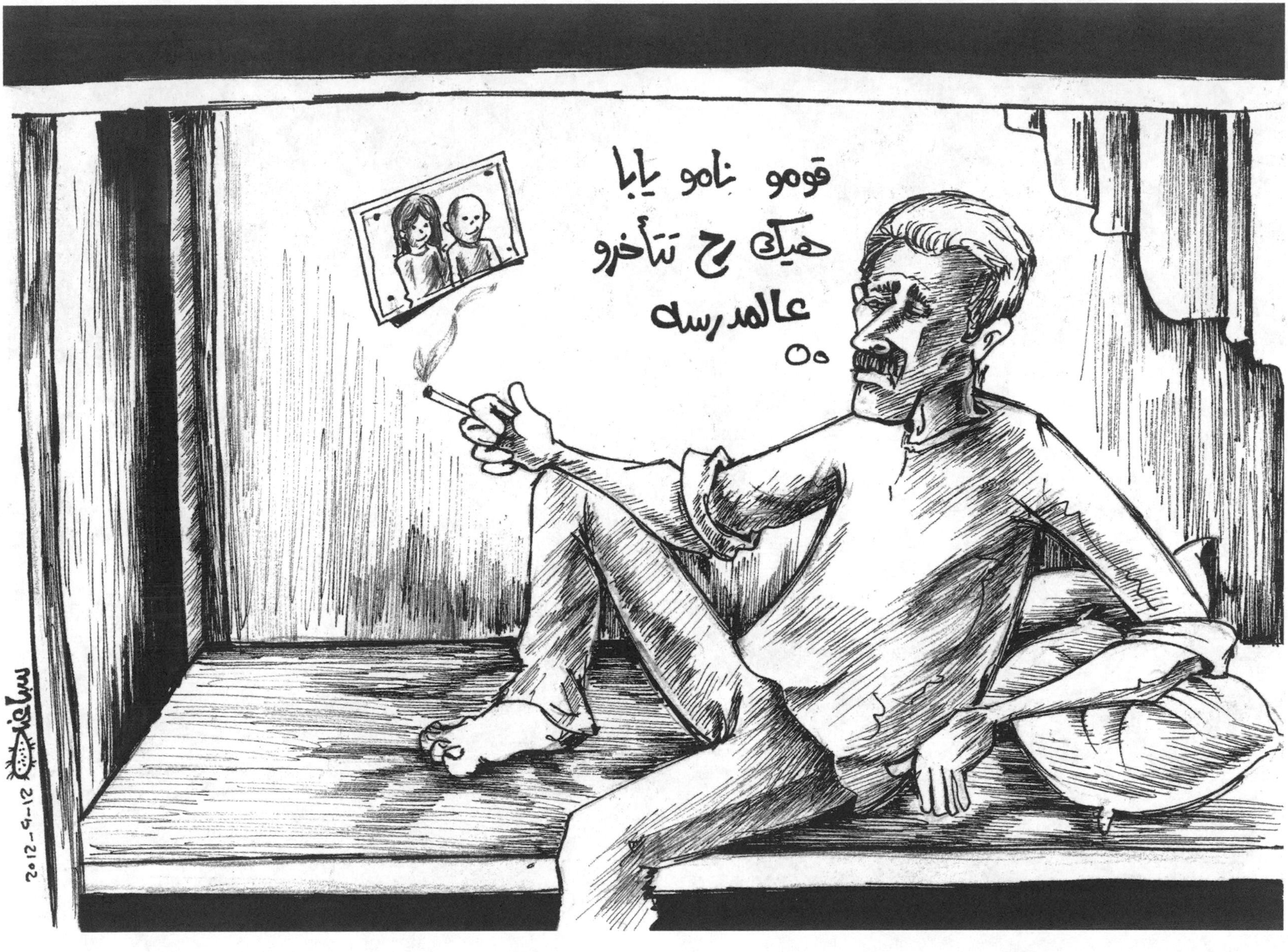
قومو نامو يابا
هيك رح تتأخرو
عالمدرسه

Go to sleep, sweethearts, or you'll be late for school tomorrow.

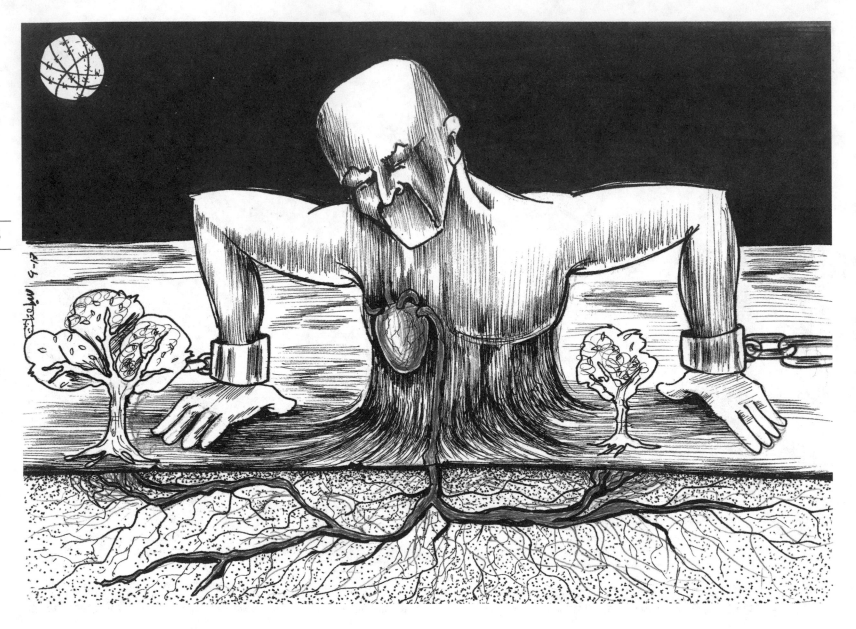

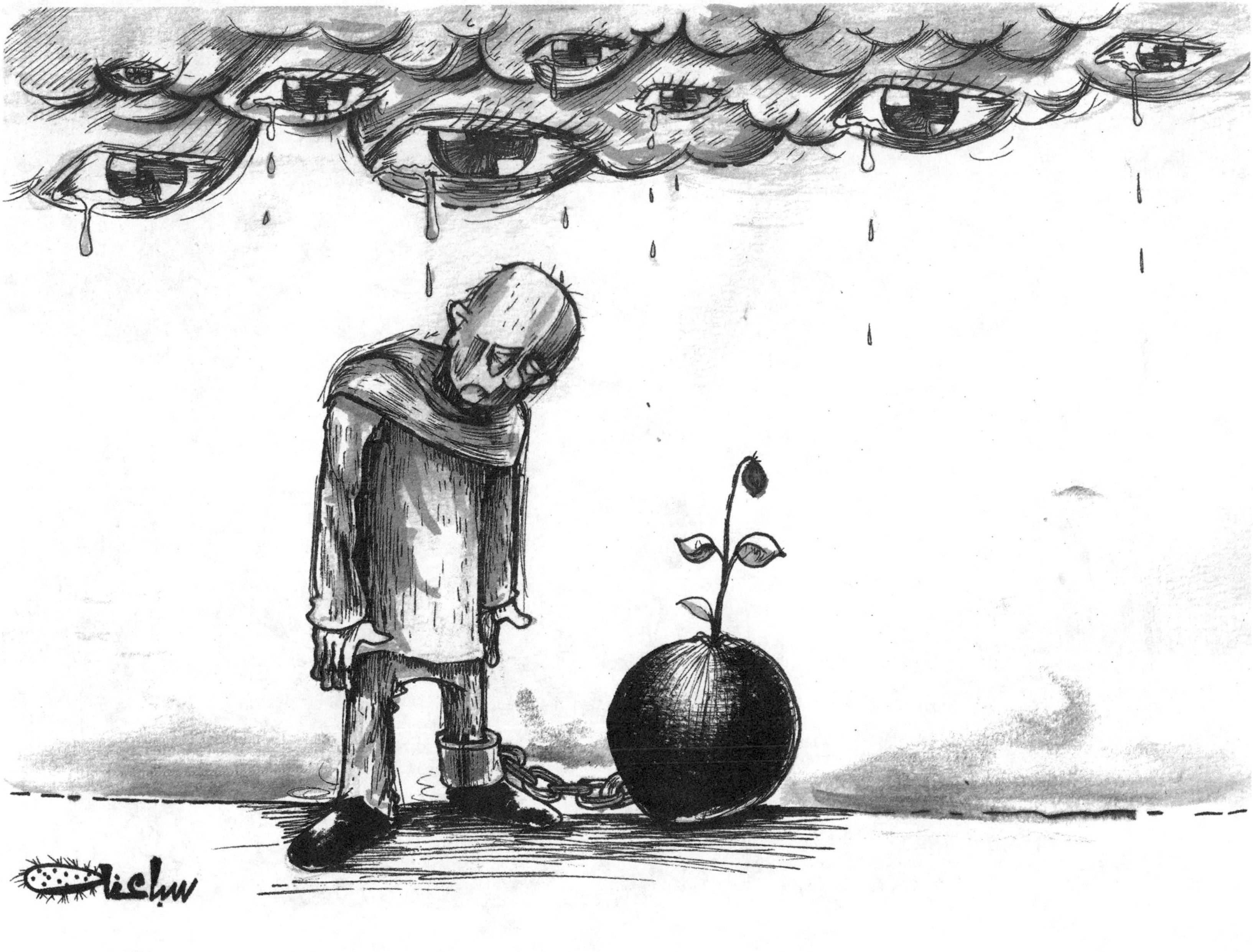

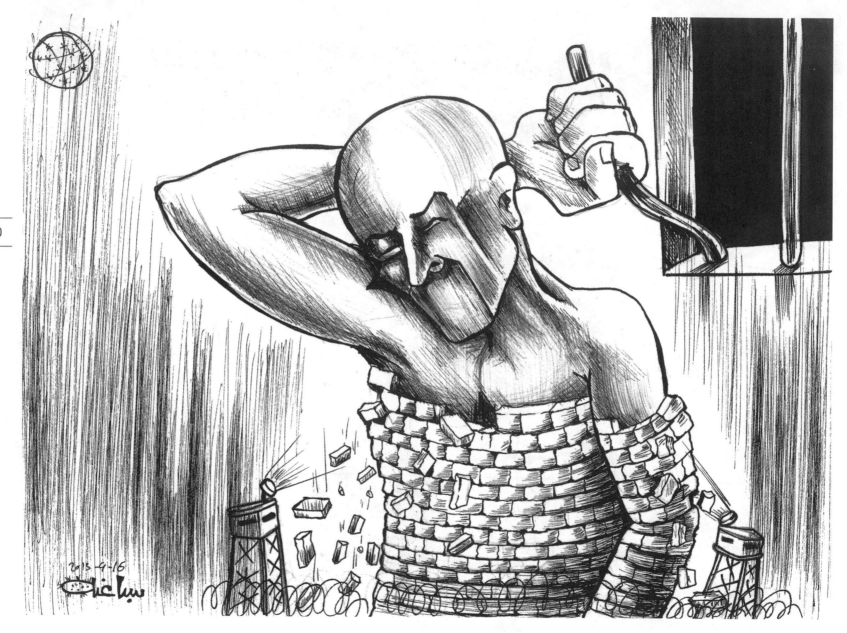

I won't become an object.

KEY TO SYMBOLS

The cactus, indigenous to Palestine, is used in Palestinian art as a symbol of Palestinian defiance and *sumud,* or steadfastness.

Checkpoints make it difficult for Palestinians to travel even trivial distances without showing identification papers to heavily armed Israeli soldiers or settlers (and sometimes being denied passage altogether.)

The Palestinian flag represents the Palestinian people. Prior to the establishment of the Palestinian Authority in the West Bank and Gaza Strip, raising the flag or using the four colors of the flag in combination (in artwork, for example) was cause for arrest by the Israeli occupation authorities.

The key symbolizes the Palestinians' Right of Return to the homes they were ethnically cleansed from in 1947–48. Refugees took the keys to their homes with them as they fled, expecting to return soon, when hostilities ended. The Right to Return is enshrined in the Universal Declaration of Human Rights.

Olive trees have great economic as well as symbolic significance for Palestinians. Olive trees, some of which date to Roman times, provide the main source of income for about 80,000 Palestinian families. Israeli soldiers and settlers have uprooted more than 800,000 olive trees since 1967.

 A house in an Israeli colony or settlement, built in the West Bank in contravention of the Fourth Geneva Convention. Many settlements are sited on hilltops above Palestinian towns; often, the settlers terrorize Palestinian neighborhoods and the Israeli army does not intervene. The settlement houses depicted here have pitched roofs. Other structures shown include flat-roofed Palestinian housing, prison cells, and watchtowers.

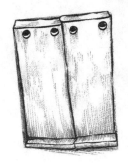 The Apartheid Wall (part of a system that includes barbed wire fencing, watchtowers, and sand patrol roads) snakes deep into the West Bank, cutting it into small, easy-to-control segments. In urban areas and elsewhere, the Wall is 25 feet high, 3 times as high as the old Berlin Wall.

ABOUT THE AUTHOR

Mohammad Sabaaneh was born in Kuwait in 1979 and has been working as a cartoonist since 2002 (currently at the Palestinian newspaper *al-Hayat al-Jadida*). His work has been published in many Arabic-language newspapers including *al-Ittihad* (United Arab Emirates), *al-Quds al-Arabi* (London), *al-Ghad* (Jordan), and *al-Akhbar* (Lebanon). Sabaaneh is a member of the international Cartoon Movement and won third place at the Doha Center Cartoon Contest in 2013. He has had solo and group exhibitions in Washington, DC, Great Britain, Spain, Germany, Norway, Holland, Switzerland, Qatar, and Syria. He has lectured about the art of caricature at An-Najah National University and The Arab American University (in the West Bank), the New School and School of Visual Arts (New York), and institutions in Spain and Great Britain. He has used the art of caricature with deaf students to help them use more than one dialogue language to express their feelings; with children who witnessed Israeli assaults to help them psychologically; and in workshops with children to develop their critical thinking. Sabaaneh has been the Middle East representative for Cartoonist Rights Network International since 2015, and in 2016, he became the Palestinian ambassador for United Sketches, an international association for freedom of expression and cartoonists in exile.